THE HOUSE & GARDEN BOOK OF
VACATION HOMES
and hideaways

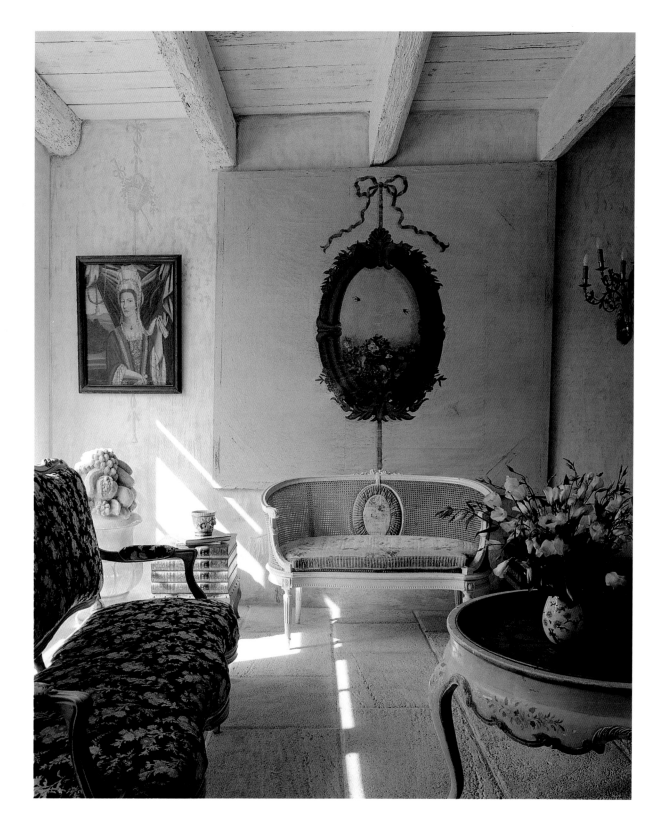

ABOVE AND OPPOSITE Two views of Tom and Diane Berger's flamboyant home in Provence. In the salon, a design for an Aubusson carpet, painted on canvas, hangs behind a canework sofa. Outside, by the pool, a topiary bird surveys a stone urn (pages 144-51).

THE HOUSE & GARDEN BOOK OF
VACATION HOMES
and hideaways

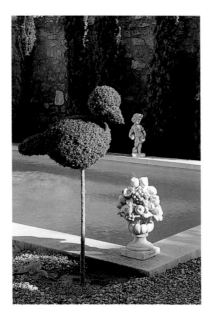

edited by

LEONIE HIGHTON

THE VENDOME PRESS
NEW YORK

First published in the U.S. in 2000 by
The Vendome Press
1370 Avenue of the Americas
New York, N.Y. 10019

Distributed in the U.S. and Canada by
Rizzoli International Publications through
St. Martin's Press
175 Fifth Avenue
New York, N.Y. 10010

Library of Congree Cataloging-in-Publication Data

Highton, Leonie
  The House & garden book of vacation homes/by
Leonie Highton.
    p. cm.
  ISBN 0-86565-219-8
    1. Vacation homes--Designs and plans.
  2. Architecture, Domestic--Designs and plans.
  I. Title: House & garden book of vacation homes.
  II. Title: Book of vacation homes. III. House &
garden. IV. Title.
NA7574.H54 2000
728.7'2'0222--dc21
00-038142

Printed and bound in Singapore

Designer: Alison Shackleton

Photographers: Anita Calero, Tim Clinch, Michael Dunne,
Andreas von Einsiedel, Brian Harrison, Richard Labougle,
Keith Scott Morton, Jonathan Pilkington, Sue Royle,
Christian Sarramon, Fritz von der Shulenburg,
Christopher Simon Sykes, Simon Upton, Peter Woloszynski.

Text contributors: Olinda Adeane, Darleen Bungey,
Victor Carro, Caroline Clifton-Mogg, Quentin Crewe,
Susan Crewe, Jonathan Dawson, June Ducas, Liz Elliot,
Anne Hardy, Carolyn Harrison, Suzanne Lowry,
Sophie Lund, David Mlinaric, Lorenza Bianda Pasquinelli,
Anthony Roberts, Caroline Seebohm, Liz Seymour.

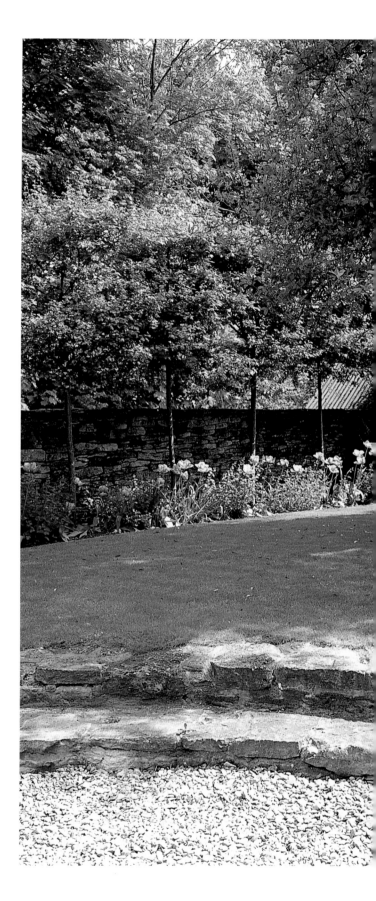

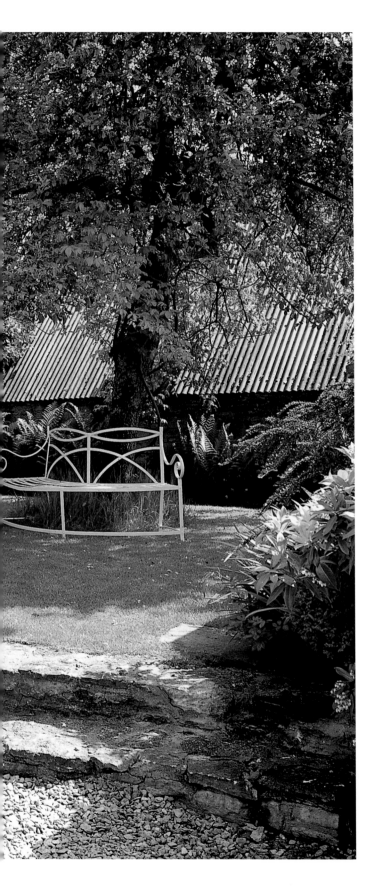

Contents

LEFT The garden of Roger Jones's Cotswolds cottage is designed as a series of outdoor rooms (pages 102-11). Here, a mature tree provides a backdrop for an elegantly curved, metal seat.

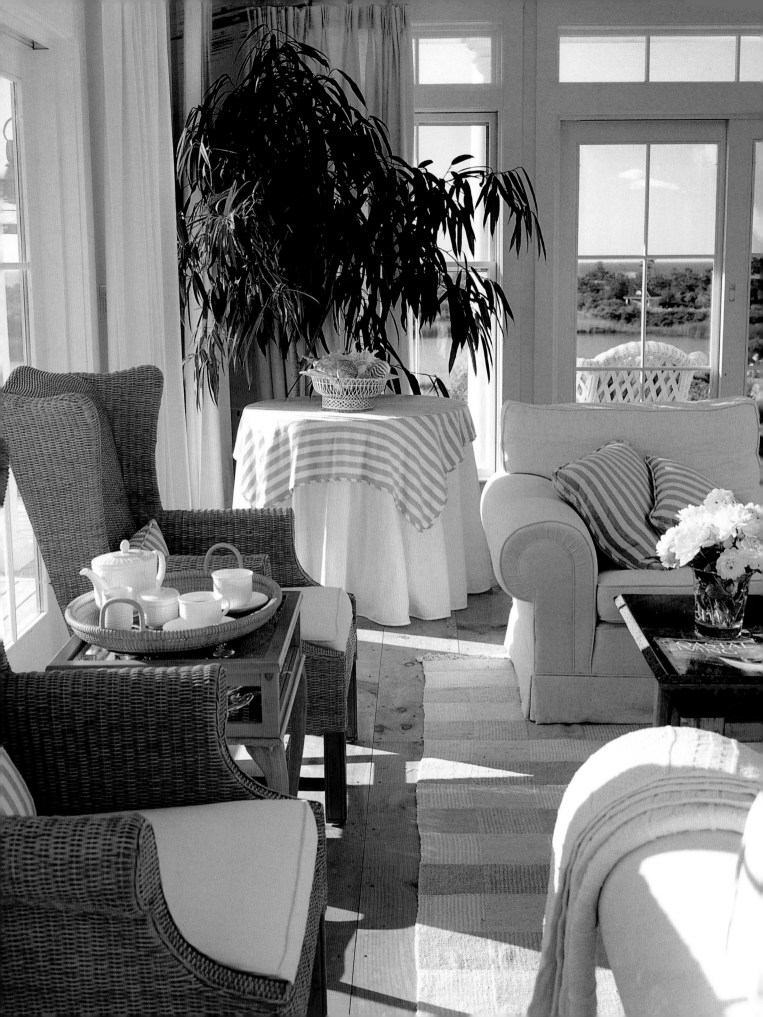

Introduction

Wherever in the world I travel, I am irresistibly drawn to the windows of the local real-estate agents. I scrutinize the rows of photographs of houses for sale, tantalized by the inadequacies of the images but convinced that, somewhere amongst them, is my dream hideaway waiting to be turned into a reality. The fantasy knows no bounds. In my mind's eye, I have bought a crumbling chateau in Provence, a croft in Scotland, a beach cabana in Brazil, a cottage in Devon, a chalet in the Alps – and a dozen more besides.

I am not alone in this. Many, many people share my obsession with buying vacation homes. But why do we have this fantasy? Why is the idea of staying in our own holiday house so much more seductive than staying in a hotel? The answer has a great deal to do with the idea of freedom. We may not want a life of non-stop leisure, but the chance to escape from the tyranny of the mundane and to convince ourselves that we are masters of our own destiny is a powerful draw. We seek a home-from-home, familiar yet different, a place where we can feel totally relaxed, unchallenged by strange surroundings and new faces. We relish the thought of being able to do as we please and only acknowledge the outside world if and when we feel like it.

But the freedom to come and go as we wish is not the only attraction of a holiday home. For those of us who love interior decoration, a vacation house has another, more tangible appeal in that it offers a fantastic opportunity to play with a building which is completely different from our regular home and to come up with all kinds of new and exciting ideas. The location of a holiday house must inevitably influence the choices – but that does not mean that everything in the interior has to echo the local vernacular. The important thing is to maintain a sense of appropriateness and informality: crimson velvet drapes are not compatible with huge windows overlooking a sun-scorched beach; and shorts do not sit attractively on deep-buttoned upholstery. Conversely, a country cottage in a cool climate can be more inward-looking, as this type of building often has small windows, creating a greater feeling of intimacy. Although simplicity and a modest style of decoration are called for here, warm textures and colours can be introduced to enhance, psychologically as well as physically, the concept of shelter from the outside elements.

A few of the houses in this book are used for more than brief weekends and vacations. They may have started out as places for occasional breaks, but such is their lure that they soon became homes for longer periods. Their locations, however, are so spectacular that most of us could only imagine them as holiday destinations. The extraordinary wooden house built amidst the jungle on Bali, for instance, seems so remote from the architectural styles and urban environments of New York, London or Paris that, for any city dweller, it is hard to envisage living there day-to-day, surrounded by exotic flowers and lush palms (pages 154-61).

John and Cynthia Hardy's house on Bali is, perhaps, the most obviously exotic of all the homes in this book, not just in its setting but also in its structure. Based on the design of a traditional Bornean long-house, it is built on poles, and many of its rooms are open-sided. The vernacular style of

OPPOSITE In the sun-room in Geo Davis's house in Nantucket (pages 48-57), white linen enhances the light, summery ambience.

Felix Dennis's pavilioned retreat (pages 170-81) is also derived largely from Far-Eastern building traditions but, in this case, the location is on Mustique in the Caribbean. Another exotic house is the one on Lamu, off the coast of Kenya, which is the subject of many local legends and has now been sympathetically restored and extended (pages 162-69).

Those particular houses are all situated in the tropics, but there are other island houses with a totally different character. These are on Nantucket, a two-hour ferry ride off the coast of Massachusetts, where the climate is not always kind. There can be chill, blustery winds on this one-time whaling outpost, but Nantucket has masses of charm, especially evident in its traditional houses faced in clapboard. They are not buildings which should be decorated with overt luxury: they look at their best when treated rather simply, almost naively, with painted floors and pretty fabrics. The floor in the hall of the house decorated by Vivien Greenock of Sibyl Colefax & John Fowler (pages 64-71) is an especially delightful example of the genre, its stencilled shamrocks picked out in colour on a soft white background. In fact, white is the common denominator in most of the Nantucket rooms illustrated here. Painted matchboarding is another consistent theme but, in spite of this being a rather humble finish, the effect in all these houses is casually sophisticated.

Roger Jones's cottage in that most English of country regions, the Cotswolds (pages 102-11), also demonstrates sophistication in that he has successfully included some quite grand pieces in a modest setting yet maintained a sense of appropriateness. In contrast, some of the other country houses featured are much bigger in scale and have been furnished with a dramatic eclecticism. The most remarkable of these is Tom and Diane Berger's home near St-Rémy-de-Provence in southern France (pages 144-51). The Bergers come from the United States but are great francophiles and, a while ago, realized their hope of finding an unspoilt, old house which they could restore and furnish in their highly

individualistic style. They are prodigious collectors and have scoured local markets for all manner of wonderful treasures – some fine antiques, others simple café items – which add up to an intriguing entity with much of the drama of a theatre set.

The Bergers' rooms are full of character, based largely on allusions to the past. A similarly reassuring note of history is seen in the house in Tuscany (pages 74-83), where the ancient stone walls are reminders of the building's venerable pedigree. In summer, the semi-enclosed terraces become outdoor 'rooms', properly furnished with country-style dining tables and chairs. The effect is as chic as the rooms indoors. In fact, the designer's whole approach to furnishing

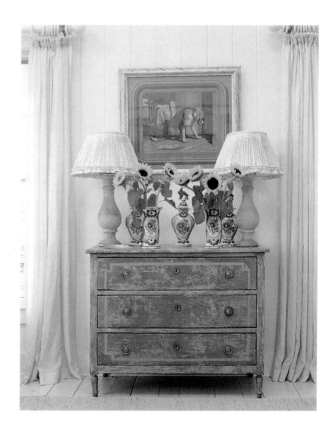

ABOVE A painted chest of drawers supports a symmetrical arrangement of lamps and blue-and-white Delftware in a seaside house on Nantucket (pages 64-71).
OPPOSITE In keeping with the simple, open architecture, Laura Ocampo has decorated this beachside pavilion in Uruguay with pale colours and streamlined, modern furniture (pages 58-63)

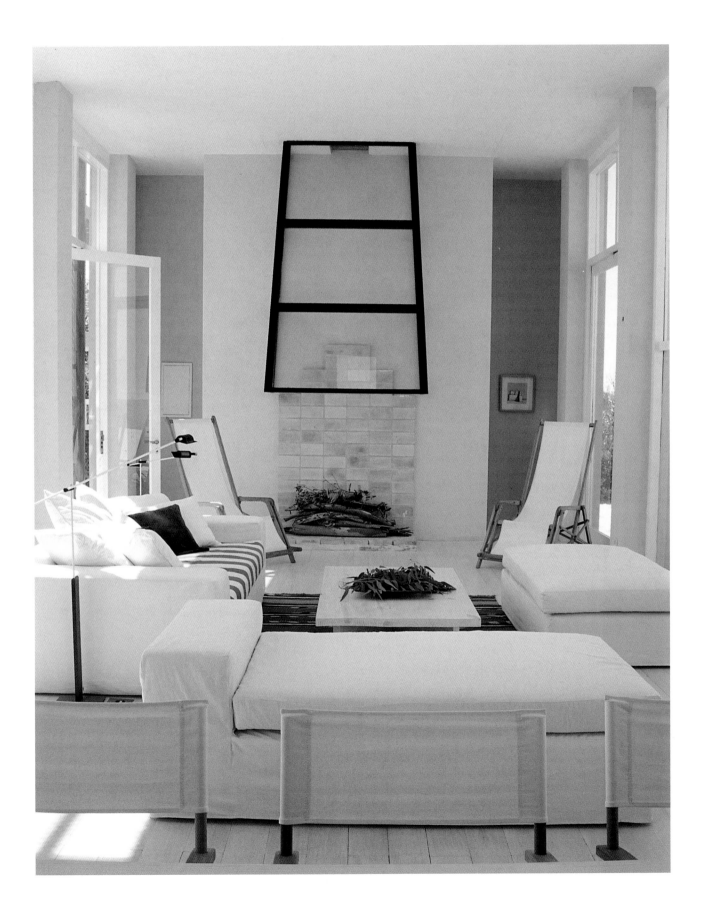

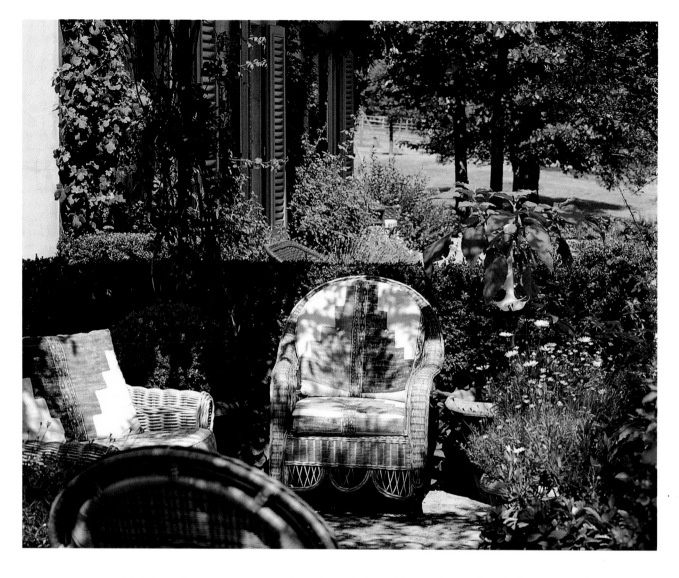

ABOVE Basket chairs on the terrace of the guest wing at Ornellaia (pages 134-43) have comfortable, ikat-covered cushions.

this house demonstrates that it is perfectly possible to use a smart style of interior decoration whilst respecting a building's intrinsic, traditional spirit. When Ilaria Miani took on the house, she did not want to fall into what she saw as the Tuscan 'trap' of trying to recreate an old, rustic style which never really existed. She preferred to be more original and, as result, ended up designing much of the furniture herself as she could not find existing, interesting pieces that bridged the gap between old and new.

Ilaria Miani's solution to furnishing her Tuscan

hideaway includes many modern touches but the house still retains an essentially nostalgic character. The interior of the house in the South of France, designed by Claire Bataille and Paul Ibens (pages 124-33), is less equivocal in its contemporary edge. Although the building is mainly old, the rooms within are serenely spare, with modern furniture, plain walls and no door architraves.

All the houses in this book have been chosen from the many vacation homes that have appeared in the pages of *House & Garden* magazine. They do not

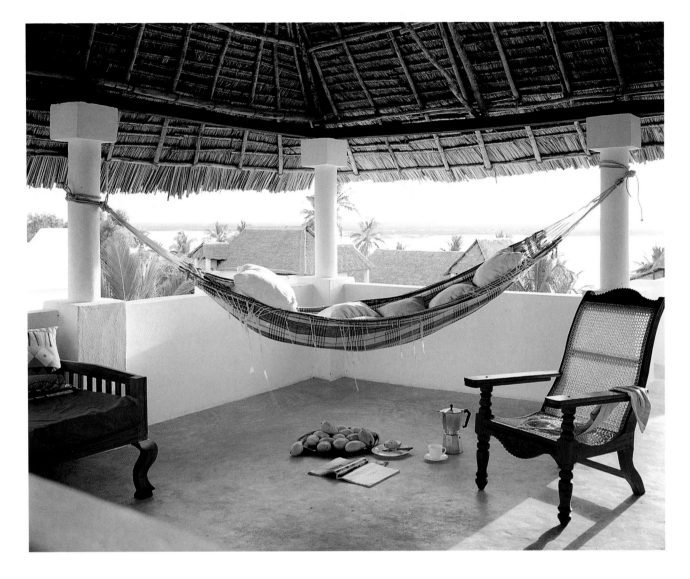

ABOVE A shaded terrace on Lamu offers total relaxation (pages 162-69).

cover every corner of the world but, in their various ways, give fascinating insights into what different people see as the perfect bolt-hole. And, without exception, they are suffused with an atmosphere of enjoyment and retreat.

The old adage that it is the journey not the destination that counts does not ring true when the destination is your own vacation home. There may be excitement and an agreeable sense of movement and change when travelling to unknown destinations, but nothing compares with the pleasure of arriving at your own front door – and staying put, surrounded by familiar scenery indoors and outdoors. Setting off from your everyday home, anticipating exactly what is in store for you when you get to your hideaway, and then finding that everything is just as you remembered, is the greatest and most reassuring of all luxuries. It is like meeting up with an old friend: however much time has elapsed since you last saw each other, you take up just where you left off and carry on as though there had never been an interruption.

SEASIDE
SANCTUARIES

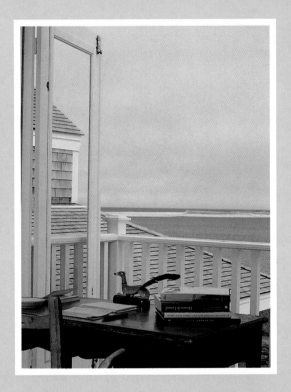

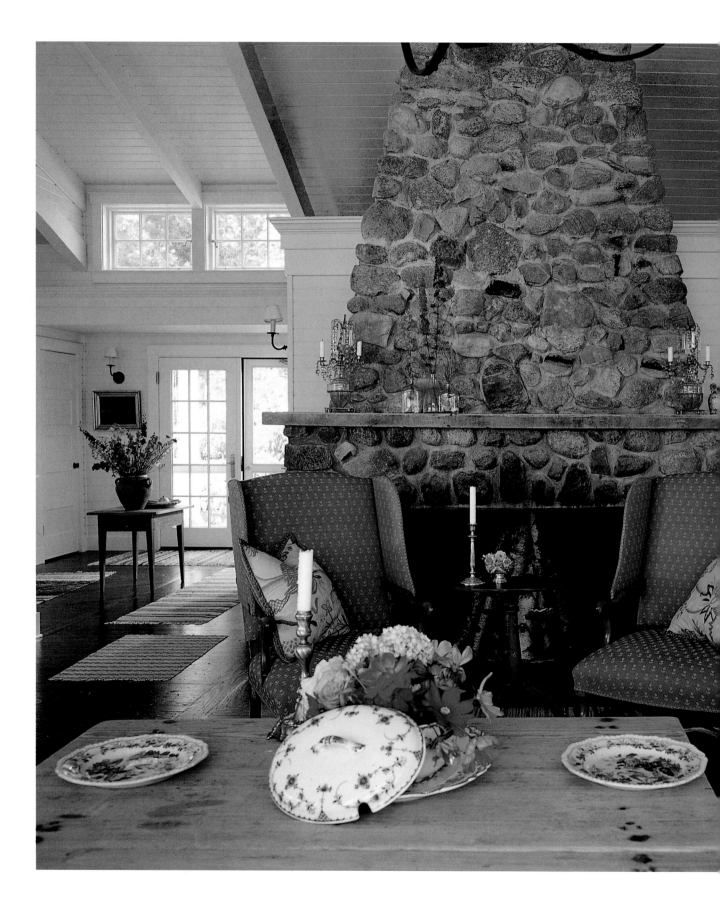

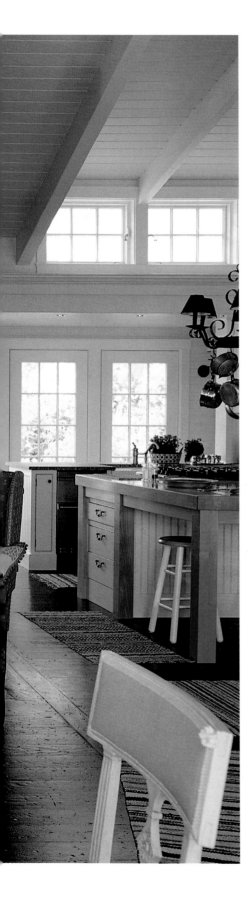

Northern influences

Although in origin separated by thousands of miles, two design cultures meet and embrace in this house in Martha's Vineyard. Its decoration is the story of a marriage – between Scandinavia and New England. Unni Kaltenbacher is Norwegian; her husband, Philip, is American. The house they have created combines her penchant for Scandinavian furniture, colours and textures, with his taste for the casual style of New England.

At the turn of the century, a cottage stood on the site of the new house. It looks out over Lake Tashmoo, with Cape Cod to the east and Woods Hole to the north. Two years ago, when, with the help of builder Robert Avakian, the Kaltenbachers decided to reconstruct the house, this glorious view dominated every design decision. The priorities were accentuating the steep hill-side site and creating a layout in which every door, deck and window would enjoy an ocean view.

Apart from a basement playroom, the house is spread out on one floor. The central module is the Great Room, which is flanked by two wings projecting at angles off the central axis – the guest wing to the north and main bedroom wing to the

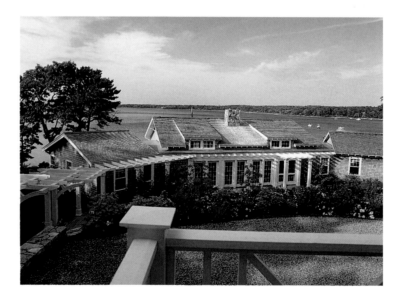

ABOVE Looking from the guest-house balcony over the main house.
LEFT The Great Room is dominated by a massive stone chimneypiece. In front of it, facing the sea, is a pair of blue-covered, wing chairs which, on winter evenings, are turned towards the fire.

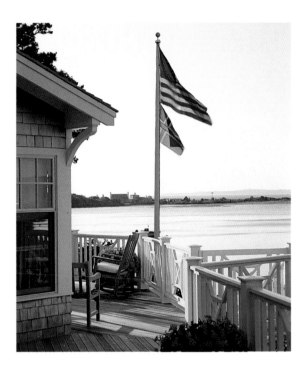

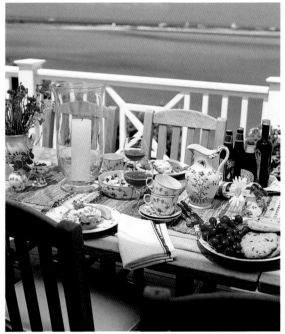

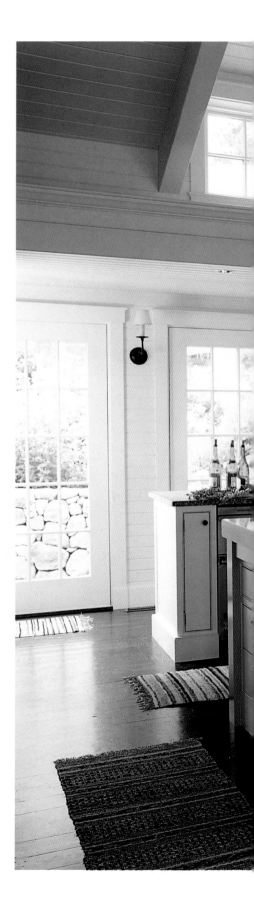

TOP *The US and Norwegian flags flutter over the terrace.*
ABOVE *A table on the terrace is laid for lunch.*
RIGHT *The kitchen, designed by William Cummings, is
contained within the space of the Great Room. The granite
work surfaces and island unit, modelled on a butcher's block,
are practical and have a country character.*

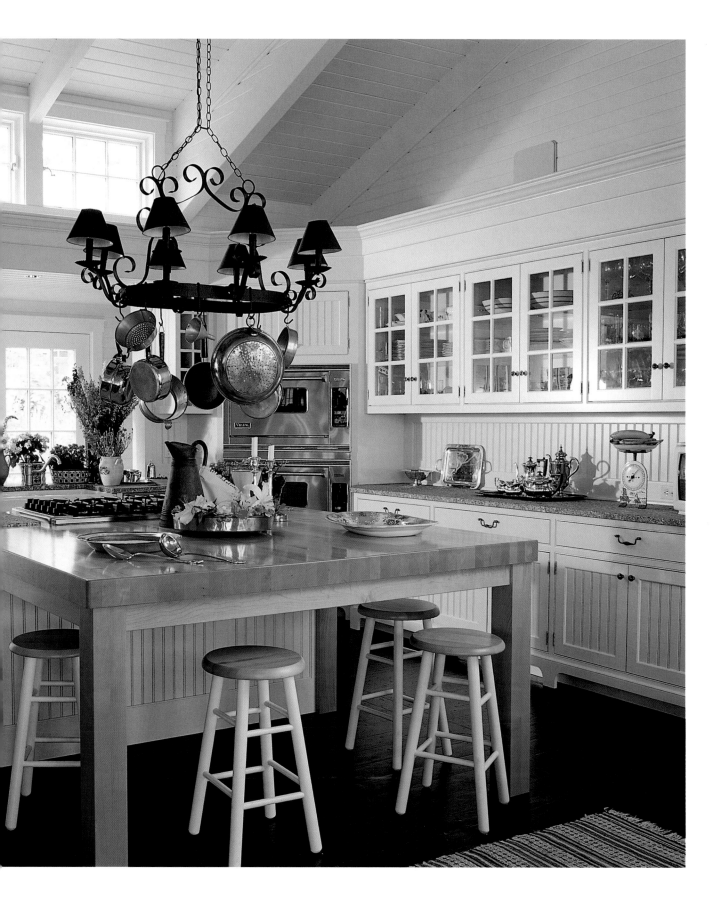

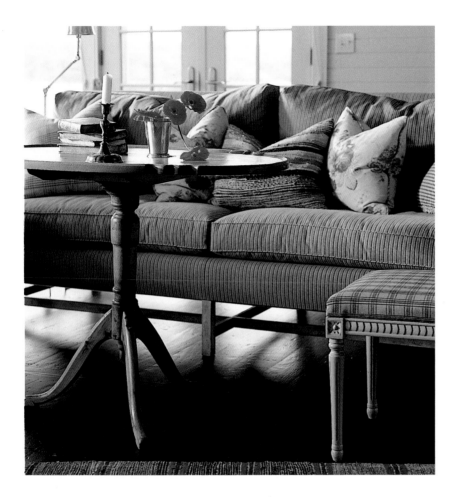

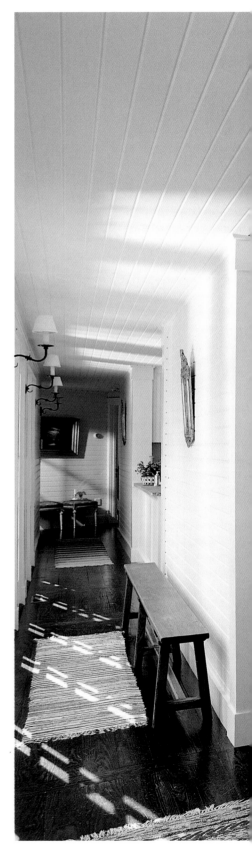

south. The effect, when one descends the steps towards the house, past the wall that encircles the garden, is of an ellipse hugging the shoreline.

The front door opens directly into the Great Room, a space of such striking appeal that even the view outside is secondary. The room was built around a huge nineteenth-century chimneypiece. Made of hefty, brownish-grey stones with a concrete mantel shelf, its weight anchors the enormous room. Sitting, dining and kitchen space are all generously incorporated into this forty-by-twenty-five-foot interior. Shimmering white beamed ceilings, matchboarded walls and a dark oak floor, with a few rag rugs, give the room a lightness, so that it seems to float like a ship above the blue horizon beyond the windows.

ABOVE A sofa covered in Swedish striped ticking and strewn with cushions is tailored yet casual in the Great Room.

RIGHT A painting that belonged to Unni Kaltenbacher's Norwegian grandfather hangs above a Vermont grain-storage chest. The stone-clad flue from the fireplace can be seen rising monumentally above. To the right is the dining area.

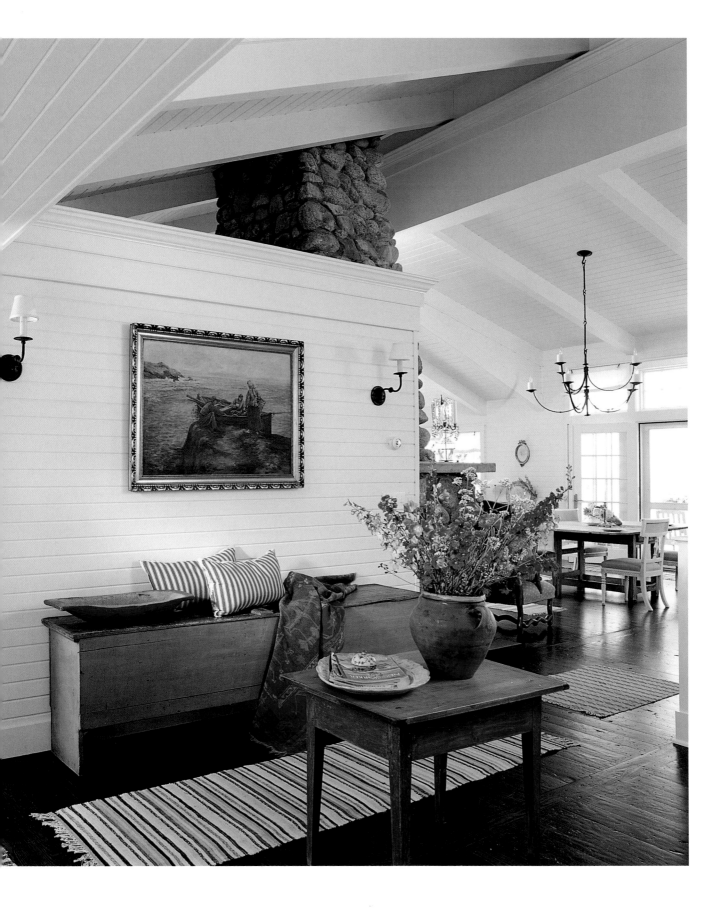

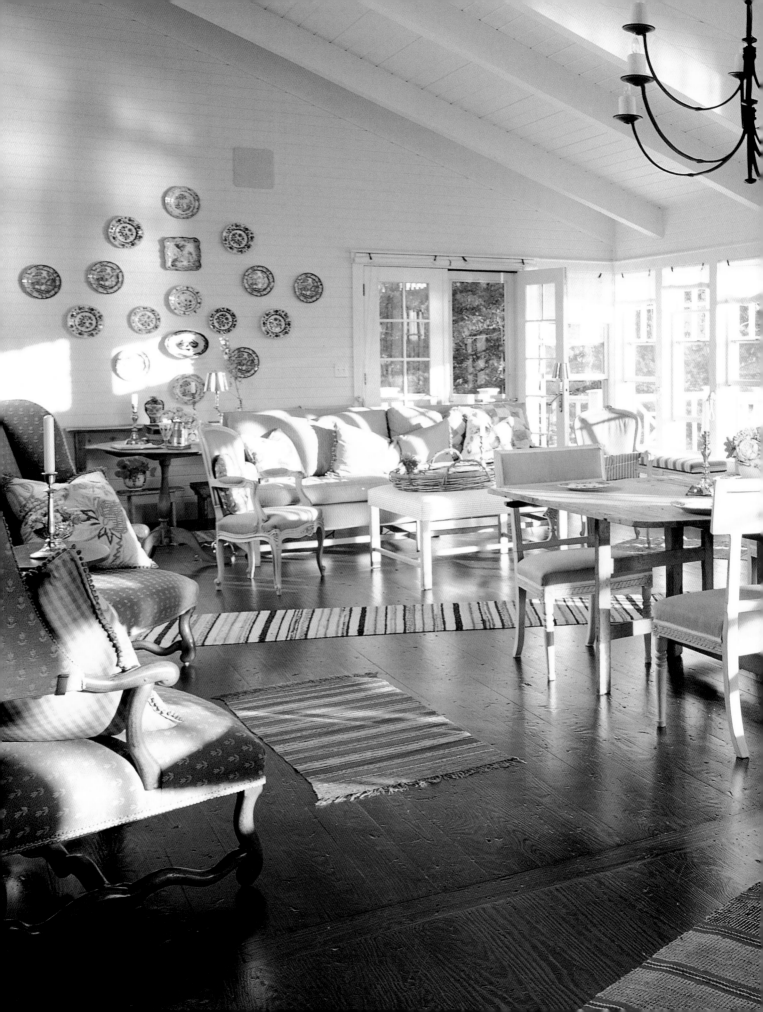

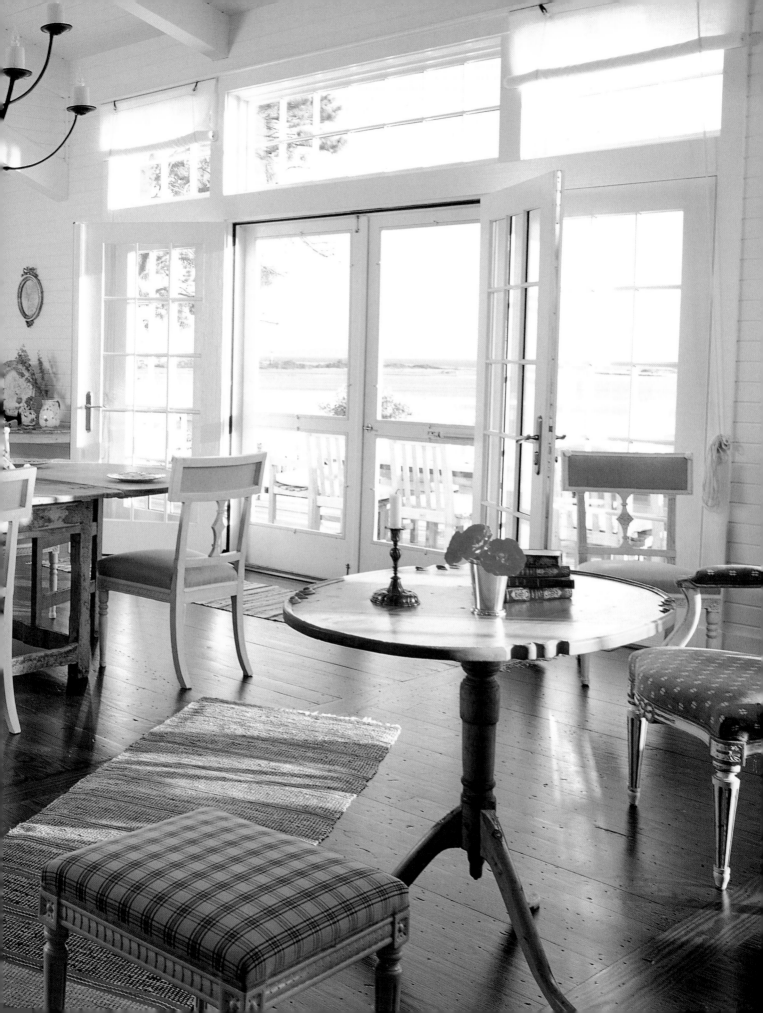

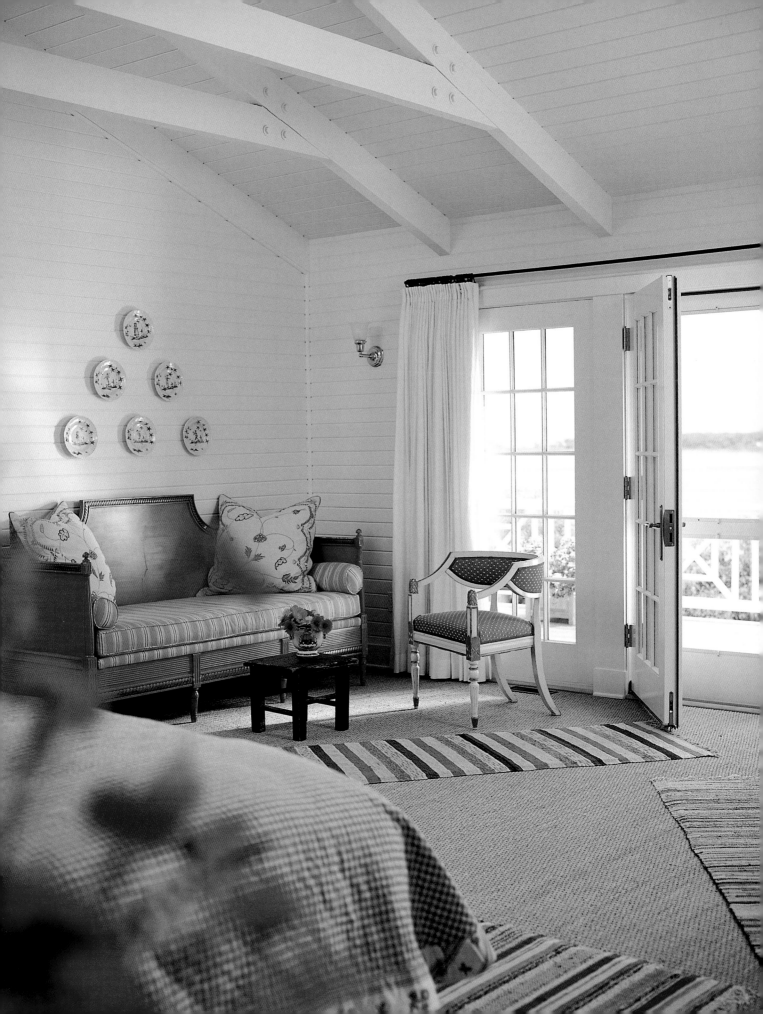

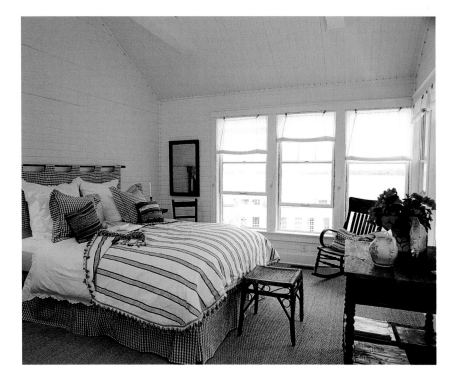

PREVIOUS PAGE The Great Room is a relaxed, sun-drenched space which incorporates many Scandinavian influences. Elegant Gustavian furniture, combined with blue-and-white china and striped rag rugs, is offset by the whiteness of the interior.
LEFT Blue-and-white checks, ticking, sisal matting and an antique American rocking chair convey an air of nostalgia in this spare bedroom.

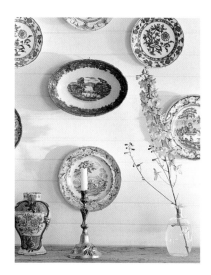

ABOVE One wall of the matchboarded Great Room is hung with a medley of blue-and-white plates.
OPPOSITE The main bedroom, furnished with a rare, painted, Gustavian bench, opens on to the terrace.

Both wings of the house lead off from the central entryway, reached by a long, window-lined gallery. 'I thought we would hang pictures here,' Unni says. 'But I prefer it simply flooded with light.' To allocate so much space to the Great Room, and to comply with local planning regulations, the spare rooms had to be quite small. There is, however, a separate guest house with two bedrooms, a sitting room and a playroom on the other side of the garden. Off the main bedroom wing, the Kaltenbachers turned an extra space – some 200 square feet – into an office-cum-study for Philip.

The furniture and furnishings in the house are almost all Scandinavian in origin, many of them brought from Norway and Sweden by Unni and her designers, William Cummings and Bernt Heiberg of Heiberg, Cummings Design. 'I love the light palette of Scandinavia,' Unni says, 'and the mixture of elegant restraint that is characteristic of Scandinavian design.' This quality is conspicuous in her collection of late-eighteenth-century Gustavian furniture, which shows the influence of French neoclassicism on provincial Scandinavian crafts-manship. Little strokes of gilding and fluting give a charming French twist to the straight-backed, plainly upholstered chairs that decorate these rooms. Unlike some collectors, Unni does not repaint any of the furniture. It is its soft, faded quality that is so precious to her.

'Scandinavia and New England speak the same design language,' says William Cummings, whose firm is based in Oslo and New York. 'Simple lines; unostentatious antiques; lots of light; pale colours; strong textiles, such as ticking, rough cottons and linens; and everything functional and comfortable. Textures are important – rustic wood planks for walls, for instance, to prevent the rooms from seeming cold.'

The two wings off the Great Room further demonstrate this successful wedding. A palette of soft greys, blues and greens is consistent. Untreated, greyish brown, speckled granite worktops (slightly rough to the touch) in the kitchen reappear in all the bathrooms. 'When I like something, I use it everywhere,' Unni says. And lest the check or striped fabrics (not a petal of chintz anywhere) and plain white-linen blinds seem a little austere, the note of French frivolity in such Gustavian pieces as a gilt mirror or footstool delights the eye.

The exterior reflects the sturdy past of the site. The house has been shingled in cedar, which weathers to a mellow grey, with white-painted

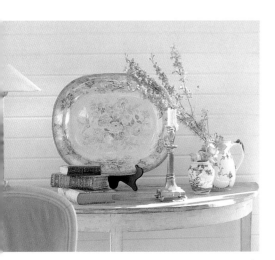

ABOVE Blue-and-white china is a recurring theme in the house. Here, an Irish plate is juxtaposed with antique Danish porcelain jugs.
RIGHT The painted, matchboard design of the cupboard doors in the bathroom links with the wall finish.
OPPOSITE Check patterns and crisp Norwegian linen are the dominant theme in the main bedroom.

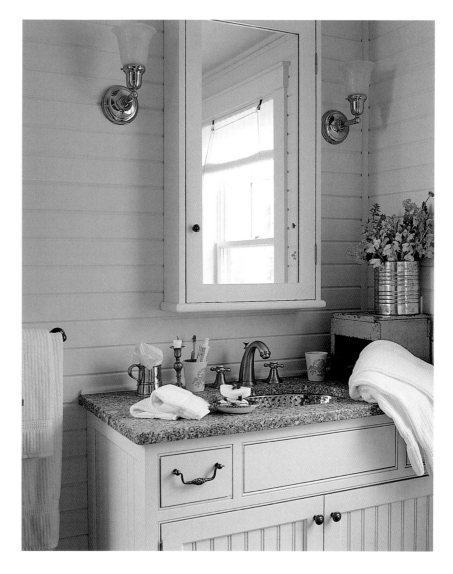

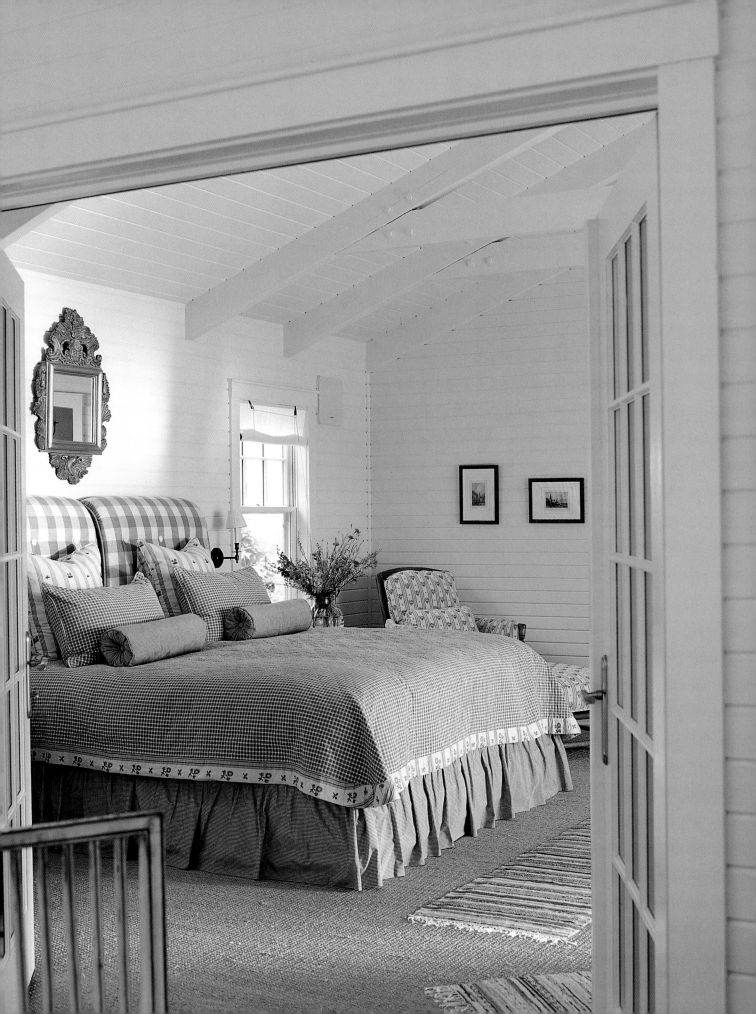

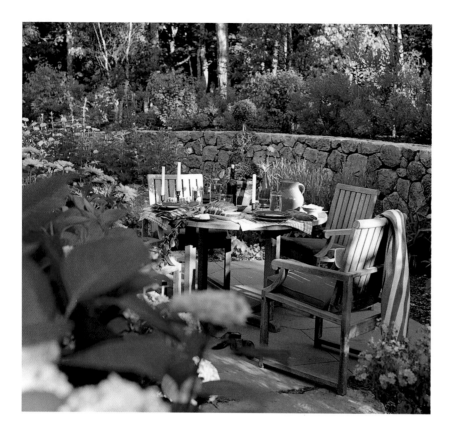

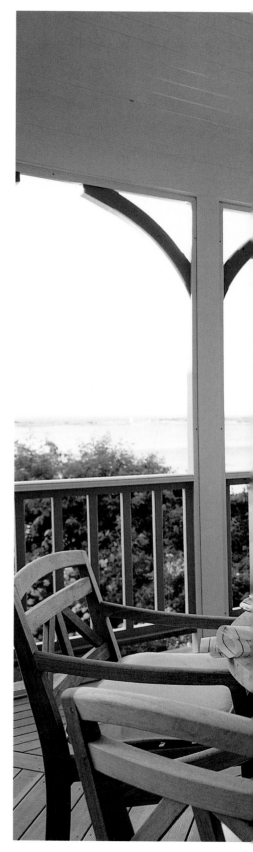

wooden balustrades and columns – local materials in this part of New England. A deck overlooking the water runs the length of the house; at the south end is Philip's folly, a screened gazebo. 'We built it as an after-thought,' Philip recalls. 'Now people sit here all night.' The guest house (elevated behind the main house so that guests can share the view) has the look of a carriage house and is linked to the main house by a pergola.

Landscape designer Chris Horuchi and gardener Chuck Minnick have preserved native trees in a wooded area behind the guesthouse. A more formal terraced garden greets the visitor at the front of the house while, at the back, steeply sloping towards the water, is a small lawn and banks of rugosa roses and weeds. When Unni declared to her gardener that she wanted weeds, he was horrified, but 'I wanted them,' she explains 'in order to suggest the abundance of an English garden.'

The most telling juxtaposition of the two worlds is found near the spa: a small Japanese-style pool garden behind the guest house is protected by a high hedge of birch, that most Scandinavian of trees, and native New England blueberry bushes.

ABOVE *A table is laid in the walled garden of the guest house.*
RIGHT *The gazebo overlooks Lake Tashmoo, with a view towards Cape Cod.*

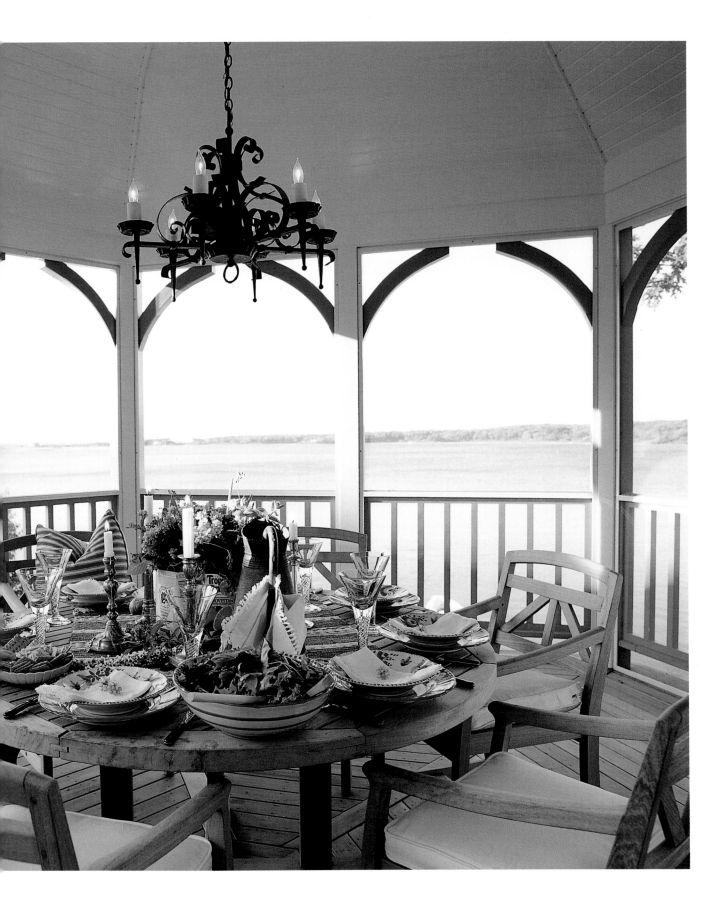

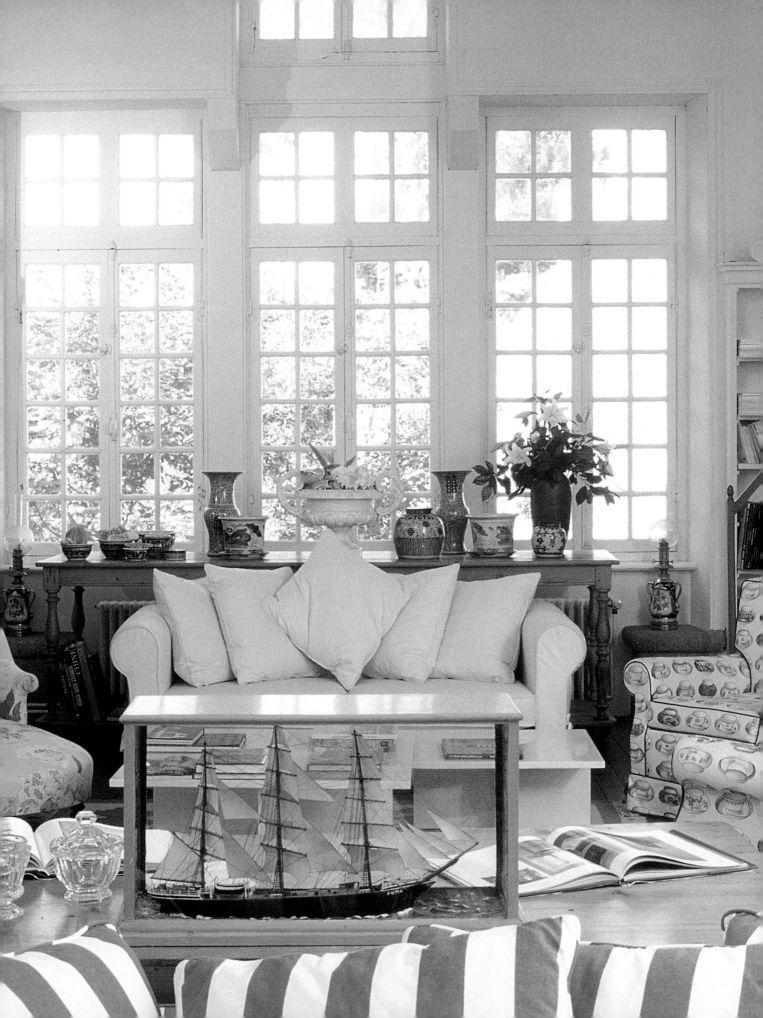

The lure of Brittany

The Côtes-du-Nord is that part of mainland Brittany lying roughly south-west of the Channel Islands, and it is the only one of France's Channel *départements* without a ferry port. It is the traditional heart of Basse Bretagne, where, more than anywhere else in Brittany, the Breton language and mores are kept alive.

The coastline is rough and rocky, with the kind of barnacled granite that razors your shoe-leather. There are pink cliffs, small islands visible from the shore, and fishing ports at the mouths of rivers. Wherever there's a strip of sand, you will find some kind of resort, with concentrations of houses that look almost unnecessarily solid – probably because they are mainly of granite construction – extending up the slopes behind. Those with the best sites and sea views date from between 1859 and 1914.

This is especially the case at Perros-Guirec, a sprawling harbour and seaside resort between the cathedral town of Tréguier and the port of Lannion at the mouth of the river Léguer. After the 'discovery' of this unspoiled stretch of coast by the Breton writer Ernest Renan in the late nineteenth century, the usual process of popularization began in the area and Perros-Guirec did not escape. Artists and writers arrived, followed by the rich and fashionable, then by masses of the bourgeoisie in quest of leisure and sea air. By 1906 there was a railway, which meant Paris was only fifteen hours away; by 1924 there was a casino. Finally, in more recent years, the town gained a spa, a waxwork museum and a marina.

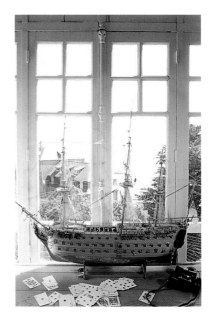

*ABOVE Ship models and other emblems of the sea feature throughout the house.
LEFT Brittany's traditional coastal resorts, with their solid-looking houses, have an old-fashioned charm.
OPPOSITE The living room is filled with light. Beneath the huge window is a nineteenth-century upholsterer's table.*

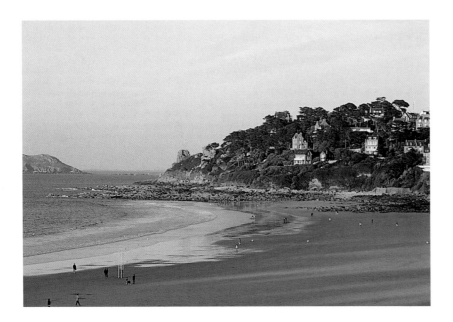

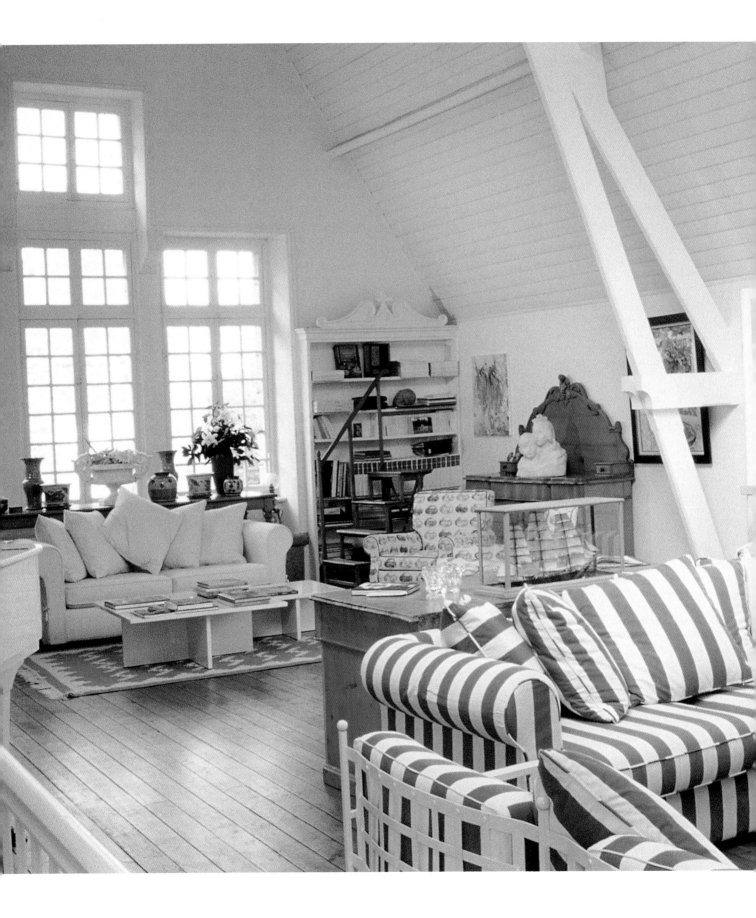

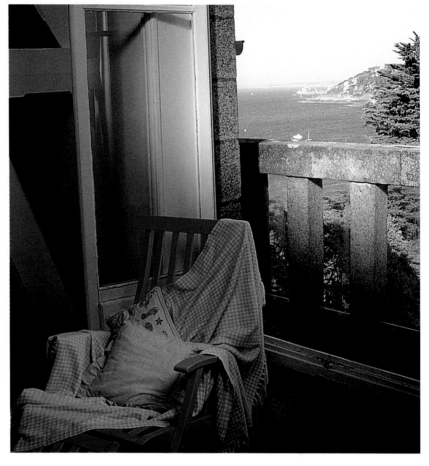

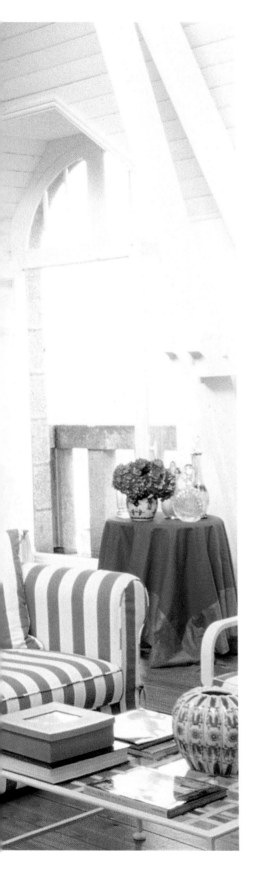

Among the pioneers of the 1890s was Charles Le Goffic, a tradition-alist Breton writer from Lannion and the descendant of a Venetian gondolier brought to France to ply his trade on Louis XIV's personal canal at Versailles. Le Goffic seems to have been a colourful character: a pious contemporary described him as 'short and squat like these Bretons are, trenchant in his speech, a smoker, a swearer of rich oaths. God for-give me, I even saw him chew tobacco like a mariner! I suspected him of taking other liberties as well...'

This reprobate, bald, bearded and unkempt, was a prolific writer who ended up with the Legion of Honour and a chair at the Académie Française. But, in the meantime, in 1900, he acquired a plot a couple of hundred feet above the Trestraou beach at Perros. On it he built the per-fect writer's house overlooking the Baie des Sept Iles, where he lived and

ABOVE Built of granite, the house and its terrace overlook the sea.
LEFT Seating in the living room is upholstered in different fabrics to generate a relaxed
ambience. Broad, blue and white stripes have a jauntily nautical character.

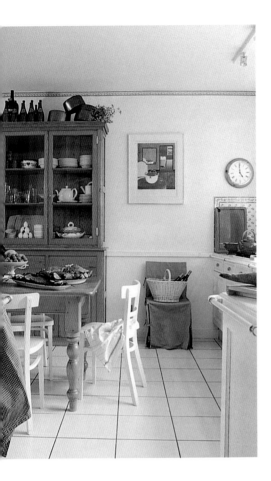

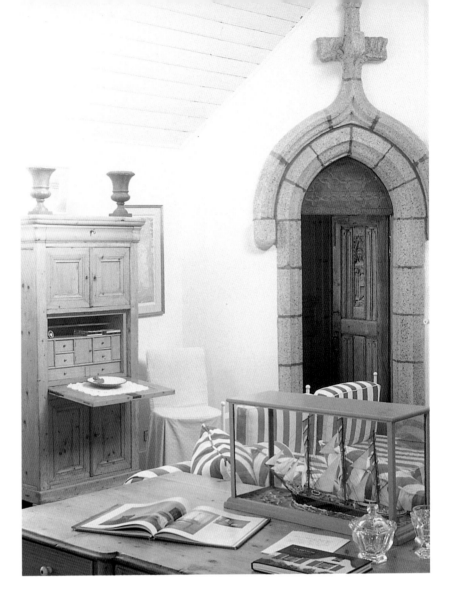

ABOVE The kitchen, with its free-standing cupboard and country table, is very much a family room.
ABOVE RIGHT The granite construction of the house is revealed in this impressive door surround in the living room.

worked between late May and early July, renting it out to vacationers for the rest of the year.

The years went by. Le Goffic died in 1930, and his three-storey, slate-roofed holiday house, with its steep garden among the pines and hortensias, passed into other hands. Eventually, the cul-de-sac in which it stood, near the old excisemen's path along the cliffs, was named after the tobacco-chewing academician by a grateful municipality. Subsequent owners did not make many changes inside the building; Le Goffic's cavernous writing studio overlooking the bay kept its varnished deal ceiling and bookcases, and year after year the small bedrooms lay empty during the *mois noirs* of winter and filled up again in the spring.

In 1992, the house was bought by Jean-Michel Queré and his wife Fabienne. Their main residence was in central Brittany, but Fabienne wanted a pied-à-terre in Perros, where she could bring their children for weekends and holidays. However, finding the existing interior decoration 'finicky and over-ornate', she completely transformed the place. 'A house by the sea, in this part of the world, should above all feel natural and be

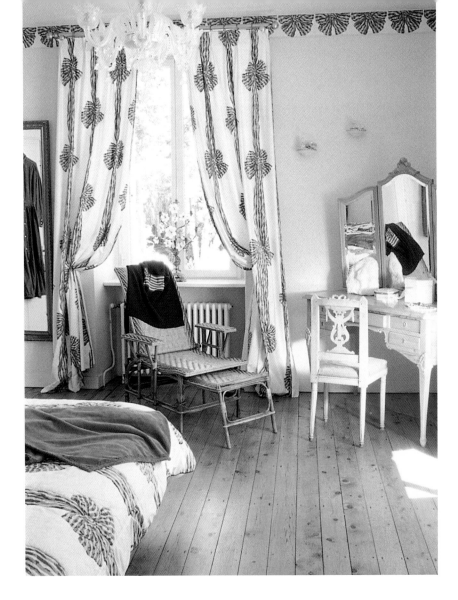

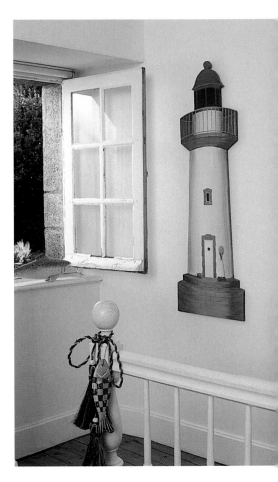

flooded with light,' she says simply. 'Essentially, all we did to the house was let in the sun.'

But there was more to it than that. She stuck to one colour scheme for most of the house. The colours she used are dark blue for the tiles and fabrics and plain white for the walls, a scheme relieved only by the original pale pine doors and floors, and by simple deal furniture collected all over Brittany. Appropriately, there are numerous references to the sea, including ship models in the living room and a wooden lighthouse on the stairs.

Charles Le Goffic's former *cabinet de travail*, with its monumental fireplace and crucifix-crowned bookcases, is no longer the cave of dark Edwardian wood and stencilled patterns it once was, but a wonderful family living room – airy, white, sunny and full of comfortable chairs; but the views of the bay are as spectacular as they ever were. It is a place of irresistible attraction. As Le Goffic once wrote: 'The sea is... a mysterious enchantress offering an inexhaustible supply of sensations, images, rhythms and dreams.'

ABOVE LEFT Ribbon-patterned chintz and a matching frieze are fresh and cheerful in one of the bedrooms. ABOVE RIGHT Continuing the marine theme of the house, a lighthouse by local artist Sylvie Guezennec decorates the staircase.

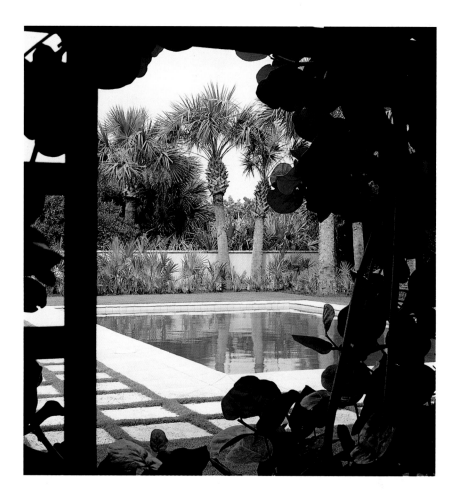

Tropical Swedish

ABOVE The paving between the lawn and pool has been interplanted with grass.
OPPOSITE The cantilevered porch, which leads off the upstairs bedroom and landing, faces the sea in traditional Caribbean style.

Think Florida, think exclusive resort, and you probably conjure an image of a particularly distinctive form of traditional Florida interior decoration – a cocktail of lime green, vibrant tangerine and vivid lemon yellow, rising from deep, cream carpet. But in the Florida community of Windsor – the location of this house – nothing could be more different.

The founders of this community were Galen and Hilary Weston, whose English house is Fort Belvedere in Windsor Great Park, once home of the Duke of Windsor. Perhaps because of this, their Florida Windsor seems very un-American: there are no ribbons of houses on wide boulevards flanking golf courses and beaches, but instead a 'village' with a distinct centre, a place in which services and social life are in walking rather than driving distance – rather like the Prince of Wales's English town-planning venture at Poundbury, in Dorset, which was one of the inspirations behind this transatlantic project.

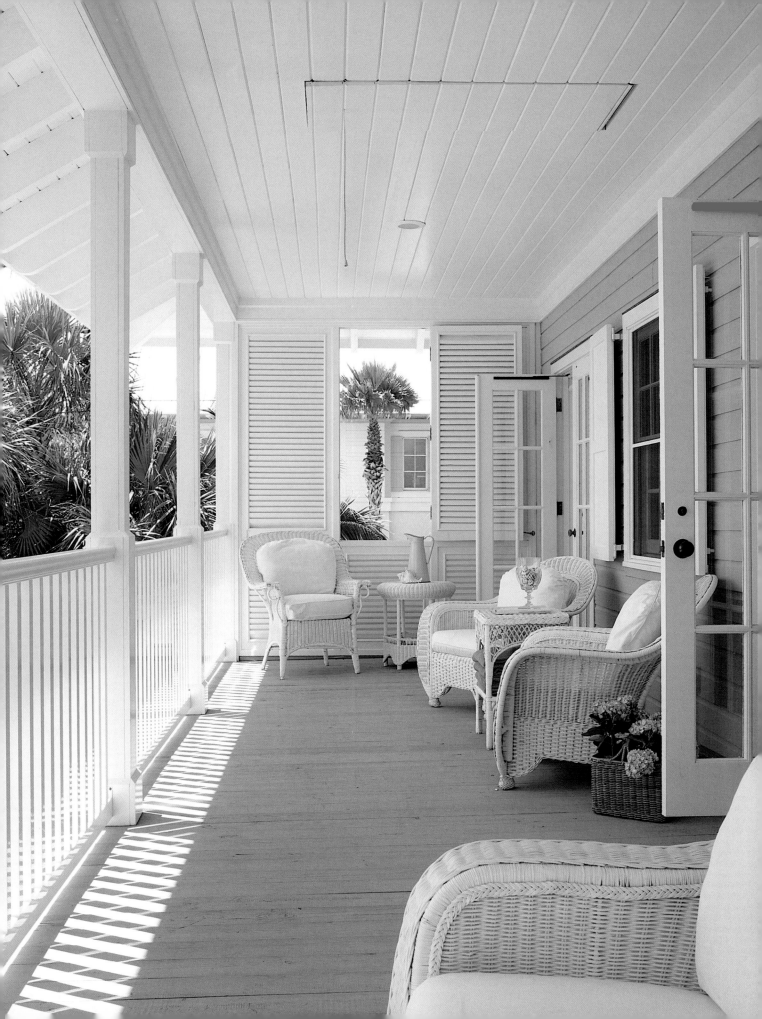

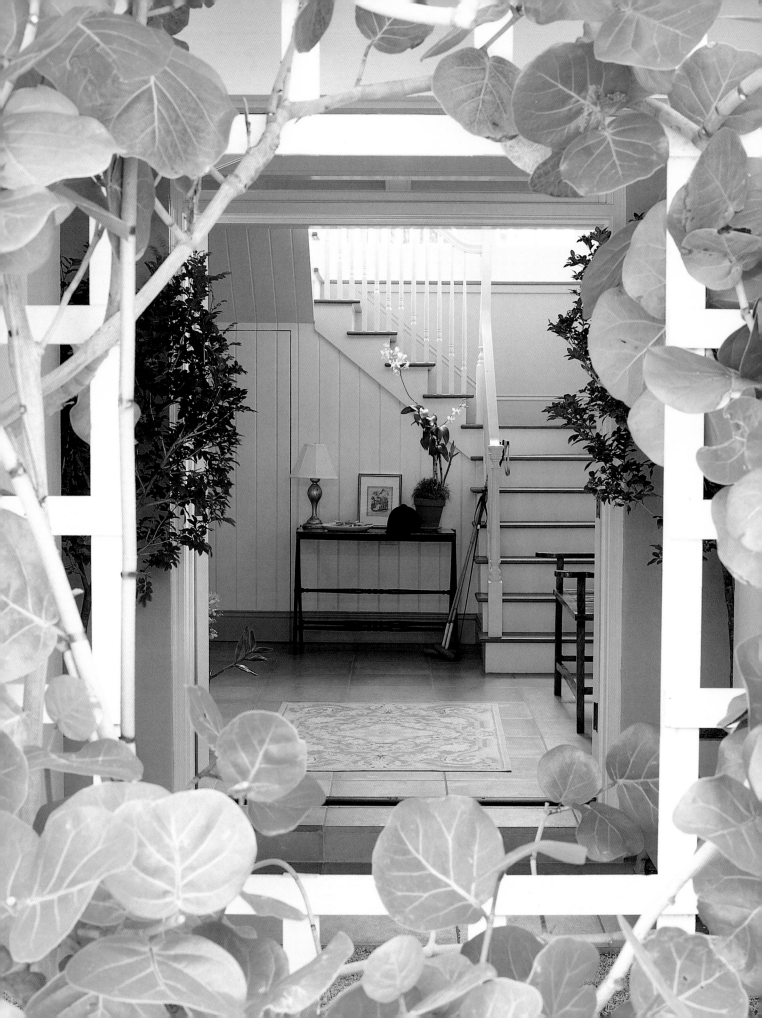

The overall planning of Windsor was conceived by Duany Plater-Syberk & Co, who not only designed the layout of the narrow streets, services and so forth, but also laid down firm general architectural rules, including the choice of building materials (stucco, clapboard, shingles) and where each house should be sited within its plot (built up to the street line and with a long balcony or porch on the street side). They also drew up specifications for a choice of several different architectural styles, including one known as 'Sideyard', which traditionally has the garden at the side, overlooked by a veranda. The all-round effect at Windsor is charming – pretty in the best sense of the word, human in scale and totally suited to Florida holiday life.

Many of the houses built at Windsor have been designed by the architect Clemens Bruns Schaub, who was responsible for the guest house shown here. Attached to one of several houses built near the beach beyond the central village, it follows the Sideyard house style, with two storeys, a full-length balcony and, significantly, an interior courtyard. For Clemens Bruns Schaub, this last element was almost the most interesting part of the project. 'It's what makes these houses successful. In the heat and humidity of Florida, a courtyard gives a sense of repose and becomes a focus.' It becomes, in fact, a cooling outdoor room – essential for hot climates, as architects have known since the days of Pompeii.

Unlike most houses, which function from the inside out, this house works in reverse – the garden suggests the style of the interior. The ground-floor sitting room opens to the light and air on three sides, so that the wall of green trellis and the sound of water from the fountain in the courtyard are part of the room. Inside, the house is deceptively simple. There is no full-scale kitchen: instead, in the living room, Clemens Bruns designed a piece of furniture which looks like a cupboard or bureau but opens to reveal an instant kitchen with, on top, a bar sink, coffee-maker and microwave oven; and, below, hidden in a chest, a refrigerator.

Architecture aside, the house posed a decorative conundrum: the client craved Swedish decoration with its cool, northern colours and textures. But how would these work in the unforgiving southern sun? The answer is immediately evident: these colours (soft 'antique' whites, grey-blue, grey-rose, grey-green) – so remote from typical Florida citrus groves – are restful and calming, not gloomy and louring. On floors of grey-blue cast concrete, white-painted furniture, much of it Swedish reproduced from traditional designs, is juxtaposed with darker pieces.

The interior decorator Susan Schuyler Smith, a veteran of many Florida houses and responsible for this house, says that it was designed to be a 'little Swedish jewel – everything we did relates to Swedish style and design.' Upstairs and downstairs the walls are painted in Swedish-

OPPOSITE A Chinese needlepoint rug adds colour and texture to the grey-blue, cast-concrete floor in the hall, seen here through plant-entwined trellis.

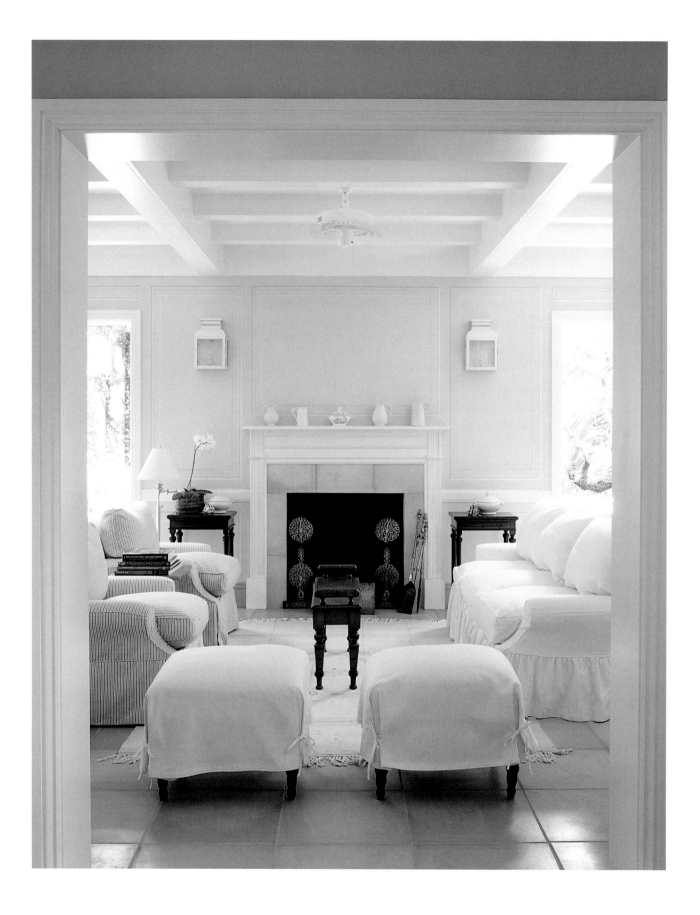

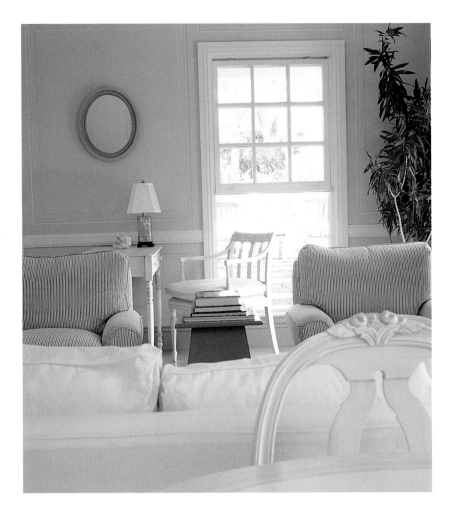

style trompe l'œil panelling. The upstairs floors are of ash which again has been stained in grey tones. 'It may sound drab,' says Susan Smith, 'but used with blues and greens, it is very refreshing.'

Climbing the stairs to the upper floor, you come upon one of the joys of the house – the 'sunset balcony' off the half landing. Here, at the appropriate hour, you can sit, cool drink in hand, and watch the sun sinking over what Floridians call a 'hammock of oak and palm trees'. Upstairs, on the main landing, is a sitting area stacked full of books, videos, drinks and all the other necessities of holiday life on the odd grey day. The two bedrooms open off this area.

The owner had very definite views about these bedrooms, particularly that they should be small enough to retain a sense of intimacy, while not becoming impractically cramped. Architecturally, each room is rather Caribbean in feeling – the ceilings are high, raftered and boarded. Superimposed on to this, the Swedish-style decoration is simple, traditional and effective – like the lightly caught transparent swag of material at the window of the 'white' bedroom. In the 'red' bedroom, the

OPPOSITE AND ABOVE In the combined sitting room and dining room, ivory-white cotton is used for the sofa and stools, while narrow-striped upholstery on the armchairs subtly injects pattern. The dining table and chairs are Scandinavian in style.

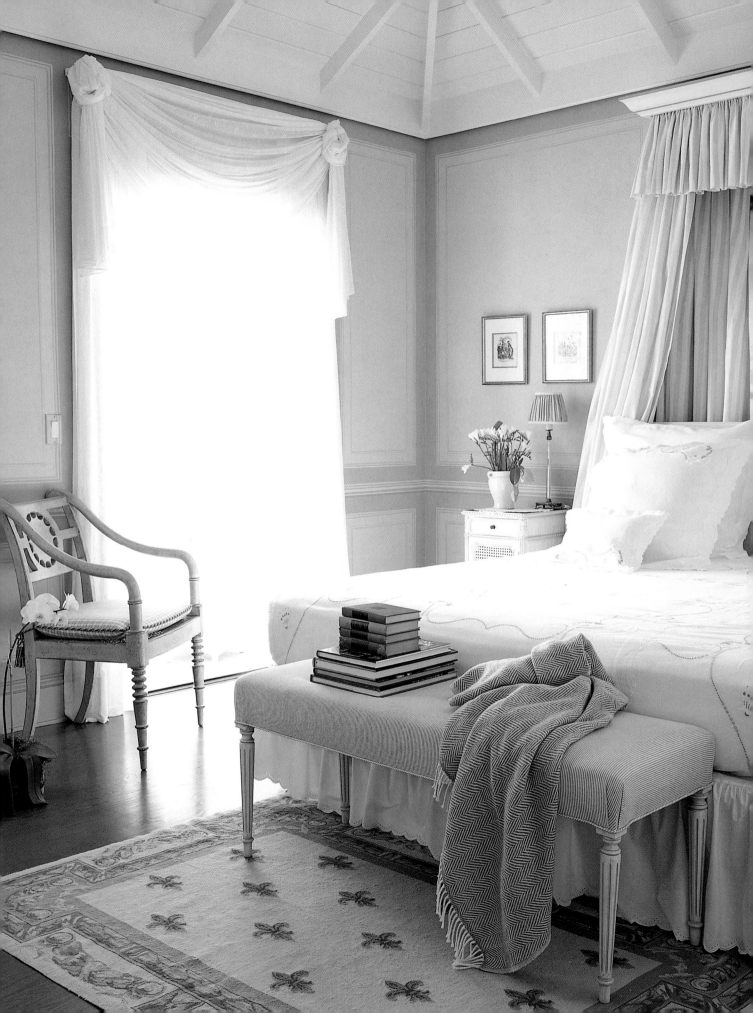

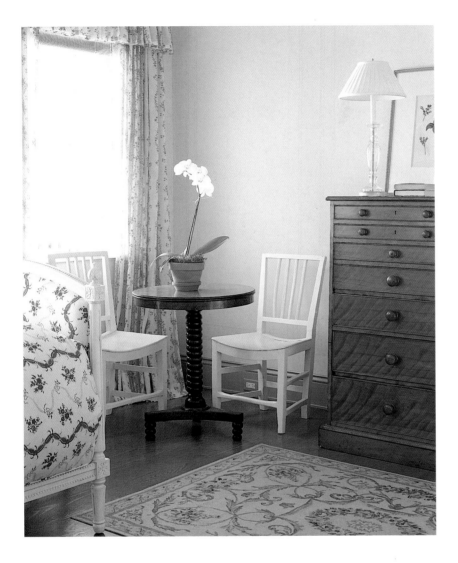

scheme is based around the red-and-white printed voile at the window.

Both rooms open on to the most important part of the building – the deep, cantilevered, sea-facing porch which stretches the length of the house and acts as its focus. This is another of the architectural requirements for Windsor and one which Clemens Bruns found especially appealing as he is passionate about verandas: 'I think they should be deep enough to use properly – big enough to sit around and talk in.'

In this tiny house, the contributions of client, architect and decorator combine to demonstrate an understanding of the strength of traditional island architecture – wooden houses with long, cool verandas and shady corners. And, although to graft a defiantly northern decorative style on to tropical architecture may at first seem a strange idea, the result – open windows, unlined curtains billowing in the breeze, and cool, airy rooms with a smattering of simple furniture – is very successful and one that every owner of a house in the sun would appreciate.

ABOVE In the 'red' bedroom, the Gustavian beds are upholstered in a floral cotton print; the curtains are of printed voile.
OPPOSITE Swagged curtains filter the light in the 'white' bedroom, where the 'panelled' walls are outlined in pale-grey. The rug is Chinese needlepoint.

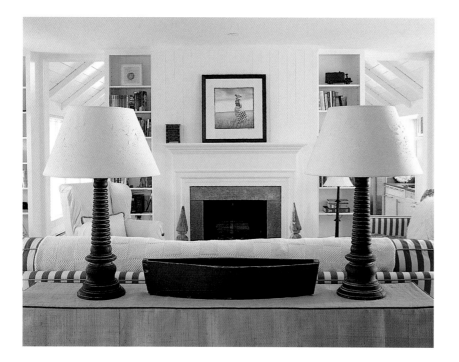

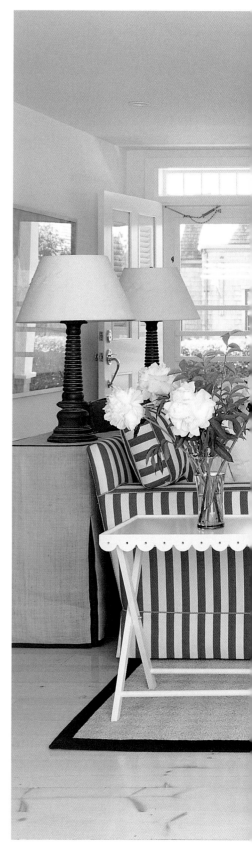

Dressed for summer

Crescent-moon shaped, and only twenty-five miles long, the American island of Nantucket looks in one direction towards the state of Massachusetts and Cape Cod; in the other, across the Atlantic towards Portugal and the rest of Europe. A two-hour ferry ride from the mainland, the island was named by its original American-Indian settlers 'Nantockete', meaning 'the far-off place', and was a whaling station long before Melville immortalized its hardy inhabitants in *Moby Dick*. Few trees rise from the sandy soil, but the wild roses grow sturdily, despite impenetrable fogs and buffeting winds, and the wildlife flourishes.

The pretty, 'tamed' scene conjured by Constanze von Unruh for herself and her family is in high contrast to its rugged, island surroundings. This small, wood-shingled cottage is the charming destination for the annual Christmas and summer holiday commute which Constanze, her husband Mark and her two children Anouchka (thirteen) and Julius (ten)

ABOVE The central chimneybreast in the sitting room is faced with matchboarding. Resting on the mantelshelf is a photograph by American photographer Laura Wilson.
RIGHT The striped covers on the sofas are used during the summer; in winter, the room is re-dressed with thick linens in deep forest greens, brown wool and leather.

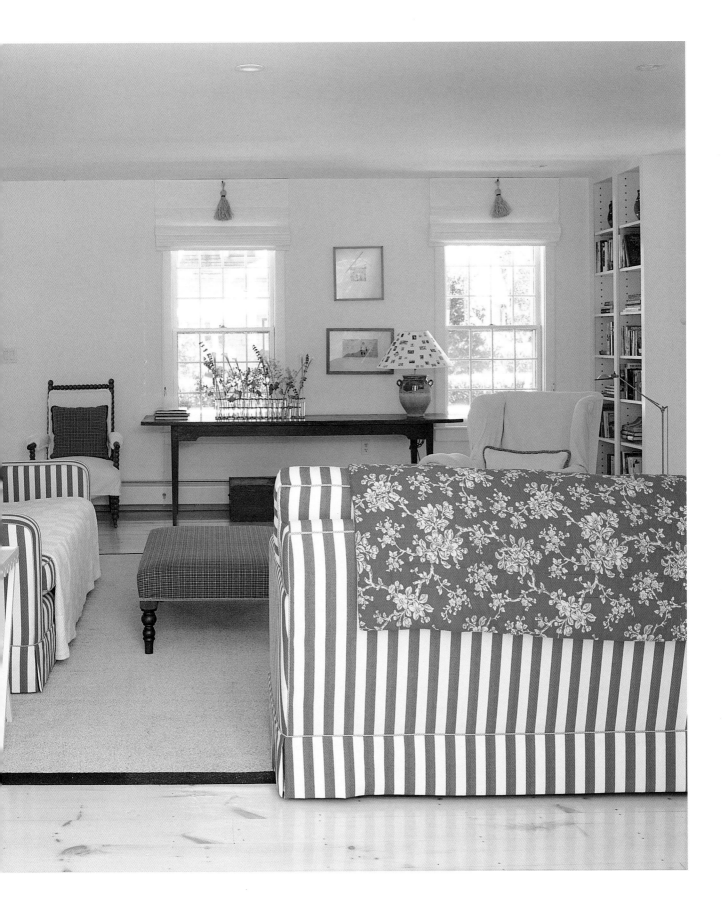

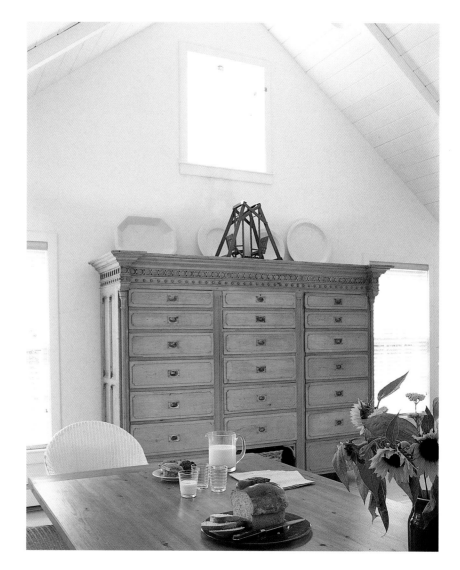

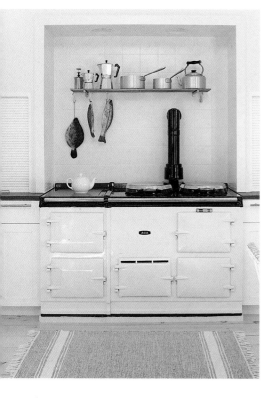

ABOVE AND ABOVE RIGHT The kitchen, with imported Aga, has a handsome, antique store cupboard also brought from England to Nantucket.
OPPOSITE Julius's bedroom is decorated in red, white and blue; the window treatment – a flat, cotton blind – is suitably plain for a boy's room.

make from their imposing Victorian house in London.

When the von Unruhs found their Nantucket house more than four years ago, it was only seven years old and, Constanze felt, without character – it had to be 'dressed and organized'. Constanze had worked with the London-based design company MC² for over a year, but this was to be her first solo job as an interior designer for her company, Constanze Interior Projects.

She enlisted the help of Boston architect Robert Paladino. Her main concern was space: she wanted a house that would expand and contract to accommodate any number of people from one to ten. Her aim was to create 'a house with a large living area for everyone to meet, and lots of private areas in which to withdraw, cuddle up, rest.' Working within the constraints of a two-bedroom, two-bathroom house, she created five bedrooms and four bathrooms by claiming attic space. The only exten-

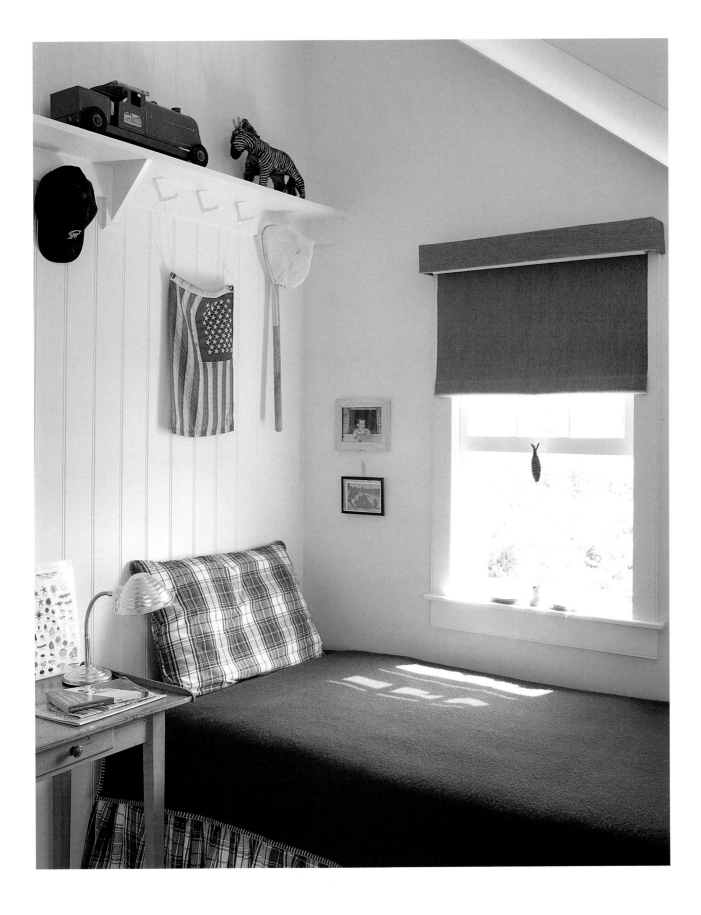

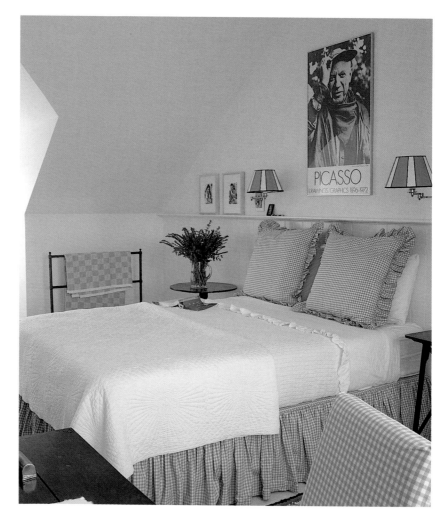

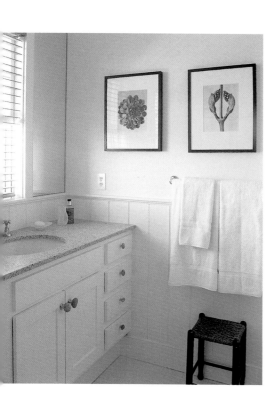

ABOVE *Thirties photogravures by German photographer Blossfeldt decorate the walls in the bathroom.*
ABOVE RIGHT *The main bedroom is a charming ensemble in blue and white. The small-scale check strikes just the right note of informality for a holiday house.*

sion came when the garage was utilized for the kitchen and the back wall was pushed out slightly.

The success of the free-flowing 'public' area on the ground floor owes a great deal to Constanze's strict and simple Shaker-inspired design. The original design had no chimney, but there is now one at the heart of the house. On one side of it stands an Aga; on the other an open fireplace. Shuttered cupboards flank the stove; open bookshelves flank the fireplace. Passageways to either side of the chimney link the sitting room and kitchen, creating a sense of balanced symmetry and movement. Throughout the house, similar mini-corridors partitioned off the rooms create transitional space and provide privacy by separating living and passage areas.

Added to the exterior, a wide, traditional front porch serves to anchor the small, boxy house within a vernacular framework. When it came to interior decoration, the notion of the beach – its colours and textures – dominated Constanze's 'dressing' of the house. Echoing the colours and

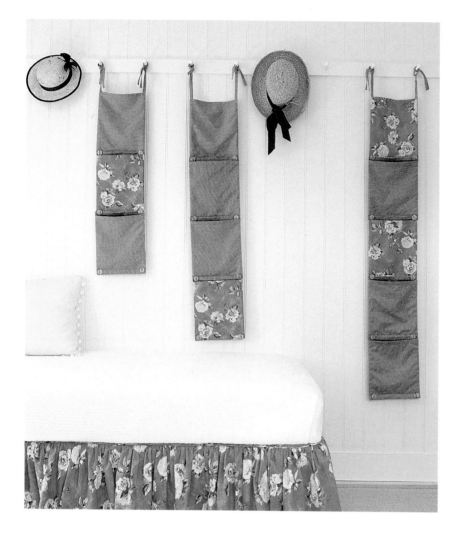

textures of the shoreline, there are off-white and grey-green shades in cottons and linens, raffia, pickled-pine floorboards, white enamel and silvery stainless steel, pebbles as drawer pulls, and granite honed to beach-stone smoothness. To offset this coolness in the freezing Nan-tuck-et winter, Constanze re-dresses the room to suit the season: she uses a combination of thick linens in deep forest greens, brown wool, leather and long-hair Mongolian lamb to make up slip covers and cushions for the warm and comforting winter wardrobe.

Back in London, if you ask Constanze's children how they feel about their house in Nantucket, they describe the rocking chairs on the porch, picnics on the beach and the numerous decorative details in their bedrooms. They talk about 'cosy' feelings, of the colours of the bedcovers, the patterns on the easy chairs, and of the space carved out of the small rooms – the neat places provided for important paraphernalia like hairbrushes and bands, binoculars and crabbing nets. There can't be many interior designers who have such appreciative clients.

ABOVE Practical, pretty storage bags are hung Shaker-style from wooden wall-pegs in Anouchka's bedroom.

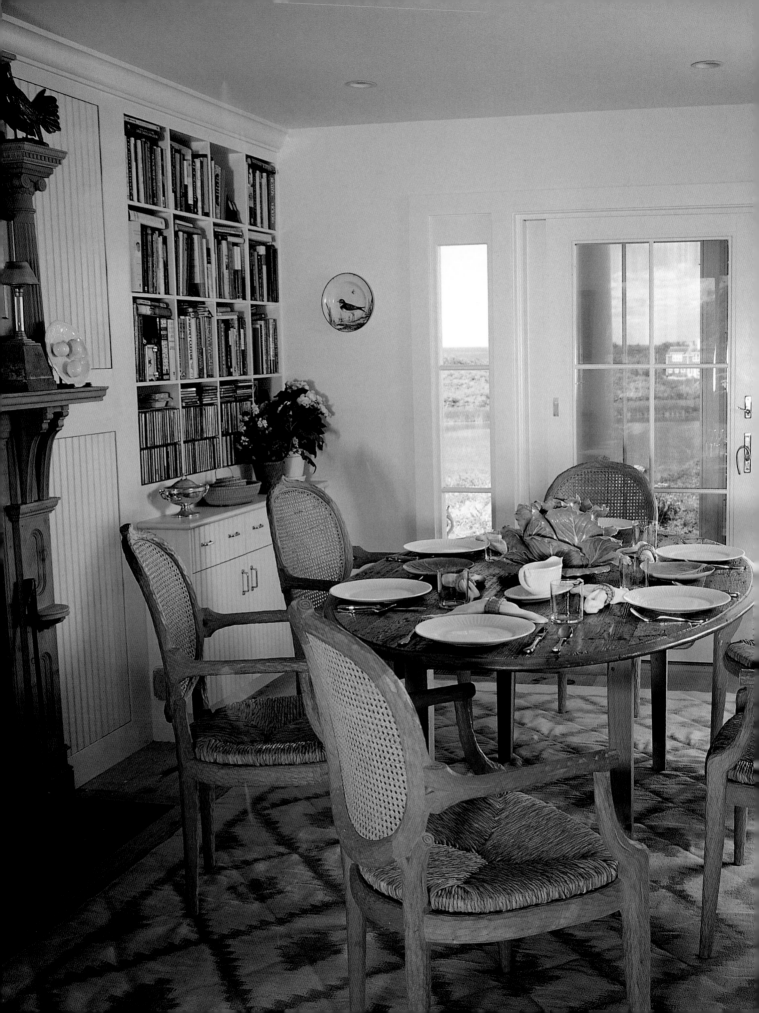

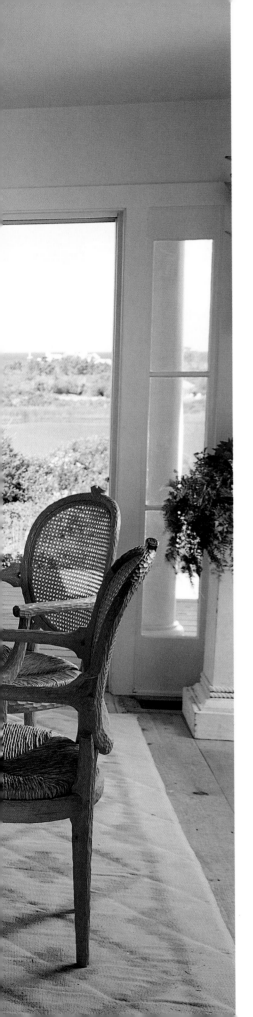

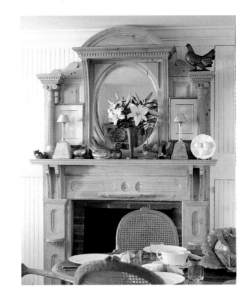

The sea, the stars...

Four years ago, American antiques dealer and decorator Geo Davis built his house on a Nantucket hill top, above that part of the island where the original harbour once stood. Earlier inhabitants had deserted the area after a storm in 1777: they picked up their houses – literally – and moved inland, away from the fury of the sea. But for Geo the changing tempers of the omnipresent sea, the bright stars and the sunsets reflected in the neighbouring pond are what this house is all about. Listen to him describe the views, the wind and the wildlife, and you, too, will feel a compelling need to drop everything and go at once to Nantucket.

Geo designed the house himself: 'The best thing about doing it yourself is that the house can be exactly what you want it to be. I had to decide whether to make it a summer house or an all-year-round house, and how many guests I might want to accommodate. Eventually, I opted for three bedrooms, with one on the ground floor with its own entrance in case I get decrepit in old age'.

The house is compact: in addition to the three bedrooms, there is a dining-cum-library area leading from the hall, a sitting room and a sun room in which Geo can sit in all seasons, reading and looking at the land-

LEFT AND ABOVE The fireplace in the dining-room-cum-library is surmounted by a chimneypiece which Geo Davis found in Portobello Road in London. It holds his collection of silver-plated chickens and is topped with a zinc pigeon.

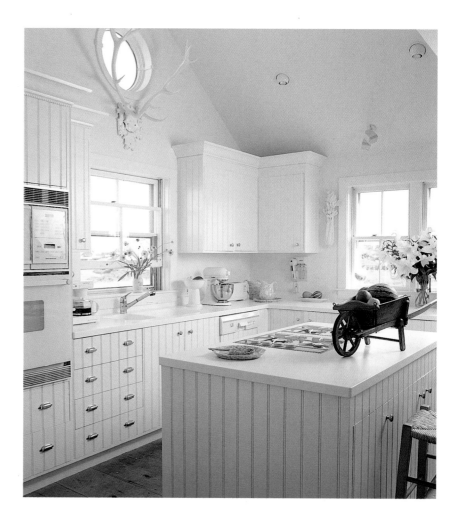

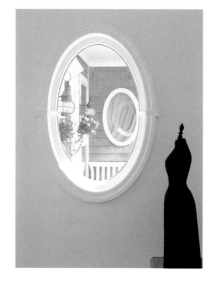

ABOVE *A miniature, French, fashion mannequin stands in the hall.*
ABOVE RIGHT AND OPPOSITE *The matchboarded kitchen has a 'mud room' opening off it. Salvaged columns are placed to either side of the doorway, creating a wittily grand entrance to a utilitarian space.*

scape. 'I never draw the curtains, there's always so much to see – the bird life, the occasional deer, the changing water; even, perhaps, at sunset, the legendary green flash as the sun drops into the ocean.' And around everything, always, is the light – cool and clear.

Indeed, light is everything in this house. The rooms have been planned around it. 'The house faces north. I put the kitchen, the bathroom and the landing all on the north-east side so that they face east for maximum light.' The quality of this clear, cold light has also influenced the way he used colour in the house. 'When I see pictures of Swedish interiors, I empathize with the Swedish sensibility; I understand why they use the colours they do. I use creams, whites and beiges because I like the sea and the landscape to penetrate and permeate everything – not to be outshone by the colour inside. People associate white with the cold but it shouldn't be thought of like that. After all, one speaks of white sand, white snow, white horses, all of which encompass warm shades.' These are relaxing, clean but unclinical tones and they all work together. 'Whenever I want to bring more colour into my rooms, I do it with candles and

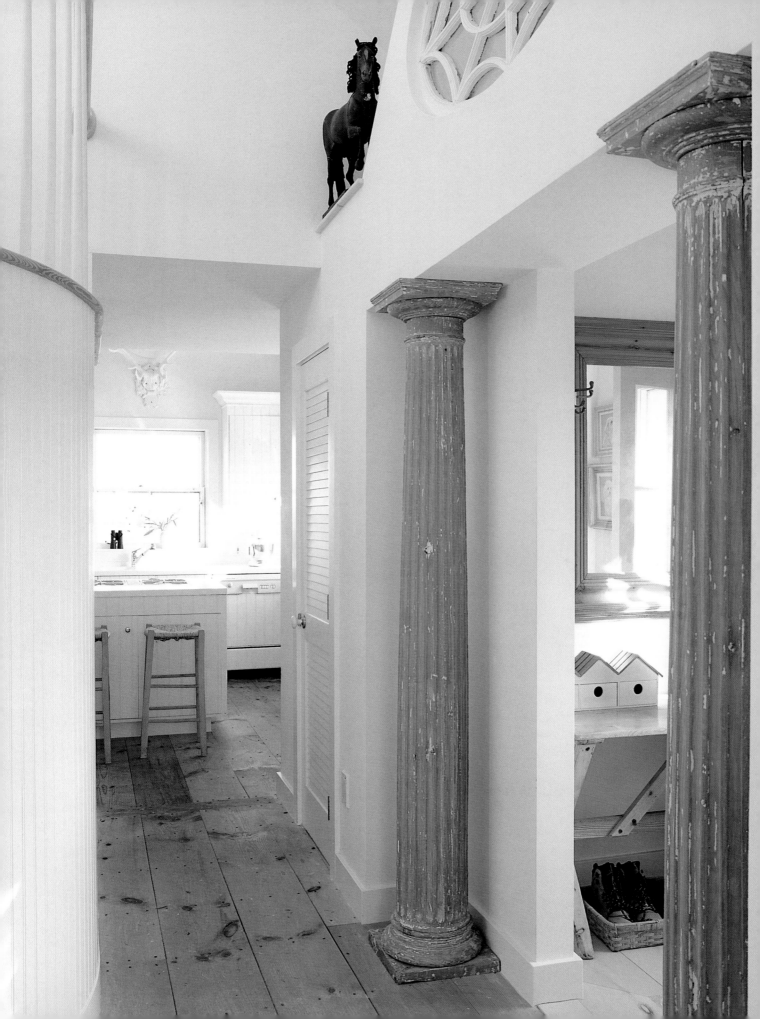

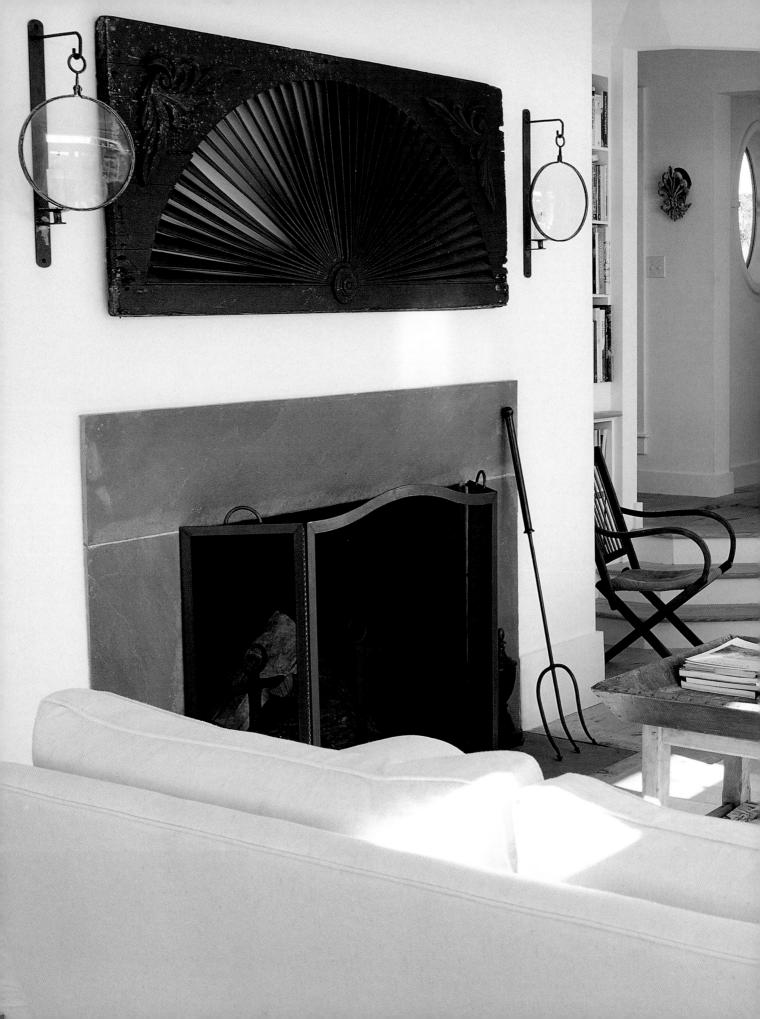

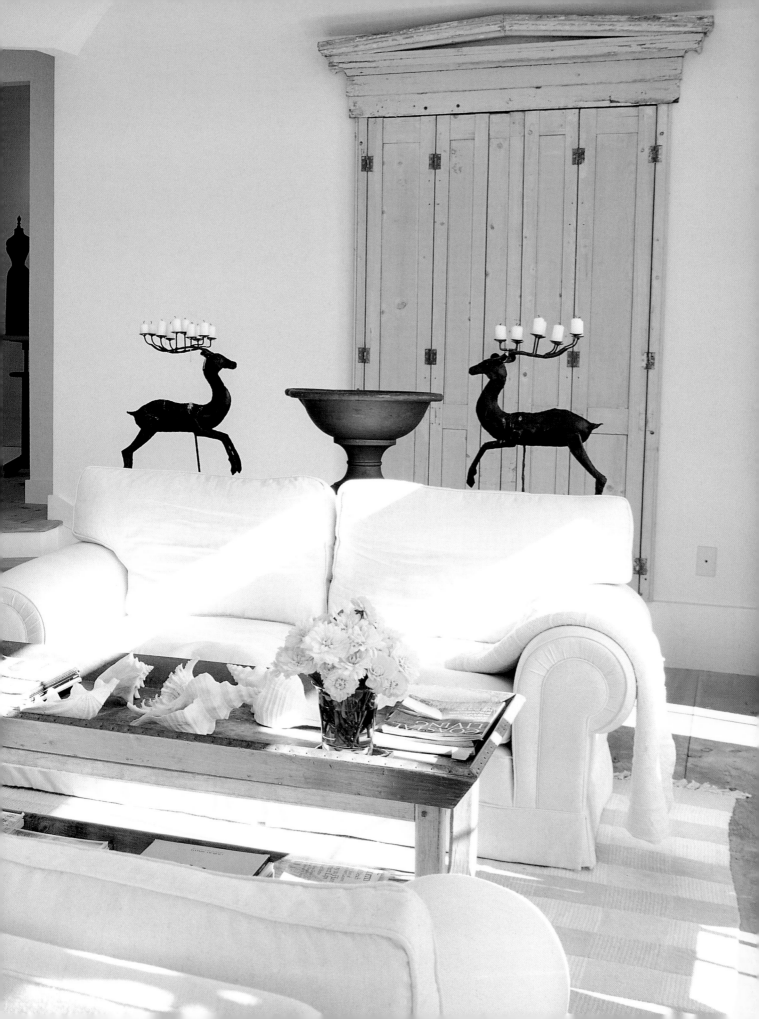

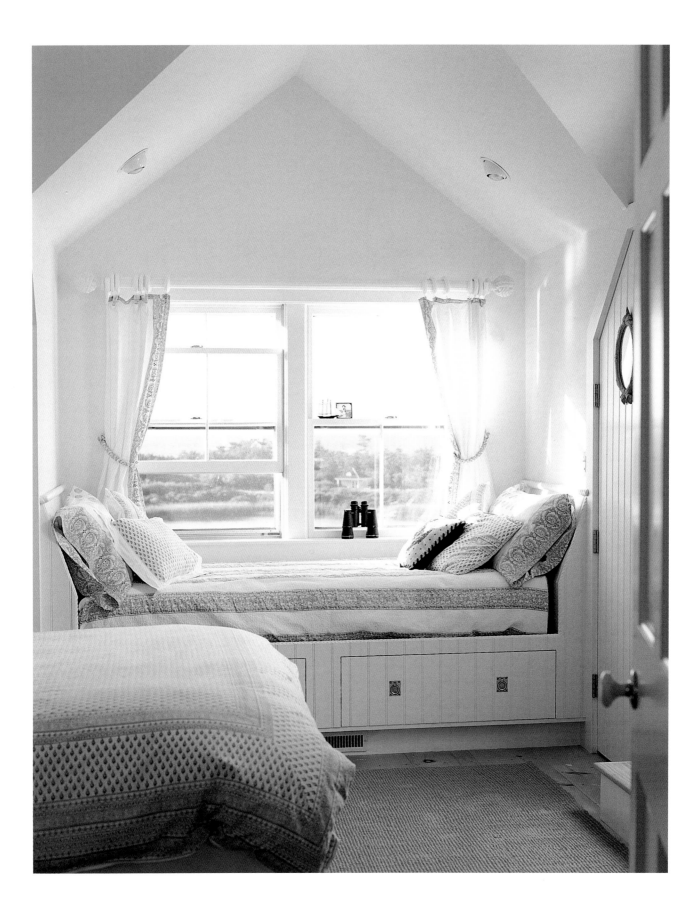

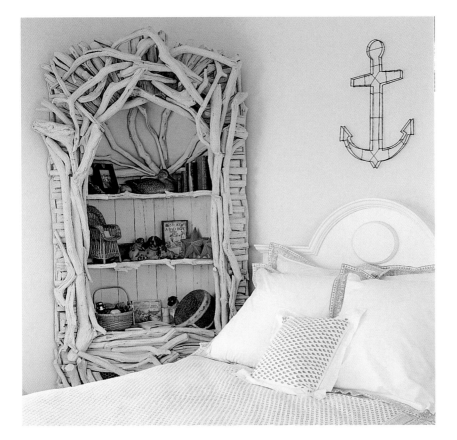

flowers.' This philosophy is demonstrated in the sun room, in which the cushions and throws are changed with the season – pale, striped linens in the summer give way to silk-velvet animal prints in the winter.

The sea and memories of the sea are foremost throughout the house. One of the bedrooms is designed along nautical lines, with a built-in 'ship's' bed with drawers underneath. Above another bed is an openwork metal anchor – a frame for a sailor's memorial wreath. Everywhere are nautical mementos and model boats from Geo's several collections.

That Geo Davis is a natural collector seems only right for a man whose successful Nantucket shop, Weeds, sells the sort of things we all like to buy – French and English country antiques, pretty, collectable trinkets and, unusually, his own white china, designed by him and made in England by Wedgwood. Called, naturally, 'Nantucket', it was based on a traditional Nantucket ship basket.

An added source of warmth in the house comes from an abundance of pale-honey pine furniture, including a fine, oversized chimneypiece which Geo Davis found in London in the Portobello Road. It was in two pieces on the floor when Geo Davis first spotted it, but it 'looked as if it might – possibly – fit around the fireplace in the dining room'. Even with the Atlantic between him and the fireplace in question, Geo Davis's eye

PREVIOUS PAGE The unusual, decorative objects in the sun room include reindeer-shaped candle holders and, on the chimneybreast, a wooden panel from above a door. French-window shutters and a pediment from a local house conceal a music system.

OPPOSITE AND ABOVE In addition to a divan bed, this room has a 'ship's' bed placed across the window bay to take advantage of the view. An openwork metal anchor, originally used as a memorial wreath for a sailor, hangs to the right of a twiggy cabinet by Norman Kemp. The idiosyncratic array of objects on the shelves is harmonized by their warm, natural colours.

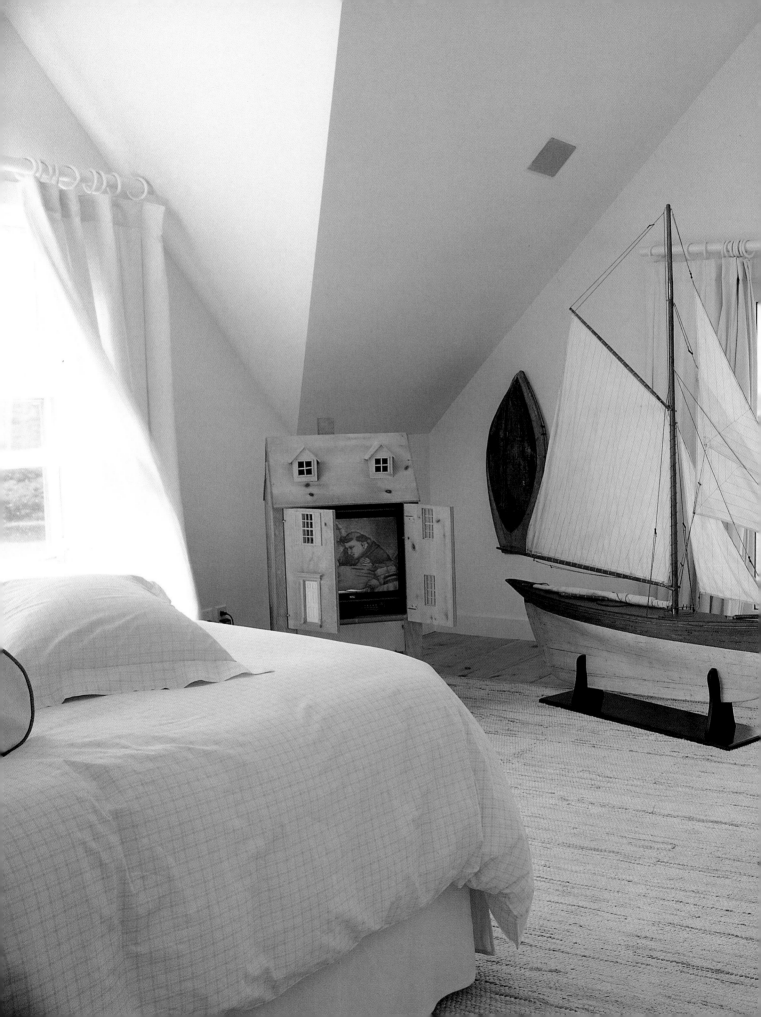

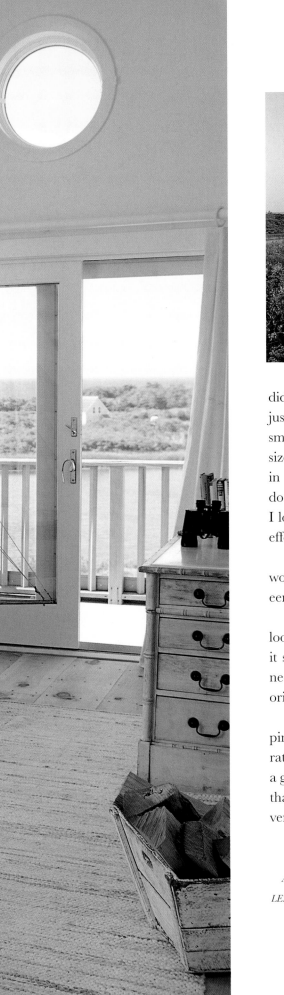

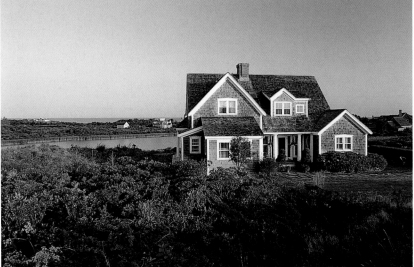

did not deceive him; the chimneypiece did fit – just – with its arched top just skimming the ceiling. Indeed, subscribing to the decorative rule that small spaces are enhanced by large furniture, Geo has used other over-sized pieces throughout the house, notably a soaring faux-pine cupboard in the sun room, and a pair of dramatic wooden columns framing a doorway. 'In too many houses everything seems to be waist high and flat. I love height – even in a small house like this one. I also love sculptural effects – hence the columns, staircase and even the niches.'

As well as pine furniture there are pine floors, pale and matt. 'I like wooden floors to be natural – unsealed and unwaxed. As in the eighteenth century, they are merely scrubbed and left to weather.

Pine in Geo Davis's eyes is generally appealing: 'I like its dried, dusty look. When it was popular in the Eighties, it was too often put in houses it shouldn't have been in, but for a beach house it's ideal: it's soft and needs little looking after. It shouldn't really be called "stripped pine" as, originally, much of it wasn't painted. It was meant for casual living.'

And when you look round the light, welcoming house, not only the pine pieces, but also the white-painted twig corner cupboard, the elabo-rate, white-plaster sconce and even the candle-bearing reindeer found in a garden catalogue, have the slightly smug air of possessions which know that someone is fond of them and that they have all come together in very much the right place.

ABOVE The house looks out over the island's original harbour towards Nantucket Sound.
LEFT Model boats form part of Geo Davis's large collection of original pieces. The model of
a Nantucket house conceals a television. The rag rug was made on the island.

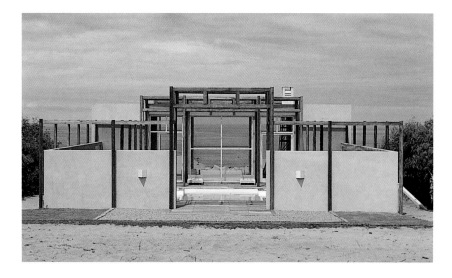

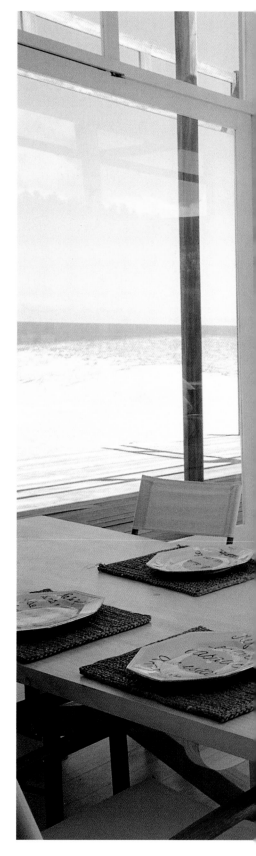

Open to the beach

A shapely limb, extended as if to test the Atlantic waters, Punta del Este enjoys the spoils of being one of South America's most exclusive, fashionable resorts. The Uruguayan peninsula's main street, a flickering collage of neon lights and plastic signs, is the Vegas strip of the southern hemisphere, while its environs seem to house over half the country's restaurants, offering exquisite food at vast prices. For those who long to see and be seen, it is a theatrical wonderland; for those who have watched the play too many times, it is a paradise without peace.

Just a few miles along the coast, however, the beaches lie empty and unruffled, with only the wash and backwash of the ocean rhythmically clocking the sun-bleached hours. Here, facing the Atlantic in a clearing where two crescents of eucalyptus trees converge, stands a spectacular beach house designed by architect Pachi Firpo.

The owners live not far from the beach, but wanted a comfortable, seaside annexe for summer lunches and swimming with friends. This, and this alone, was their brief to the architect; within it, he was free to

ABOVE Seen from this aspect, the symmetrical design of the building leads the eye beyond the pool to what seems to be a single wall of glass overlooking the Atlantic. In fact, there are two walls of glass; sandwiched between them is a pavilion with an open-plan room combining sitting and dining areas and a kitchen.

RIGHT The interior of the pavilion is furnished sparely, with white canvas used for all the seating. At the opposite end from the kitchen/dining area is a simple, modern fireplace.

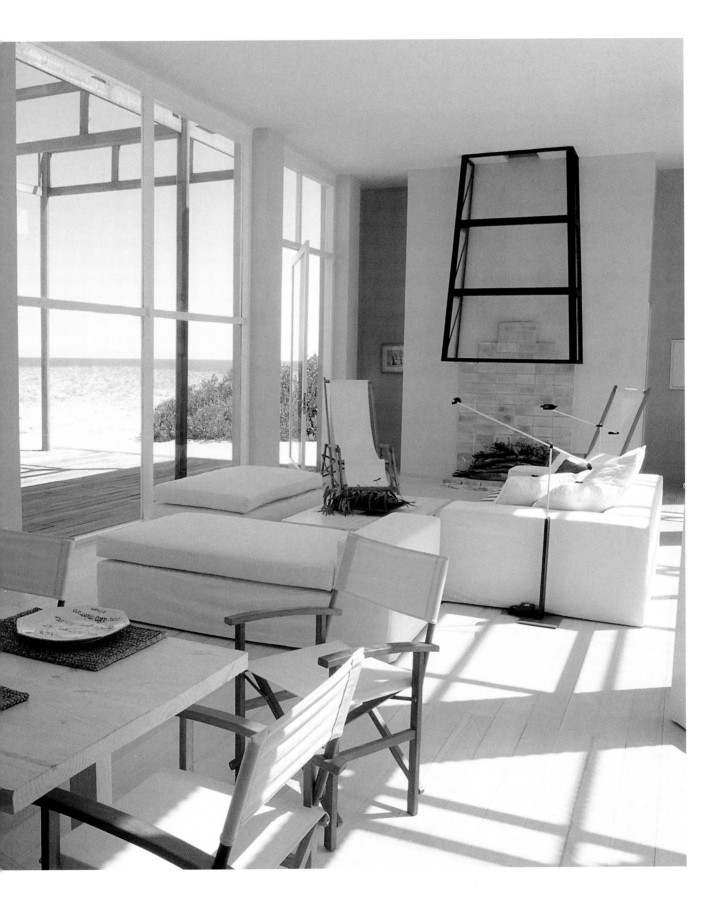

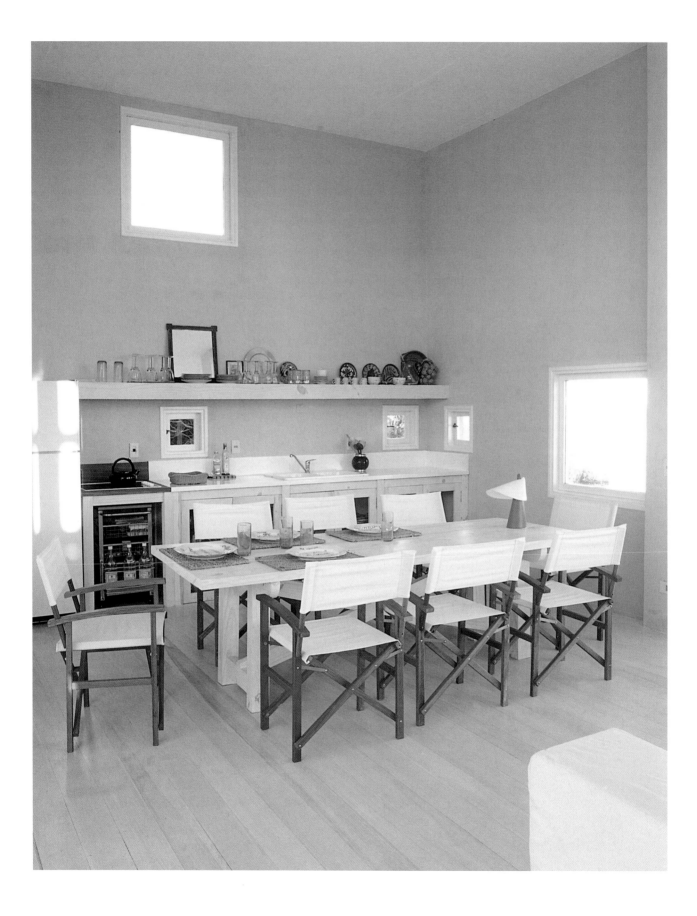

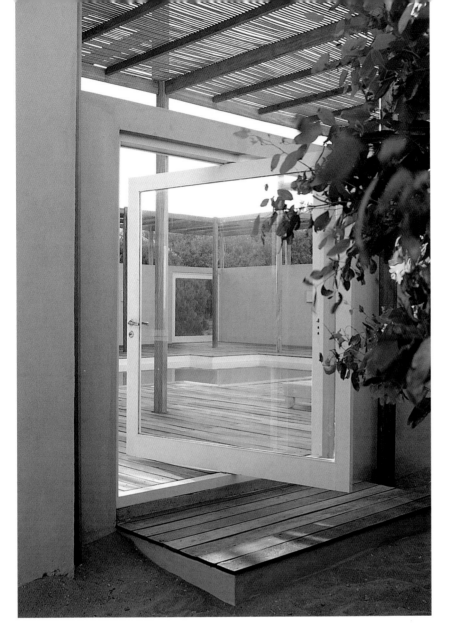

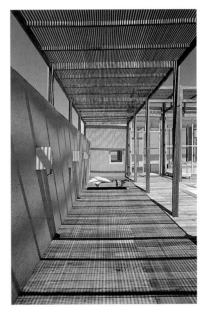

stretch his imagination and exercise his technical virtuosity. The result is an architectural 'lens' which focuses the eye on the unencumbered land-scape and the vast sapphire of the ocean beyond.

The tall, symmetrical, one-storey structure comprises front terrace, open-plan living-dining-kitchen pavilion, and, behind, a swimming pool. The pool is surrounded on three sides by brick walls lined with sandy-toned render, pierced at irregular intervals by windows; these windows frame the landscape in natural vignettes, which flourish and wither with the seasons. Around the inner perimeter of the walls runs a cloister of tough, dark Paraguayan hardwood (*curupay*) canopied with bamboo; in the full glare of the sun, it casts vibrant, zebra-like stripes on the decking – again *curupay* – which runs to the edge of the cross-shaped pool. The inspiration for this semi-covered area was, says Pachi, the impluvium of classical Roman times, the opening in the roof of the atrium at the social centre of the town house or villa.

ABOVE LEFT AND ABOVE Decking and a bamboo-covered cloister surround the cross-shaped pool. The lining of the pool is painted white but the water, reflecting the pure colour of the sky, appears blue. In each corner, large glazed doors lead straight to the beach.
OPPOSITE Director's chairs surround the table in the kitchen / dining area. In order not to appear too intrusive, the kitchen units are low: there are no wall cupboards, only a single shelf across the width of the room.

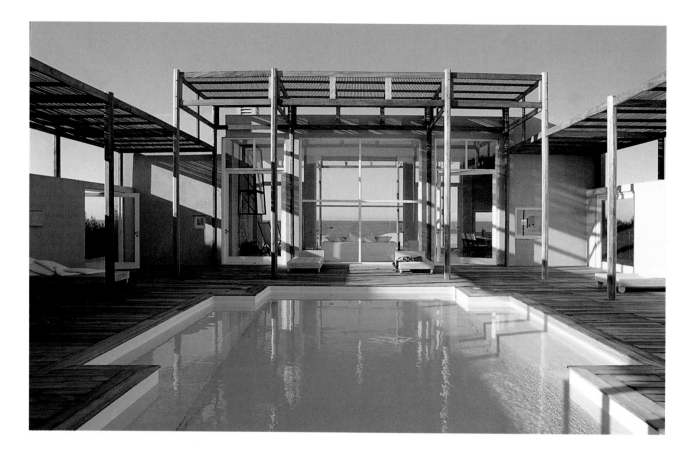

ABOVE The cloister framework around the pool creates a skeletal geometry. Seen between the pool and beach is the seating area in the glass-walled pavilion. OPPOSITE A Turkish kilim and green-and-white canvas on the sofa bring dashes of colour to the seating area.

Pachi's latter-day, South-American atrium leads to the pavilion itself. Contained within glass walls lies an interior of comfortable, luminous simplicity – the result of a close understanding between architect and Argentinian interior designer Laura Ocampo. Here, again, tactile, natural materials tell a cool, eloquent story. Between a fireplace, with a metal and glass mantel, at one end, and glazed, wooden kitchen cabinets at the other, stretch limed floorboards which look as though they have been bleached by the salty air and insistent light.

The open space is divided into a dining area with a pine table and a set of white canvas director's chairs, and a living area with a sofa, day-bed and ottoman, all covered in canvas. Tucked behind the fireplace wall is a bathroom with a marble floor and a shower with views towards the waves. Glass doors open from the pavilion on to a terrace surrounded by a pergola, which extends into the sand with, beyond, the Atlantic.

The front and back walls of the pavilion are pierced with floor-to-ceiling, square windows. As you approach the beach house from the back of the swimming pool, these windows line up and blend into one opening, dissolving the space within the pavilion and creating what resembles a huge telescopic sight focused upon the southern horizon where the ocean swell meets the sky.

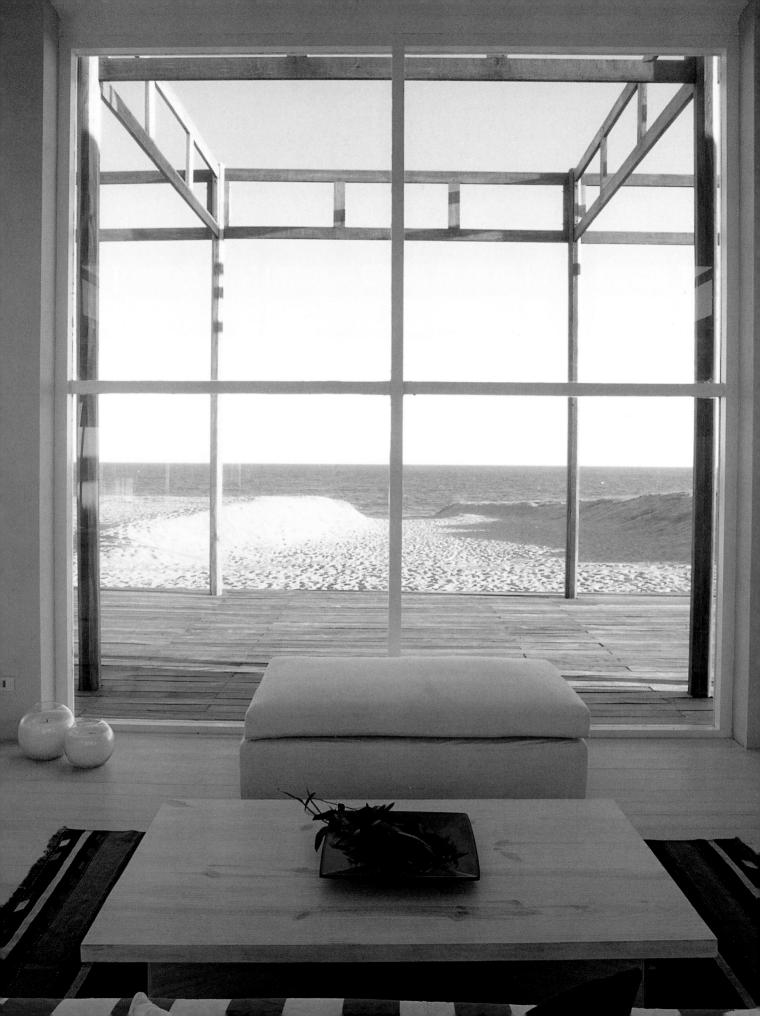

Bringing in the light

When a full moon rises on the ocean's far horizon, this small, three-bed-room house on the island of Nantucket is suffused with pale, silvery light. The moonlight outlines the contours of the Sesachacha Pond that lies on the seaward front of the house and, beyond, the line of tapering dunes which separates the pond from the sand and sea.

Nantucket, on the American east coast, is dubbed the 'old grey lady' because its quaint nineteenth-century brown-shingle cottages turned hoary grey in the briny air. Built ten years ago, in the vernacular, this alluring house, with white-painted woodwork and a traditional picket fence leading up to the main door, sits as contentedly in its surroundings as if it had been there always.

Its joy is twofold: the water is visible from all sides and, because of the many windows, there is no need to use electric lighting even on the gloomiest of days. The brightness is augmented by lashings of white paint on the woodwork throughout, including the treads of the staircase, tongue-and-groove walls, and, in particular, the gallery in the double-height drawing room which is lit by skylights.

'We wanted the decoration to be ultra simple, cut to the bone, not in the least bit grand,' says the owner, an author and columnist for a New

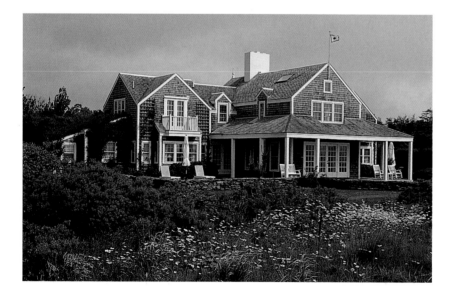

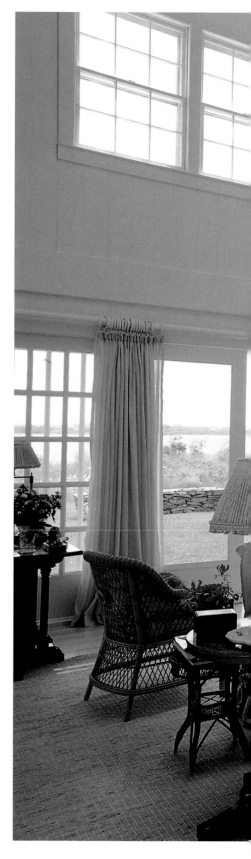

ABOVE Built in the distinctive Nantucket vernacular, the house has weather-greyed shingles, white-painted woodwork and a covered porch.
RIGHT The walls in the double-height drawing room are clad in matchboarding. Irish-linen curtains do not impede the light which saturates the airy interior.

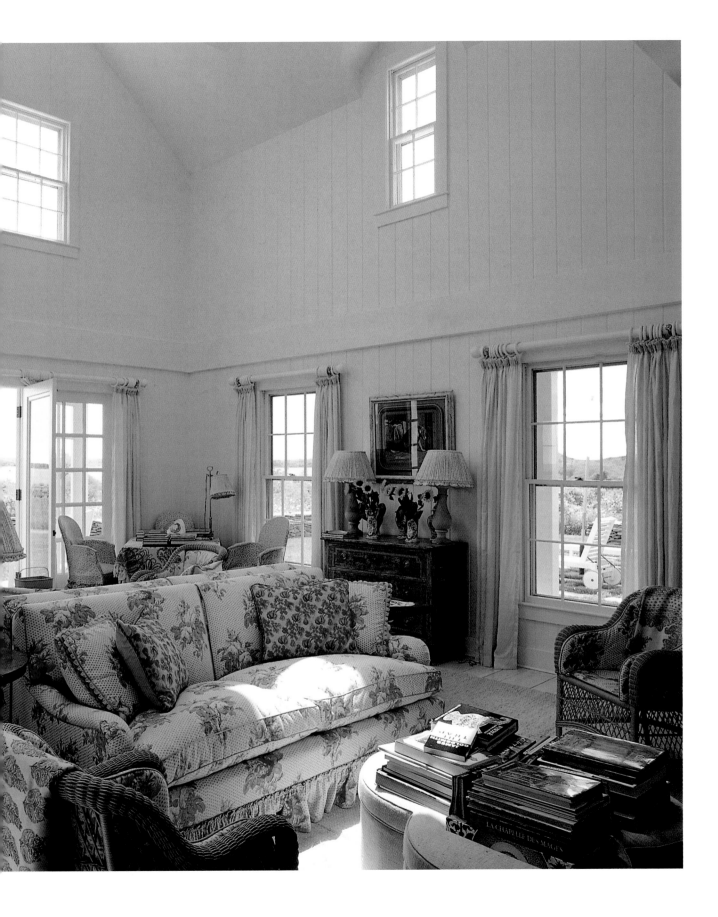

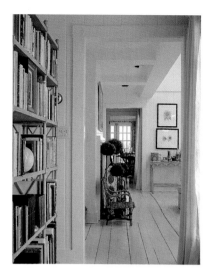

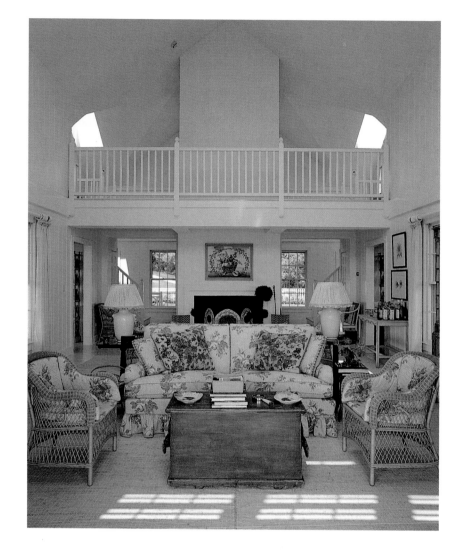

ABOVE The corridor into the drawing room is lined with open bookcases painted fresh green.

RIGHT French matting, dark-wood furniture, wicker chairs and pretty chintz combine happily in the drawing room. Seating is centred on a chest which serves as a coffee table. Needlepoint cushions add an extra note of traditional comfort.

OPPOSITE Tongue-and-groove boarding, white-painted stair treads and a stencilled floor with shamrock motifs imbue the hall with a bright, clean simplicity.

York paper, and retired publisher. 'Nantucket is low-key, laid-back, the reverse of the society merry-go-round in the Hamptons. I come here with my wife for several months in the summer – to potter and be alone.'

Of course, that is not strictly true, since the couple have four grown-up children and six grandchildren who stay nearby in rented houses. 'Our house is a gathering place for the family,' says his wife. 'They come here to swim, to picnic with us, or even stop over for the night.'

Since the owners are great anglophiles, and admire the unpretentiousness of good English decorating, they asked Vivien Greenock of Sibyl Colefax & John Fowler to decorate the house. Having decorated a New York apartment for the same clients, Vivien was familiar with their needs and taste. 'My brief can be summed up very simply,' she says: 'Suitability, simplicity and easy upkeep.' Certainly, the place remains as prettily spick and span as the day she finished it, which is now over a decade ago.

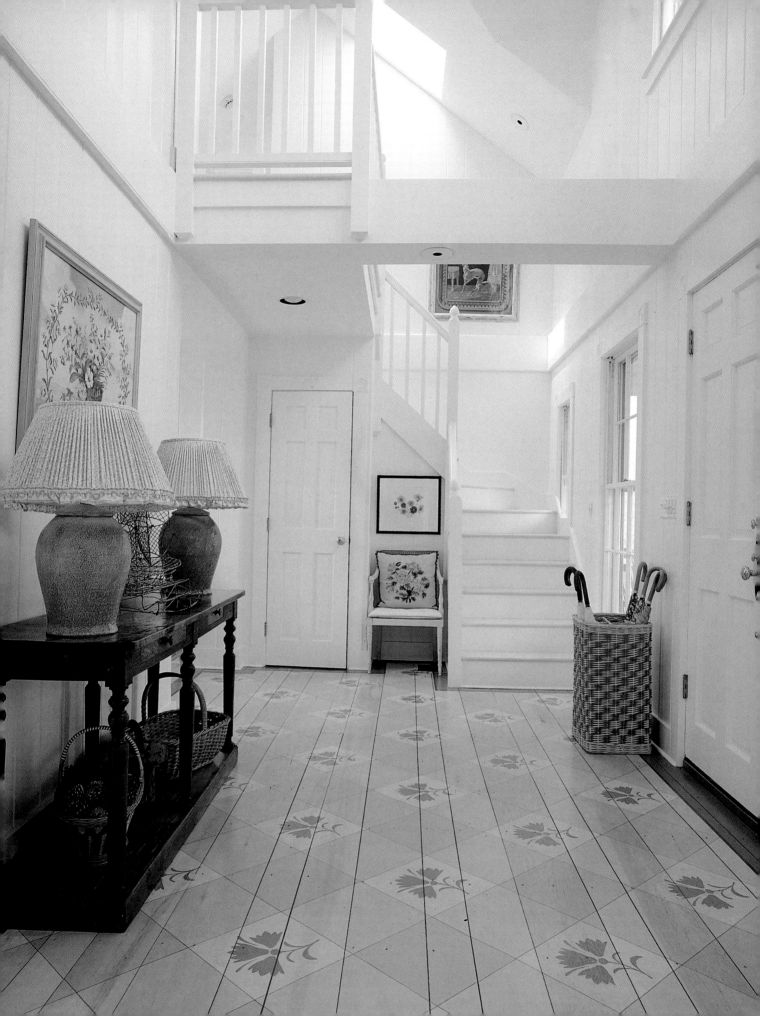

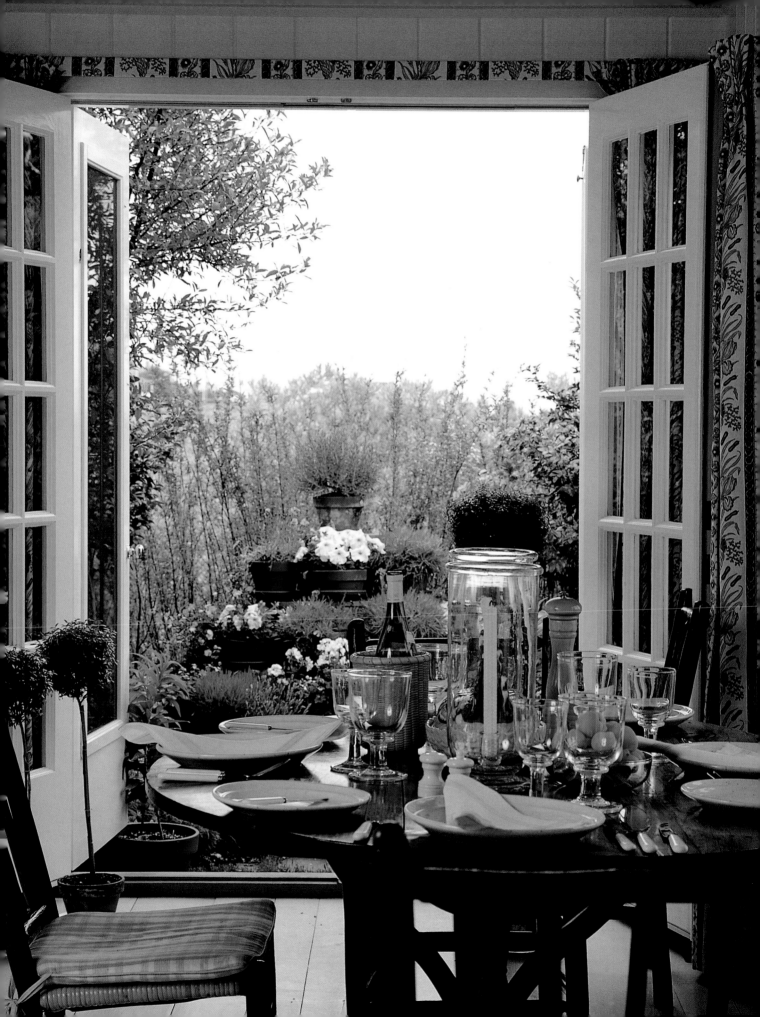

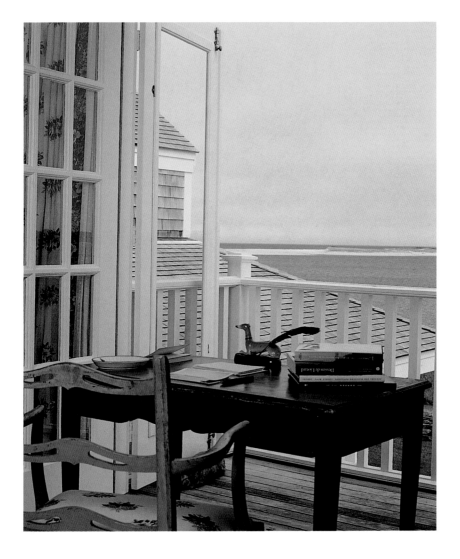

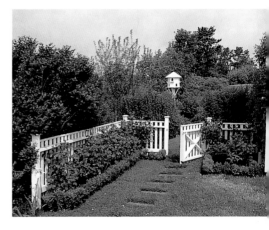

Together, they chose the flowered chintzes on clean white backgrounds for the bedroom curtains: fresh, delicate grey roses with mint-green foliage for the main bedroom; charming but unostentatious floral posies in pink and green in one spare room; fuchsia-laden trellis in the other. Battening the walls with the same chintz makes each room appear both more commodious and cosy – for the evenings here are chilly. Four-poster beds draped in unlined muslin trimmed with white cotton pompoms have a colonial air, which adds a touch of romance.

'Often the fog rolls in within two minutes,' says the owner, 'enveloping everything. I find that romantic, too.' He enjoys the eerie sound of the foghorn, and the sight of the nearby lighthouse flashing signals to the sailing boats and fishermen on the choppy and often icy Atlantic waters. Swimming can be a bracing experience in Nantucket but, undaunted by the fickle weather, devotees of the island return year after year like migrating birds.

ABOVE LEFT A tiny upstairs balcony
overlooks the sea.
ABOVE RIGHT A white-painted picket
fence is lined with rose bushes.
OPPOSITE French windows in the
informal kitchen / dining room open onto
the garden with a tiered staging of plants
in terracotta pots.

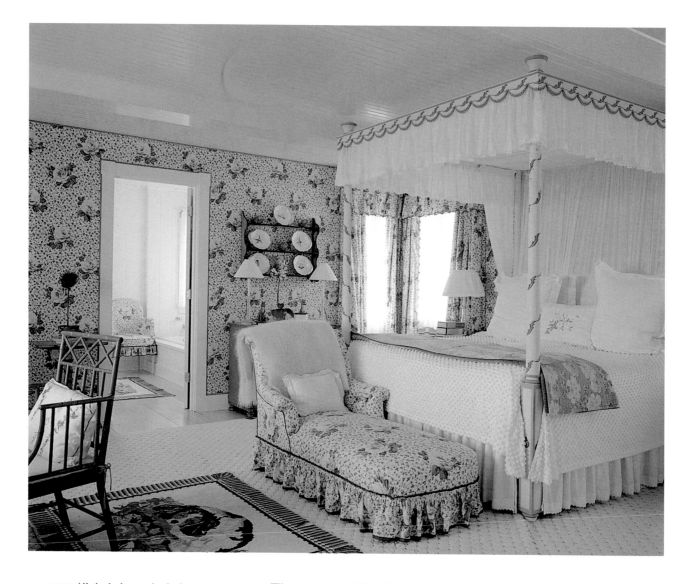

The owner's wife, who is a painter, holds dear the scrubby vegetation of the dunes where, scenting the air, wild rugosas and dark red dog roses thrive. She has created a garden of box filled with nothing but roses, and a cutting garden of species roses. Her husband loves the variety of bird life – herons, hawks, yellow finches and red-winged blackbirds abound – though he is infuriated by the wild geese which swoop in from Canada and eat his grass.

Aware of her clients' delight in nature, Vivien has brought the garden indoors – in the manner of John Fowler, the founding father of Colefax and Fowler – with flowered needlepoint rugs, sap-green leaves stencilled on to the wooden floor of the hall, pleated cotton lampshades with a fern motif and chintz cushions on rattan chairs. 'I used ornaments sparingly to ensure an uncluttered look,' Vivien says, 'along with colours that are never loud, and Irish-linen curtains, plainly hemstitched.'

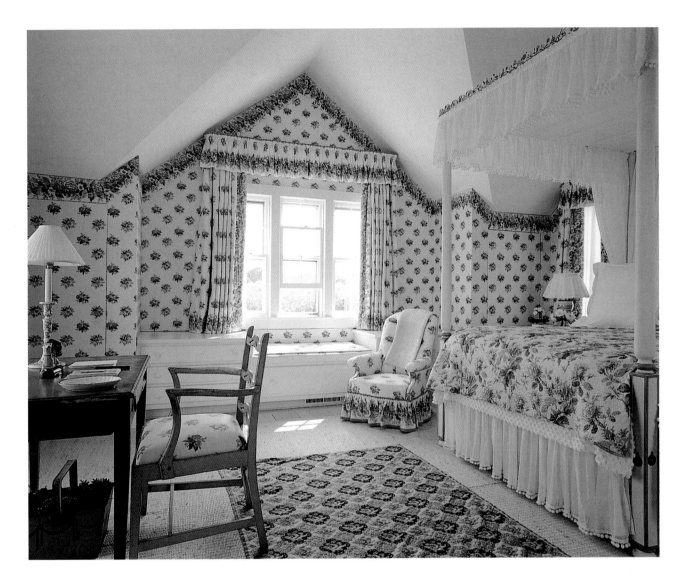

Painted wooden floors, sometimes covered with marvellous French matting interwoven with strands of string, provide the perfect canvas for these picturesque, but never twee, interiors. Decorative, but not showy, pieces of furniture – a faux-bamboo chest of drawers, a cupboard with wicker panels, a square blanket chest with rope handles – do not distract the eye but, rather, enhance the restful atmosphere.

Resembling a pantry, the kitchen is also the dining room. French provincial chairs with rush seats encircle a handsome, oval, fruitwood wine table. 'This is where we tuck into an old-fashioned English-style tea with ginger cake stuffed with raisins and nuts,' says the owner.

If you look back when walking down a path made from crushed clam shells that leads towards the road, the house is smothered in the pale pink rose, 'New Dawn'. The delicate shade of its petals melds well with the silvery-grey shingle. Nothing fancy, you understand, but perfect.

ABOVE The picturesque shape of this feminine, spare bedroom is emphasized by the decorative border.

COUNTRY
RETREATS

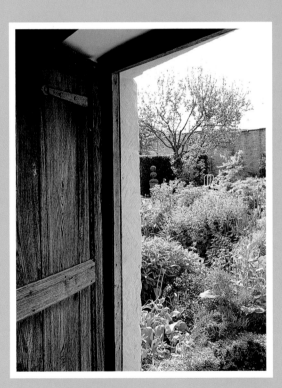

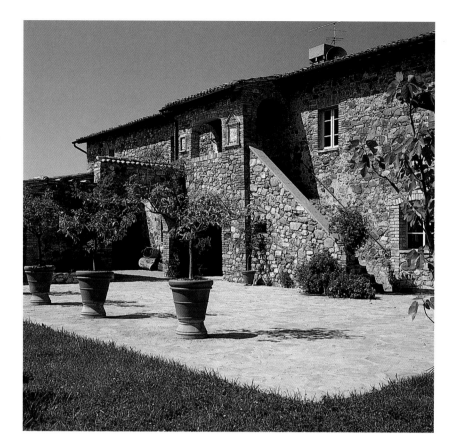

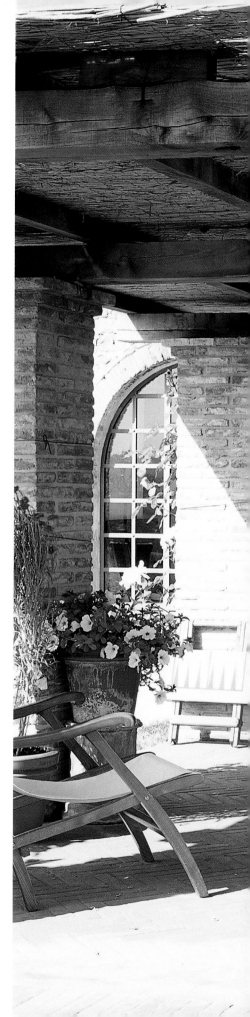

In the footsteps of the pilgrims

In the year 853, Sigeric, Archbishop of Canterbury, crossed the Orcia Valley in Tuscany, heading for Rome. The diary he kept during his travels contains the earliest-known reference to the Via Francigena, the great medieval road from France to Rome that led pilgrims to the heart of Christianity. More than twenty castles and rest houses (*ospedali*) crowned the valley bordering the road, stopping points for tired travellers. One such place occupied what is now the Buonriposo ('Good Rest') estate, owned by decorator and designer Ilaria Miani. When she and her hus-

ABOVE AND RIGHT Offset by the colour of Buonriposo's rugged stone walls, plants grown in terracotta pots punctuate the outdoor and covered terraces. Simple, canvas-and-wood, folding chairs furnish this semi-outdoor sitting area.

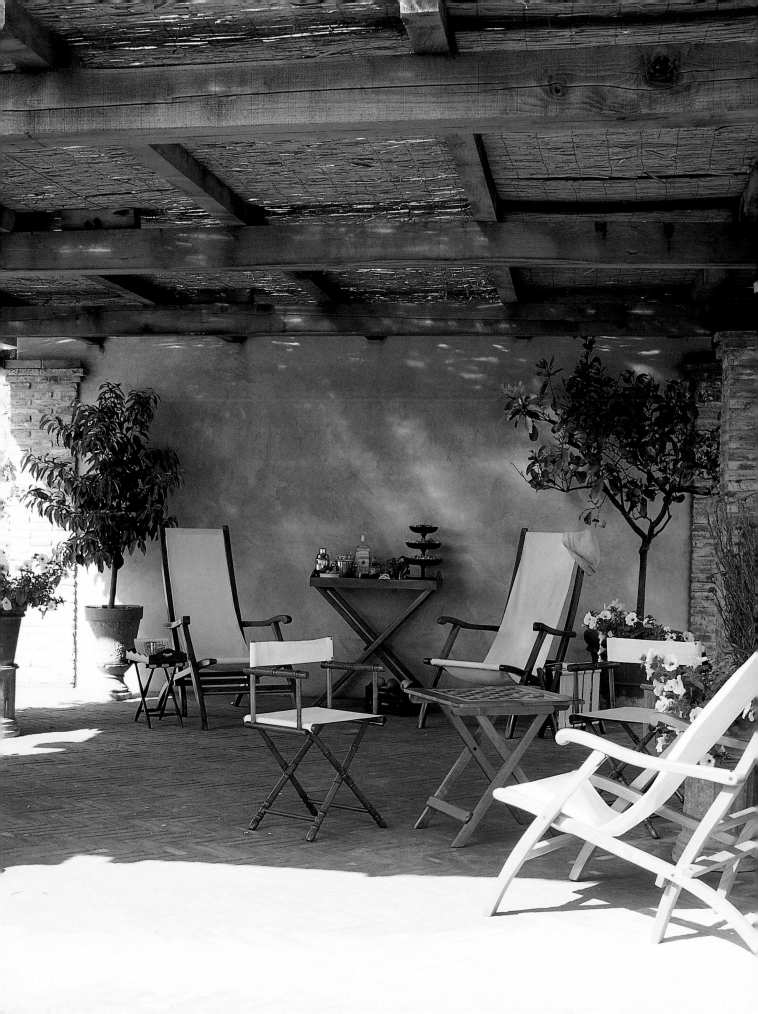

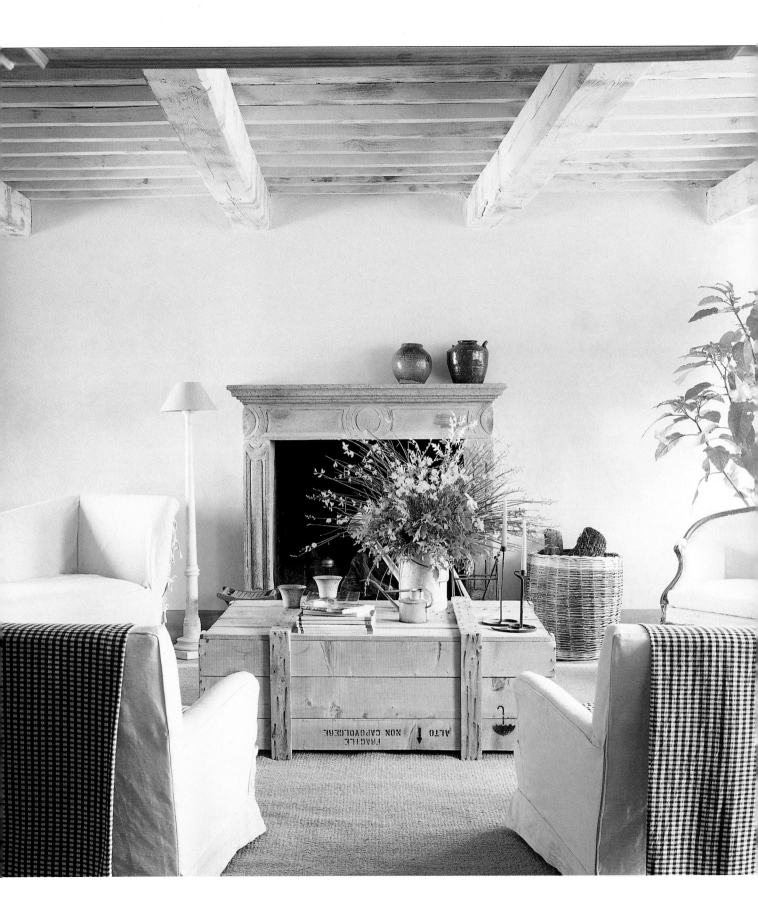

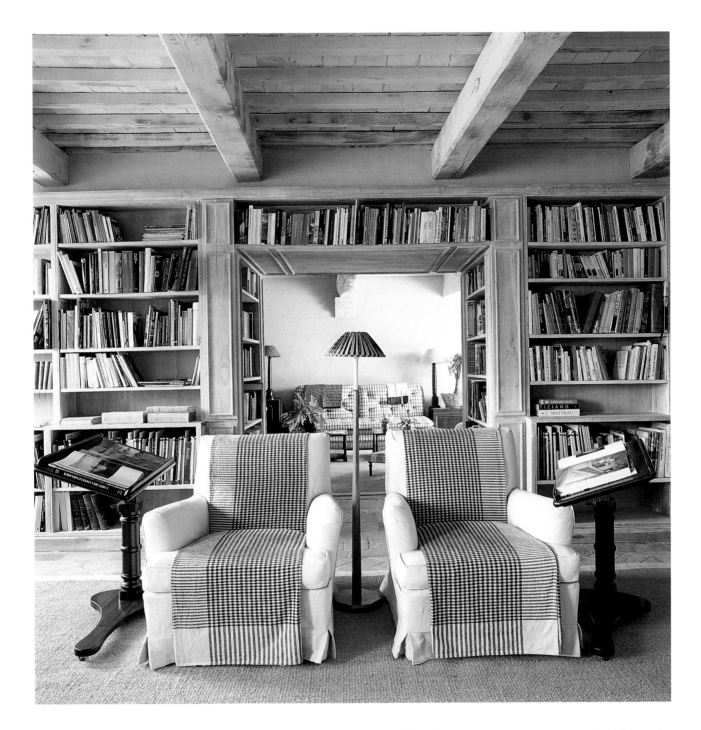

band Giorgio first visited the Orcia Valley, they were captivated by the beauty of the landscape – the same painted by Ambrogio Lorenzetti in the thirteenth century. In the expansive views of hill-top castles, baked fields and gorse thickets, dense oak and beech woods, and flourishing crops – the hard-won result of a century-long battle against the aridity of the soil – time seemed to have stood still. Even the mountain air had a special, indefinable quality about it.

OPPOSITE AND ABOVE Divided in two by a wall of books, the sitting room demonstrates Ilaria Miani's skill in mixing different styles within a neutral framework and in creating a sophisticated look without destroying the building's essentially rustic character.

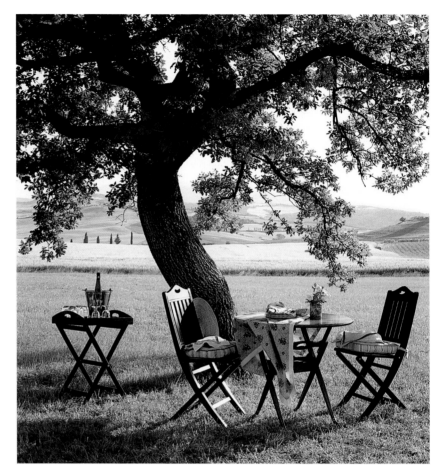

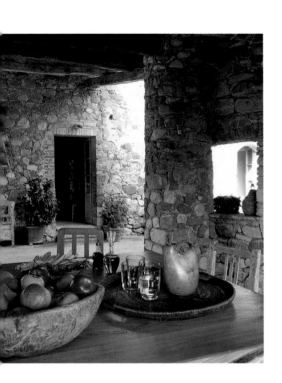

ABOVE AND OPPOSITE In summer, the covered terraces are furnished as rooms and used for dining. Here, an antique painted bench stands against one of the venerable stone walls and old ladders are used as decoration.
ABOVE RIGHT The house is surrounded by extensive, rural vistas. Folding furniture is set up beneath the shade of a tree to enjoy the panorama.

Entranced by the natural wonders of the area, Ilaria and her husband started, nearly twenty years ago, a hunt for a country estate. Buonriposo appeared at first sight as a ruined peasant's house; it recommended itself on account of its manageable size, and also the sense of history Ilaria found there – the layers of architectural accretion, including original tiles, legacy of a sixteenth-century furnace that produced bricks and tiles from local clay.

In restoring the house, the Mianis' main aim was to treat each space individually, respecting the various periods of the building, and avoiding the current tendency among Italian architects and decorators to unify buildings with fake 'rustic' interiors. Instead, Ilaria and Giorgio have maintained and made a feature of the many successive additions that characterize Buonriposo: the sixteenth-century nucleus has been restored as closely as possible to its original state, as have the eighteenth-century modifications, and building undertaken in the Thirties. A fresco in the nearby Villa la Foce, owned by the Marchioness Origo, former owner of Buonriposo, represents the house in the mid nineteenth century; it proved invaluable to Ilaria and Giorgio in their restoration.

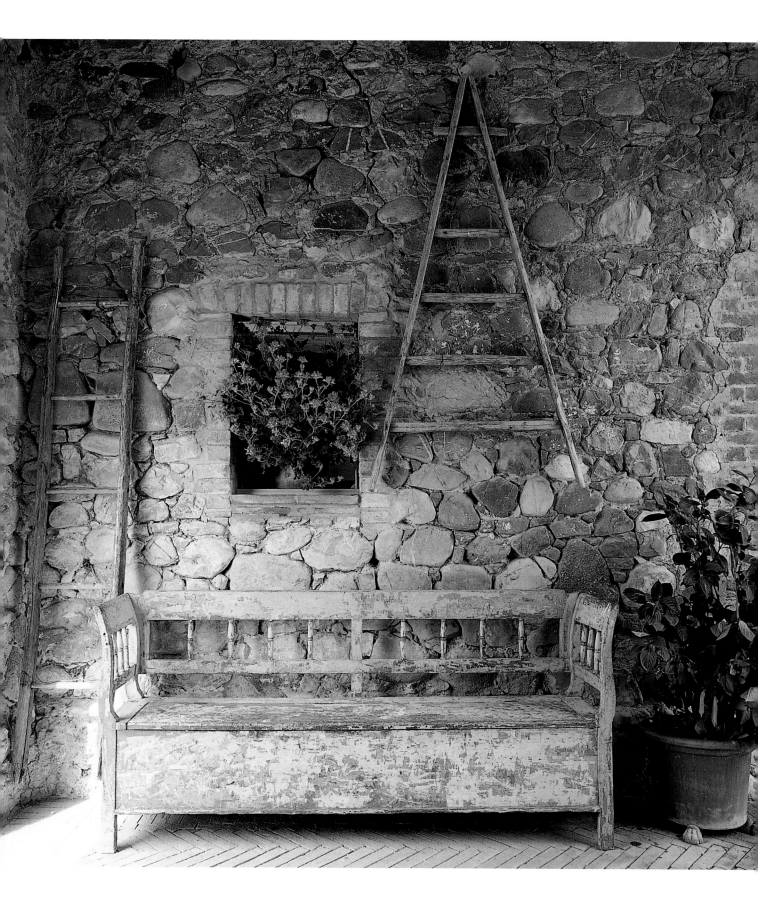

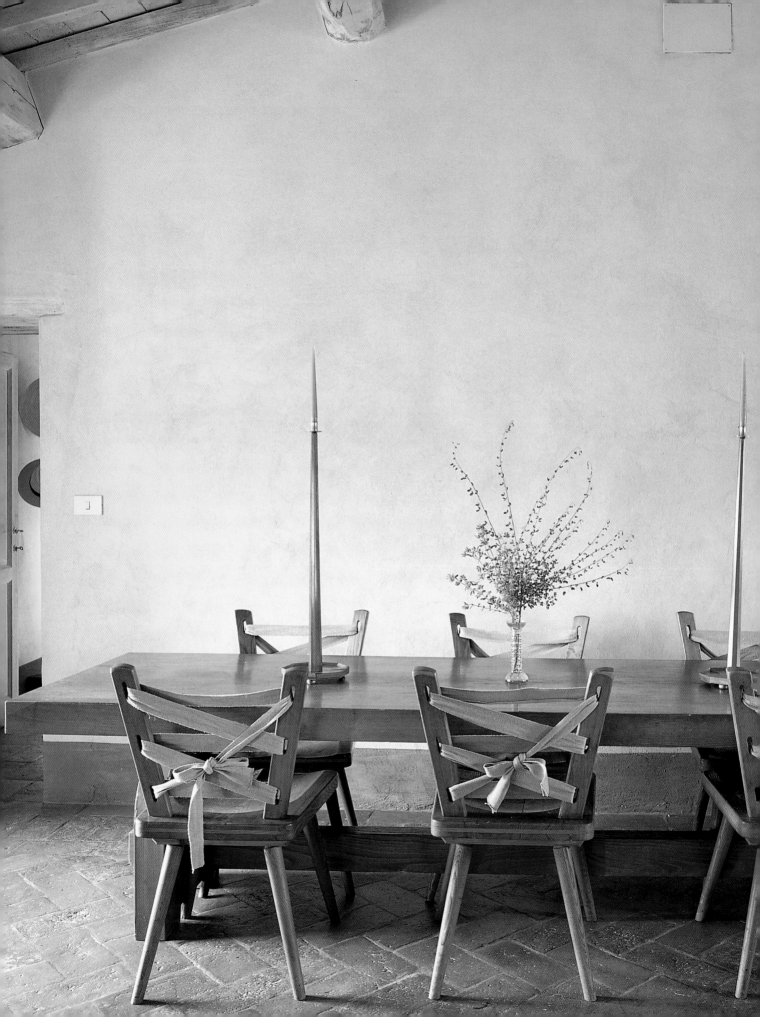

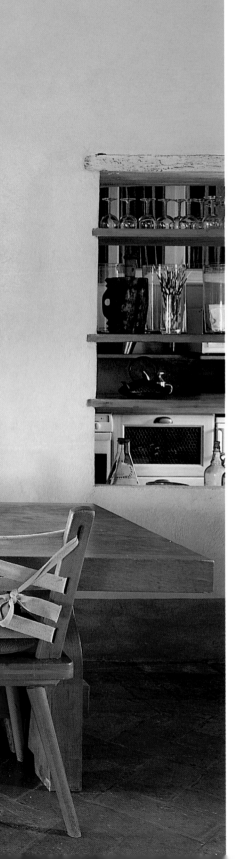

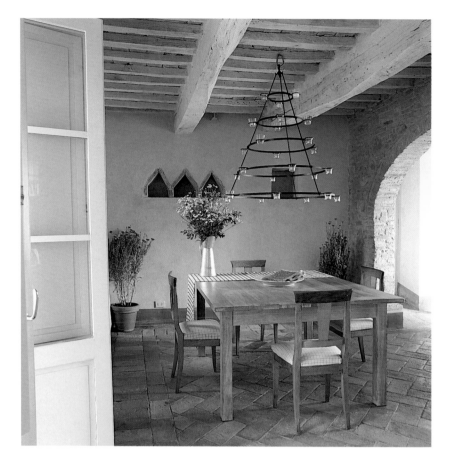

Rooms inside the house are well sized and lit by many windows, with beamed ceilings and rendered or exposed stone walls. In furnishing them, Ilaria was convinced that only the very minimum of furniture was required. 'I wanted the scenery of the Val d'Orcia to play the main role; I hoped that the neutral, stone-coloured walls would suggest the soft tonality of the local clay, the famous terra di Siena.'

She decided to avoid the sort of 'peasant' furniture popular in restorations in Tuscany, feeling that the bucolic idyll it evokes never in fact existed. Instead, the interiors of local houses were more or less primitive and predominantly bare, the furniture being limited to a bed or two and a table with a few chairs in front of the fireplace. The kind of furniture Ilaria was looking for could not be found; she realized that she would have to design it herself. And so, with the help of local craftsmen,

ABOVE This semi-outdoor dining area opens off the kitchen.
LEFT In the dining room, a herringbone brick floor and Forties, fruitwood furniture have a graphic simplicity. Seen against the plain, rendered walls, the elegantly tapered candlesticks designed by Ilaria Miani are like outsize punctuation marks.

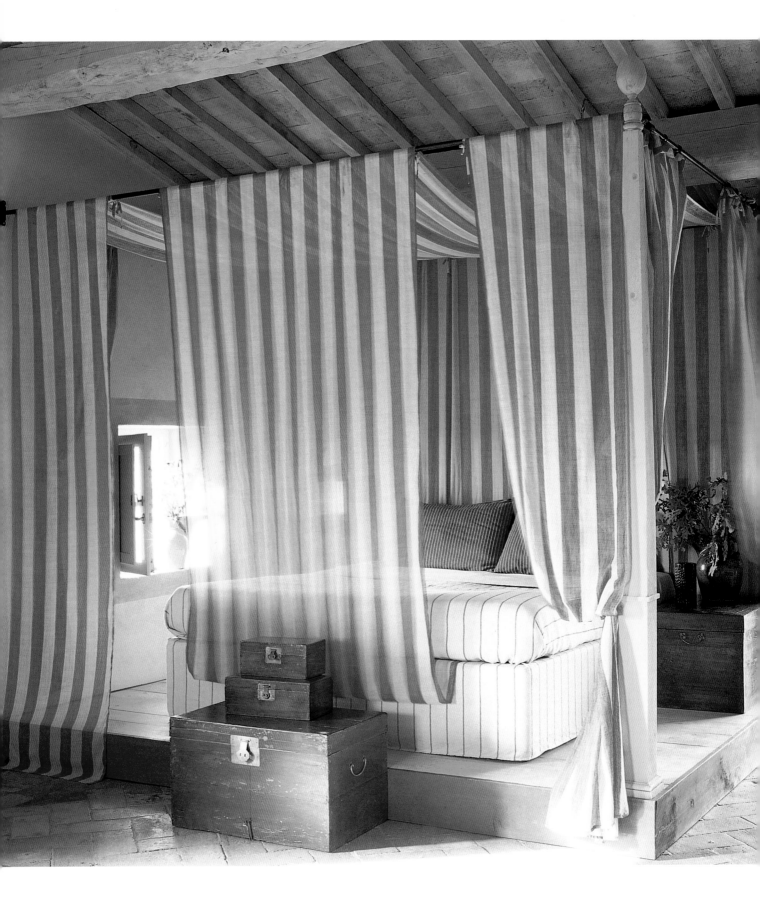

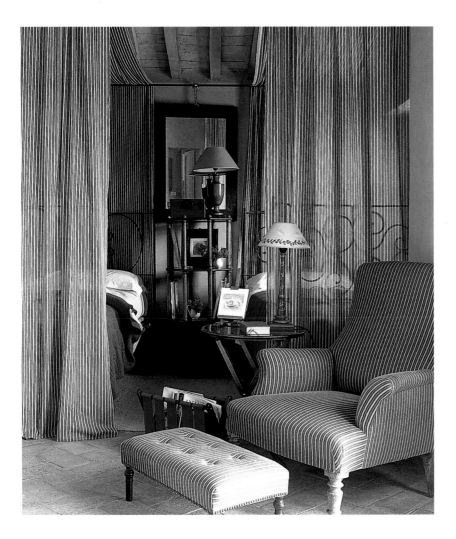

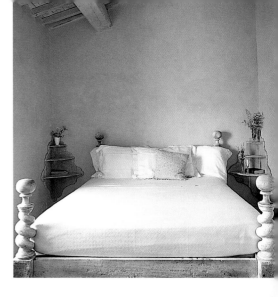

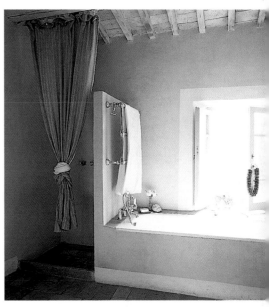

she designed book shelves, beds, lamps and accessories – more than 200 pieces. Long before its final transformation into a comfortable family house in the country, Buonriposo became Ilaria's workshop, a testing ground for comfort, practicality and good design. The message soon spread and friends and acquaintances began to place their orders. They saw in the simple wooden furniture, which makes no obvious reference to any precise style or period, something adaptable to houses both in the city and the country, and a link between old and new, rustic and sophisticated. Ilaria's designs are now available in Europe and North America. In addition, Ilaria has evolved a style of decorating that, apparently instinctively, mixes up objects and furniture from a number of periods, against a tranquil, neutral backdrop. In a spare bedroom, for example, a neoclassical bed inherited from Ilaria's Florentine grandmother stands alongside a nineteenth-century Chinese wedding cabinet, pieces from the Forties, and elegant candlesticks designed by Ilaria. Buonriposo is a perfect example of just how exhilarating such a mix can be.

ABOVE LEFT Metal canopy beds and an octagonal bookcase, all designed by Ilaria, are reminiscent of campaign furniture. Striped fabric, similar in effect to that used for for tents, enhances this impression. ABOVE RIGHT The spiral bedposts are virtually the only decoration in this monastically simple bedroom. BELOW RIGHT The bathrooms are designed to be practical and in keeping with the simplicity of the building. OPPOSITE A bold red-and-white striped canopy frames the bed which is raised on a dais in the main bedroom.

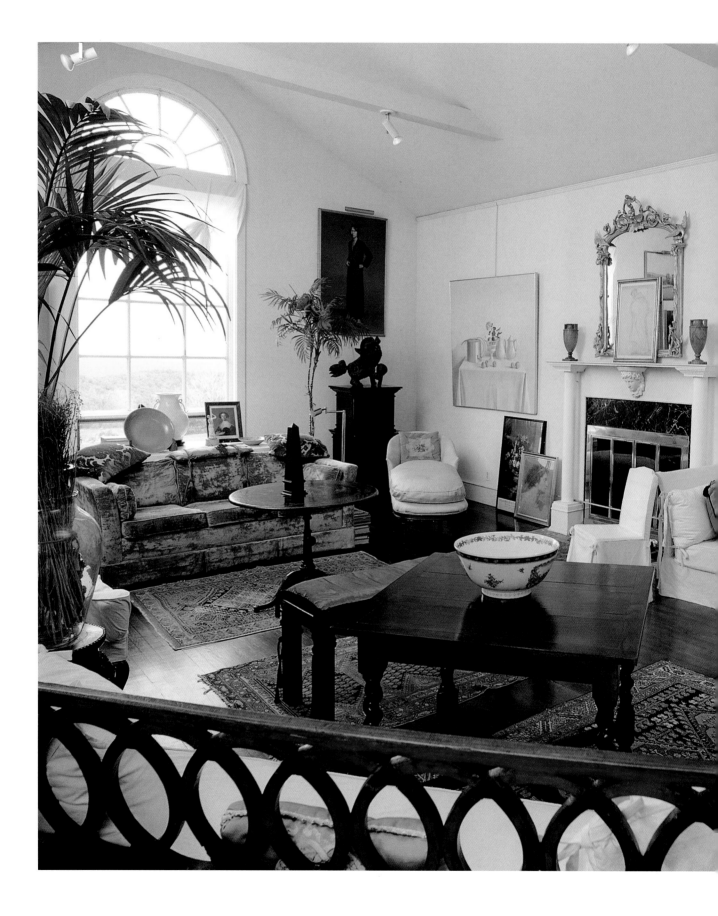

An oasis of pale, artistic calm

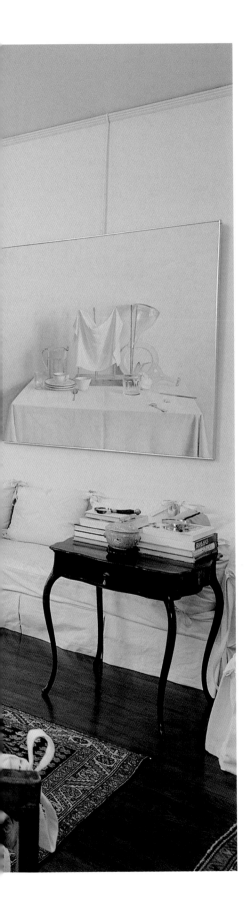

For two men whose creative lives lead them in very different directions, the country home of Paul Kellogg and Raymond Han offers precisely the right blend of serenity and simplicity. Paul's days are filled with the high-stress demands of running two opera houses, while Raymond, a successful artist, requires peace and light to produce his extraordinarily meticulous and elegant still lifes.

They moved to this remote stone house on top of a hill in upstate New York in 1972. Three years later Paul Kellogg took over directorship of neighbouring Glimmerglass, a fledgling summer opera festival in Cooperstown, N.Y. Under his guidance, the now highly successful festival has become known for its high artistic standards and for its innovative repertoire. In 1996, Paul assumed a far bigger mantle as general and artistic director of the New York City Opera; meanwhile, Raymond Han's work has become more and more sought-after. Now, more than

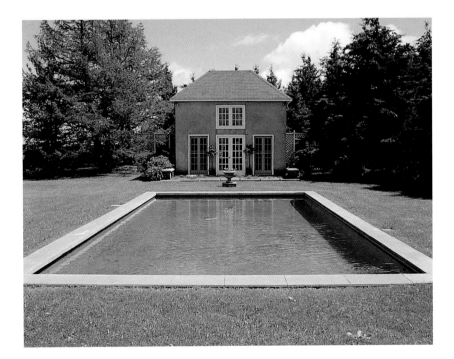

ABOVE The pool house, originally built as a studio, takes the form of a small cottage.
LEFT This room was added to the house as a studio for Raymond Han but subsequently converted into a music room and entertaining area. At the other end is a grand piano.

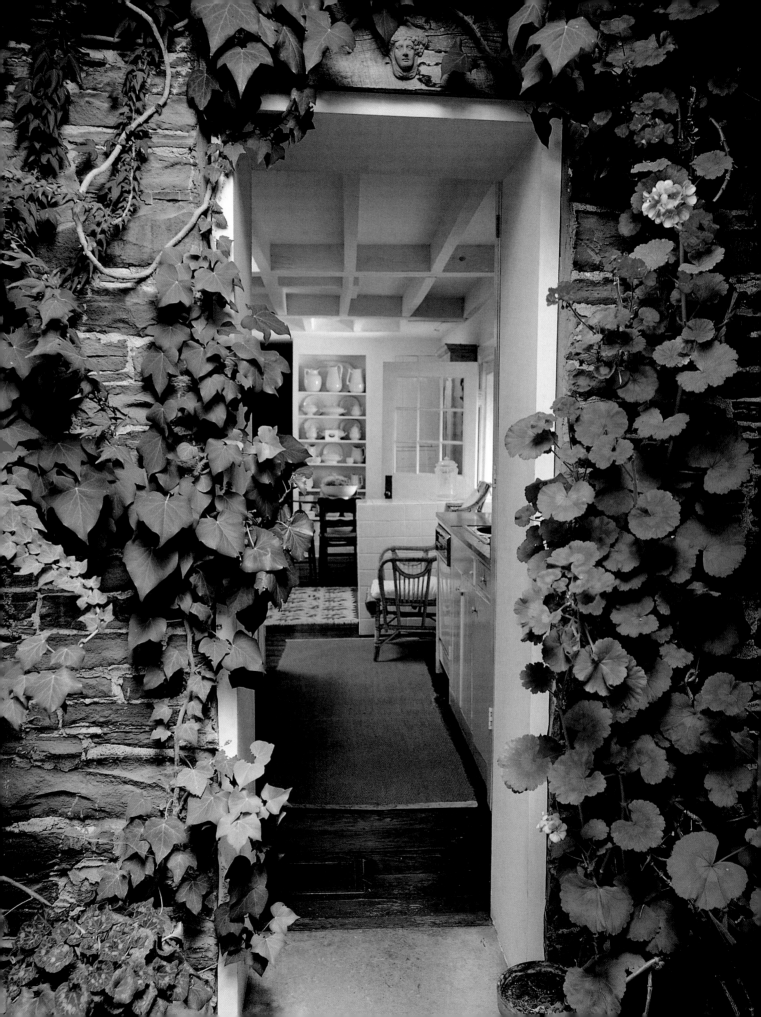

ever, their country house plays an essential role as an oasis in the midst of creative frenzy.

The house is surrounded by 100 acres of green hills and fields; inside, its almost completely white decoration, like Raymond's paintings, seduces the visitor into a kind of tranquil trance. It was not always so. 'The place looked as bleak as Wuthering Heights when we first saw it,' recalls Paul. Raymond, whose visual sensibility was equally offended, describes a nondescript interior, with little rooms, plasterboard ceilings, dark paint and poky spaces.

Work on the house started immediately. Raymond was the designer, architect, mason and gardener, Paul the construction overseer and carpenter. That was the team. There were no other helpers. They removed the downstairs plaster ceilings to reveal the old beams; they tore out the central wall in the hall; they removed with a sledge-hammer an oversized fireplace made of boulders. They ripped out the kitchen cabinets; they sanded the floors; they heightened all the doors, added fluting to the

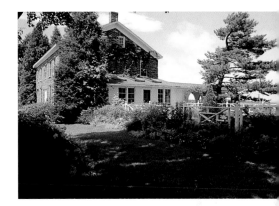

OPPOSITE AND ABOVE An arched loggia extends from the side of the house. From it, a door framed by ivy and climbing pelargoniums leads to the kitchen. LEFT The passage leading to the stairs and front door was created when a wall was inserted at right, between the hall and sitting room. The shelves make a useful resting place for hats.

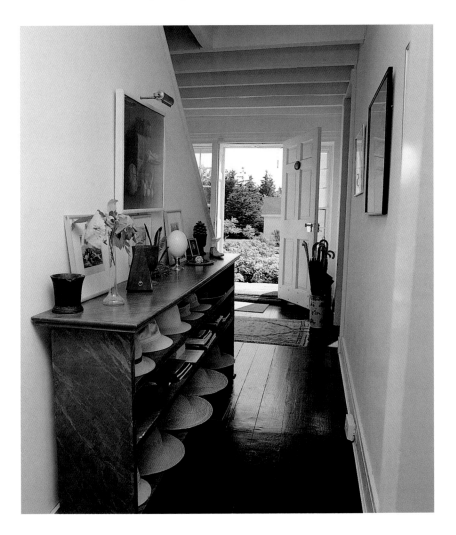

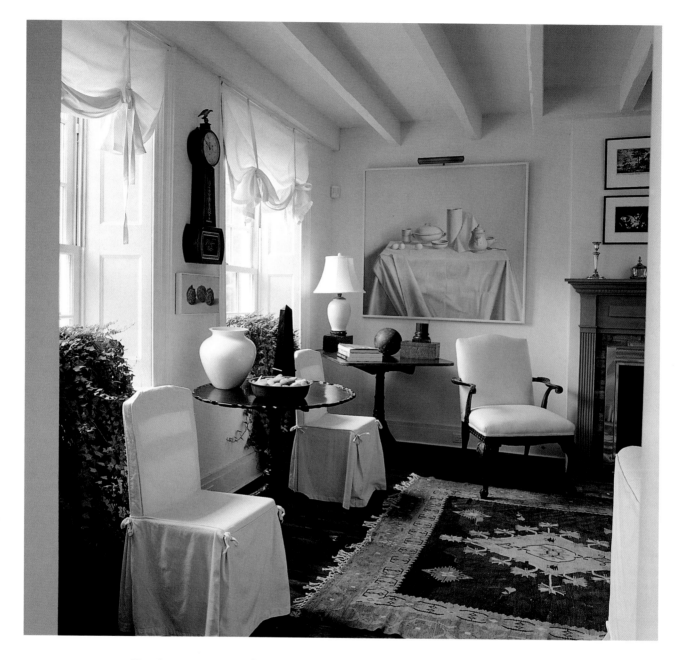

ABOVE AND OPPOSITE Two views of the sitting room. The sofa and chairs are slip-covered with heavy, white cotton, which is also used at the windows. The still-lifes here and in the dining room, seen through the doorway, are by Raymond Han.

doorcases and built a wall to separate the sitting room from the hall.

Such a massive programme of destruction and reconstruction sounds drastic, but it was carried out slowly and methodically, and the house gradually revealed its true character. The house had its own architecture, which was always respected. When the structural changes were complete, Raymond took his preferred palette of white and mixed a subtle series of white shades for every wall in the house. The result has a translucent glow creating a harmonious interplay of light and shade.

Decorative touches came later, such as the new fireplaces installed in the dining and living rooms, trompe l'œil in the bedrooms and study,

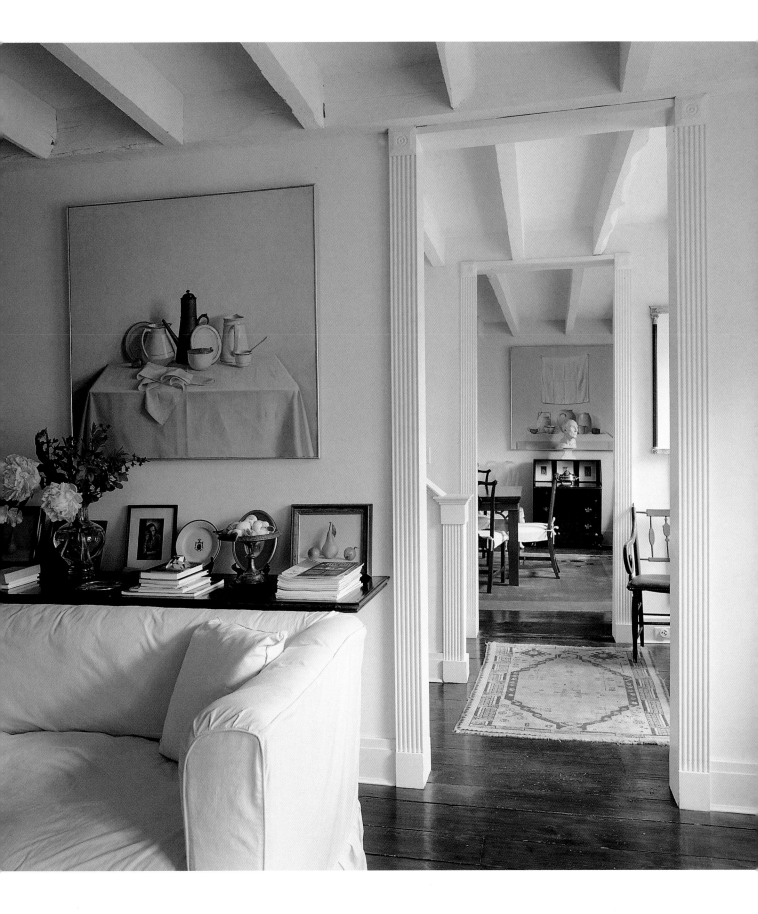

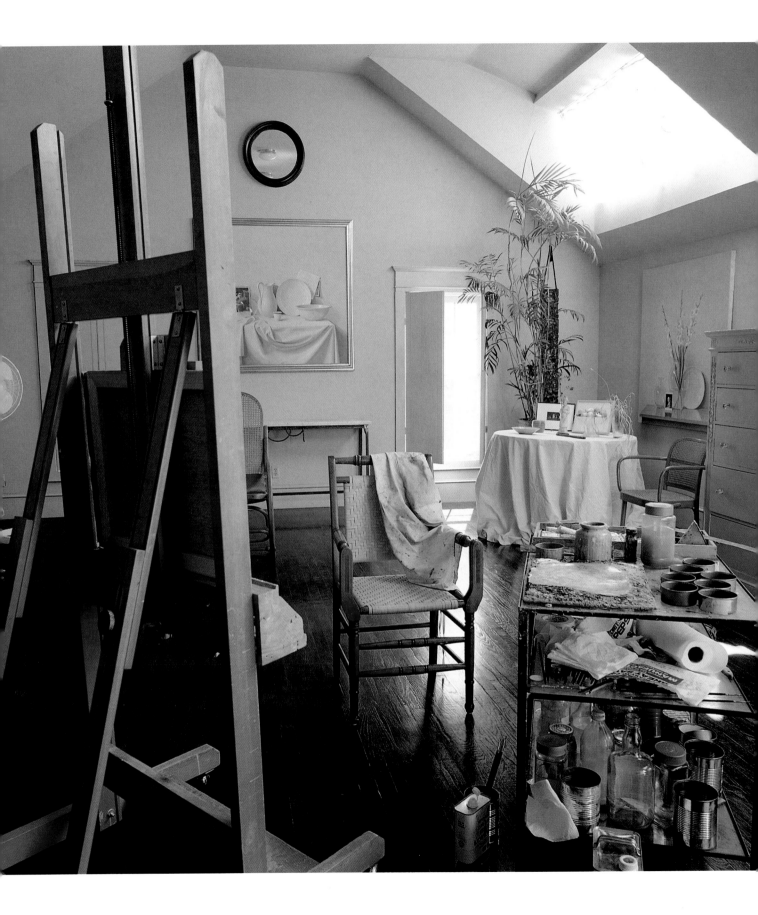

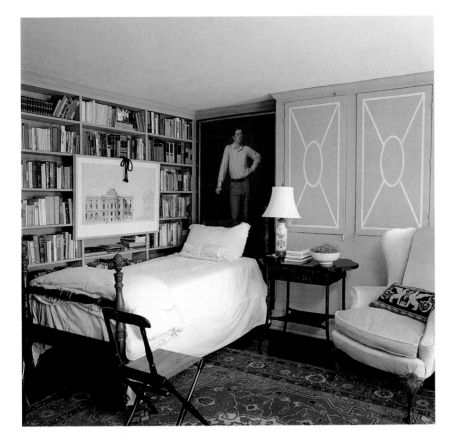

an old door given a new lease on life as a kitchen cabinet, rich but subtle colour from Chinese rugs, and display shelves for Raymond's collection of white ironstone china.

Simple furnishings throughout the house, mostly hand-me-downs and finds from antiques shops or auction houses brought from their former house, fit the unpretentious mood. (Raymond's habit of painting furniture adds to the spirit of wit that permeates the house.) Another room was added, originally as the artist's studio, but later converted into a music room and entertaining area to accommodate Paul's ever-expanding operatic commitments. Raymond now works in a large, light-filled space above the new garage.

Outside, the austere façade of the house is softened by a winding path and beds, designed by Raymond, that overflow with flowers and shrubs. To the side of the house an arched loggia has been added, with stones cut, laid and pointed by Raymond. Off the back terrace, the artist has designed two tall obelisks (their dark colours look particularly striking when the ground becomes parched in the summer) to punctuate each side of the garden, leading the eye from here to the horizon beyond. Away from the house, past a sloping lawn, is a swimming pool and a pool house which was originally built as a studio, but found not to be light

ABOVE The terrace, with plants spilling over the paving, has magnificent views across the countryside of New York State. OPPOSITE Raymond Han's new studio above the garage is painted pale grey. Though minimally furnished and very much a work-space, it has elegance.

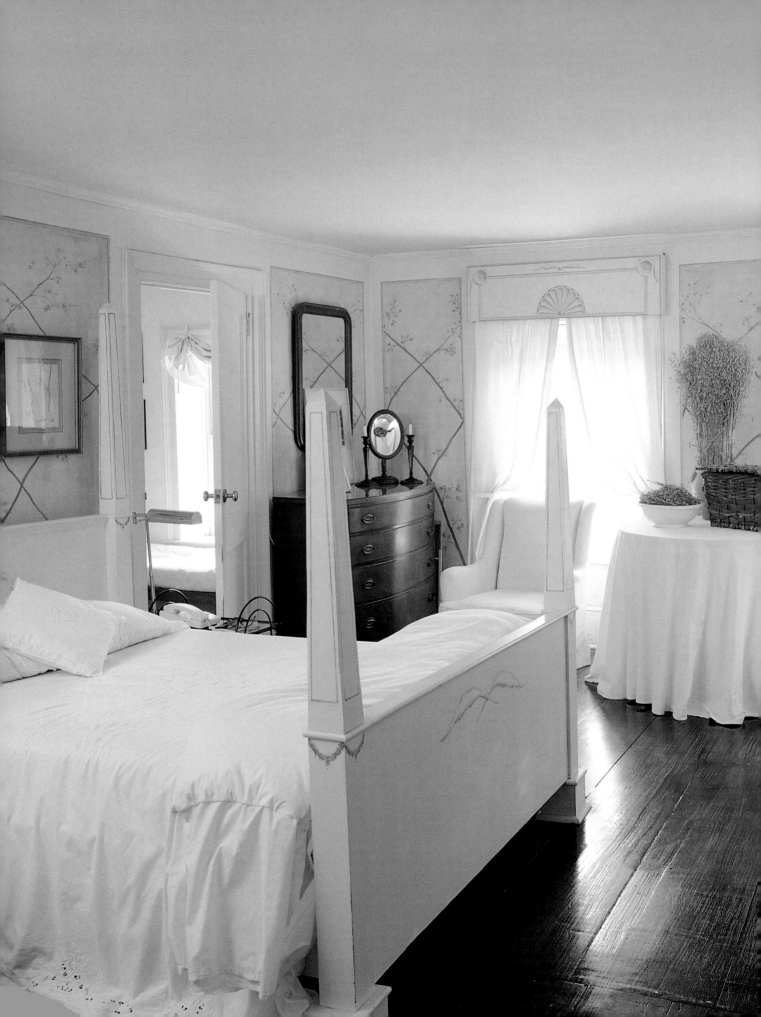

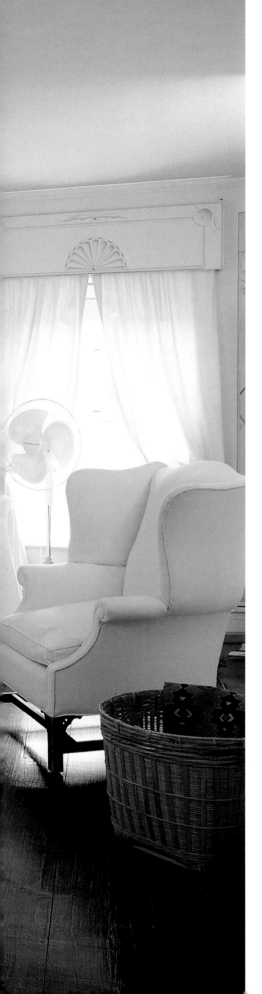

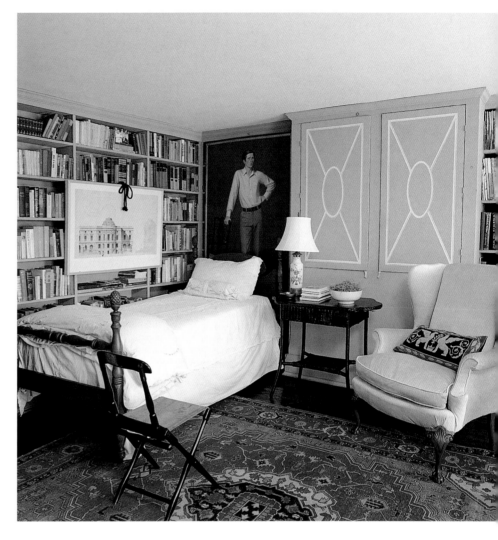

enough. Always conscious of space, the musician and the painter have placed a *tempietto*, or small temple, in front of the house to form a little vista, complete with crab apple trees.

This hill-top eyrie will never be more than a simple, sturdy, nine-teenth-century stone house, and the rooms inside will always be small, lacking girth or grandeur. But, nevertheless, the impression within is one of fluid space, and the views outside from the terrace and loggia add their promise of peace and privacy.

ABOVE The cupboards in the upstairs study have been painted with trompe l'œil mouldings. An antique oriental carpet picks up the colours of the book spines.
LEFT Raymond Han constructed and painted the wooden bed in the main bedroom; the paintwork on the walls and pelmets is also by him. The wide floorboards are left bare, while the curtains and tablecover lend softness to the room.

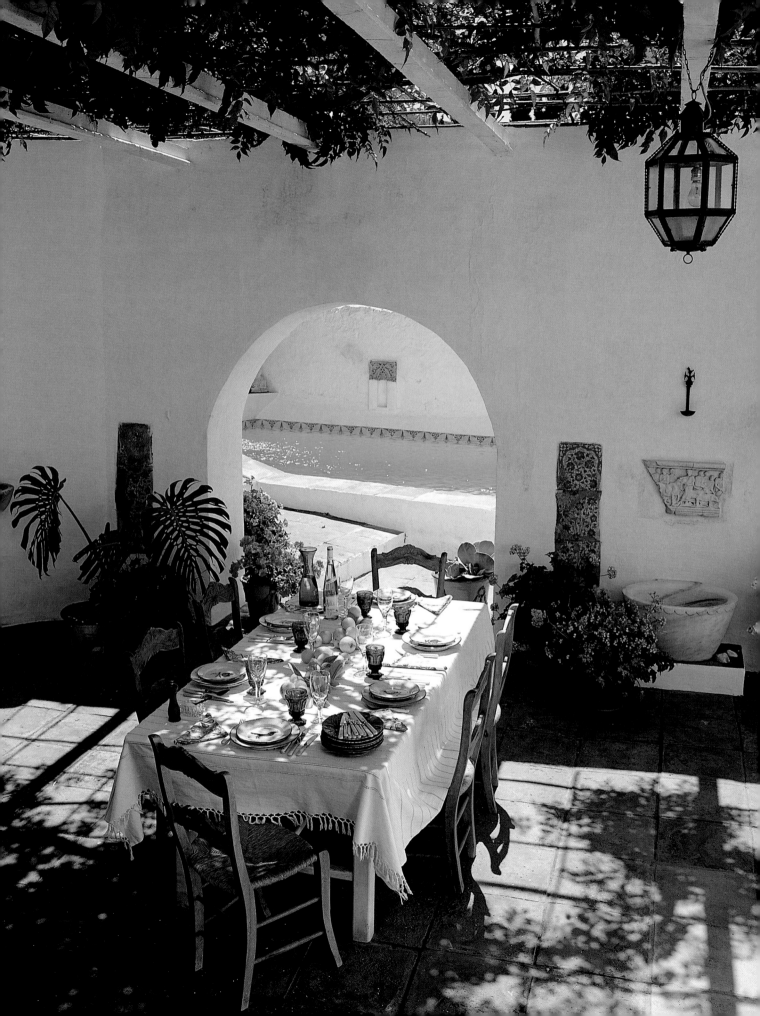

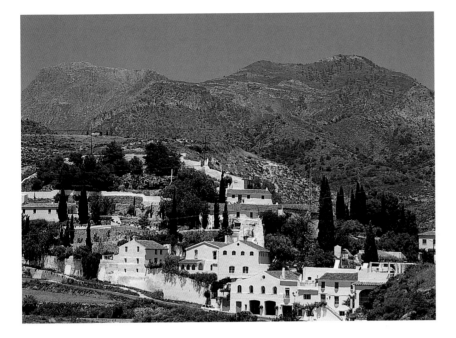

On a hillside in Andalusia

Thirty-five years ago, in Andalusia in southern Spain, the road from Nerja to the village of Frigiliana wound uphill through fields of sugar cane. A lone bus trundled up and down and occasionally someone passed by in a car, but mostly the traffic consisted of mules. La Molineta, a disused sugar, flour and paper mill dating from the seventeenth century, stood halfway along the road, on the right. A sizable complex of near-derelict buildings, it occupied an ancient, possibly pre-Roman, site. Funerary jars dating from 600 BC had been found during excavations nearby and, in the grounds of La Molineta itself, an elegant little Roman doll was discovered.

Sir Peter and Lady Wakefield bought the complex in 1965 during a short break between diplomatic postings. Rose Marrable, Felicity Wakefield's mother, had chanced upon it at the end of a long search for somewhere less crowded than the Côte d'Azur, where the family had been sharing a house. Summoned urgently to Spain, the Wakefields flew to Malaga and instantly succumbed to La Molineta's ruined charm and wild, rugged surroundings. In comparison with France, it felt as if they had gone back some fifty years in time. Nerja was still an unspoiled fishing

ABOVE From a distance, the mill complex appears like a classic bone-white Spanish village against the hills beyond.
OPPOSITE The lunch table on the terrace is laid with Granada china and locally-made green glass. On the wall to the right of the arch, above a Turkish marble bassin, there is a Lebanese stone carving. Beside it are tiles which were once in Rudyard Kipling's house in Sussex.

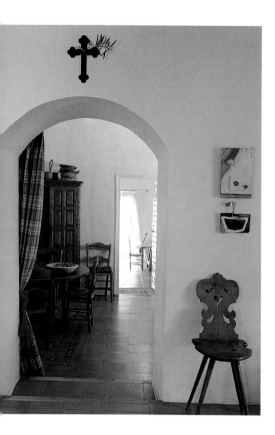

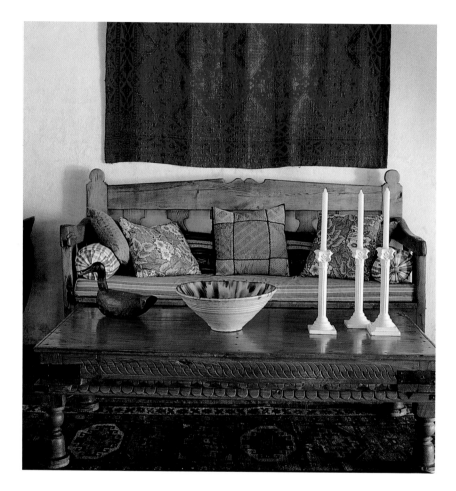

ABOVE Looking from the sitting room through the kitchen to the Big Room at the far end. A Lebanese iron cross hangs above the arch.
ABOVE RIGHT A nineteenth-century wall-hanging from Aragon is seen here above an antique walnut seat. A Nijar pottery bowl and a set of Staffordshire candlesticks stand on a table from India.
OPPOSITE The Big Room, with majestic tiled ceiling and high-level windows, has banquette seating on one side and a dining area on the other. Decorative objects include Syrian copper dishes, Nijar pots and, on the low table, a Granada bowl.

village, with narrow cobbled streets and goats in every yard. A group of returned political exiles, Federico Garcia Lorca's brother and sister-in-law among them, had settled there, prompting the newspaper El Pais to dub it 'the town of intellectuals and fishermen'. In the same article, Peter Wakefield, newly installed amid the perfumed splendour of his many terraces and courts, was singled out as 'the diplomat with a patio for every hour of the day and for every day of the week'.

Perched at different levels around La Molineta's industrial core – a great barn of a place filled with boulders, pigs and rusting machinery – were fifteen ruined houses, which were home to several peasant families. The only house that was habitable (and which the Wakefields were to occupy for the next eight years) was the Panificadora – the old bakery attached to the mill. It was inhabited by an old lady who kept a little shop. 'We didn't turn anybody out,' Felicity Wakefield explains. 'The old lady moved to the basement and had her shop there. A couple called José and Carmella were living in the bread ovens with their children, and there was Frasquito and Vicenta – these were the ones who stayed on. We got to know them well. They must have been with us for five years.'

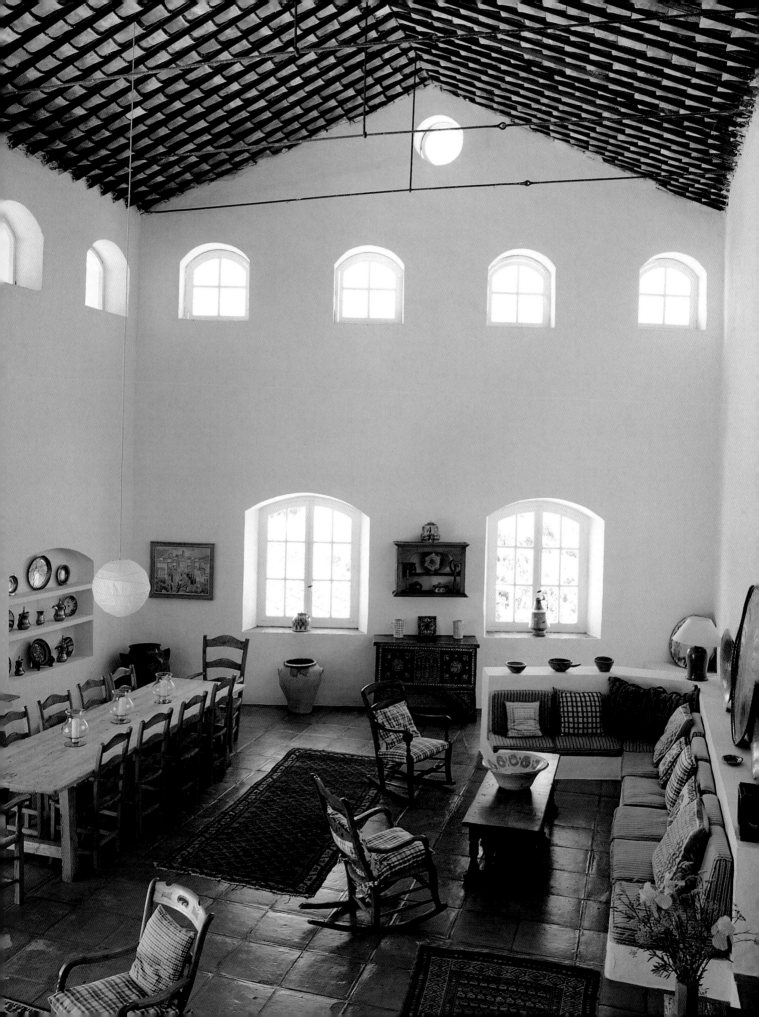

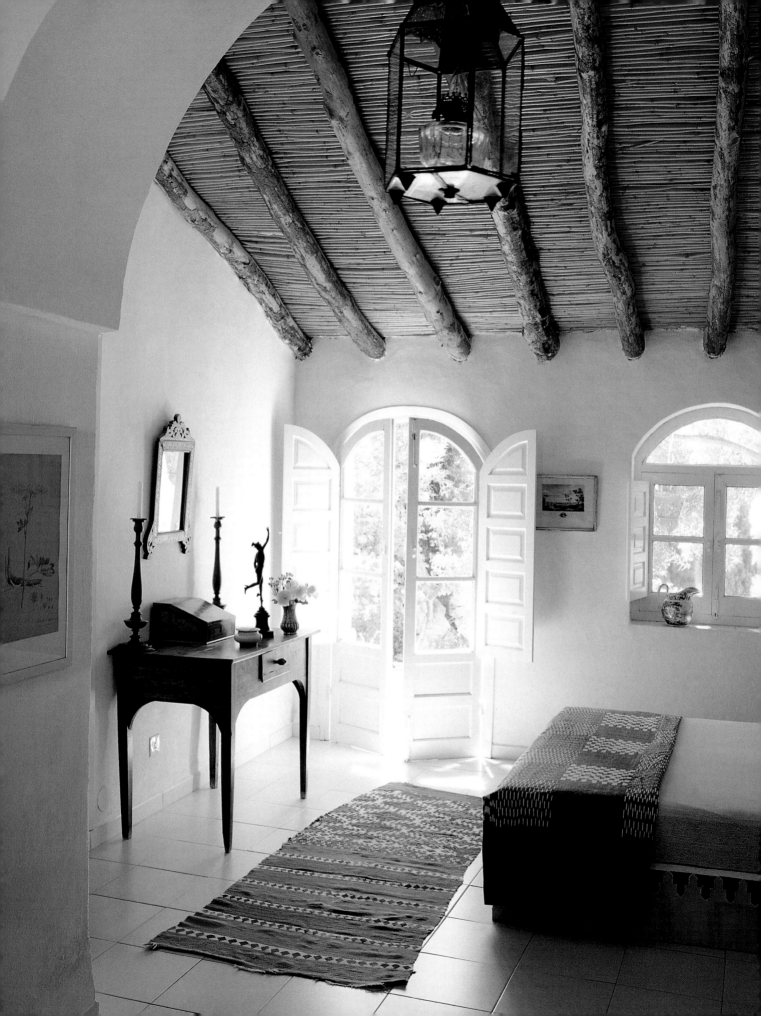

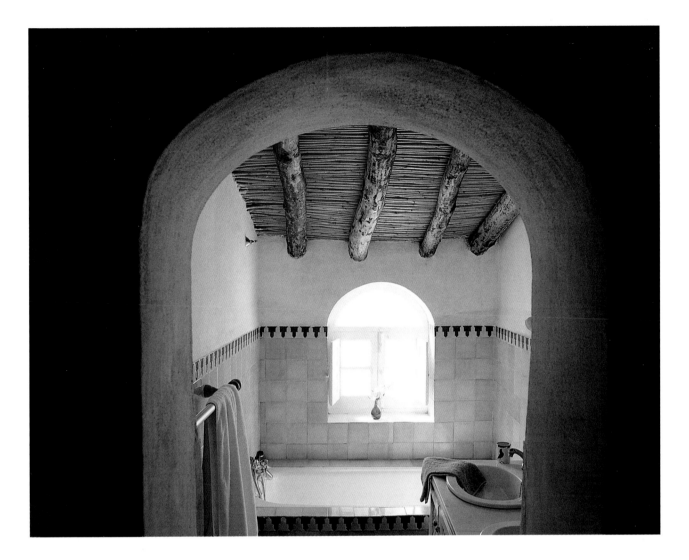

Work on the other houses in the complex started straight away. The Wakefields decided not to employ an architect; instead, that first summer, their friend Tim Bruce-Dick, an architecture student in London, came out to join them and drew them an enormously helpful ground-plan. The first house to be completed was the Casa Rosa, belonging to Felicity Wakefield's mother. She moved in that autumn but, sadly, died in the December of that year.

Soon the original fifteen houses had been whittled down to nine. What could be propped up had been saved; the rest were allowed to disintegrate into romantic courtyards or secluded patches of garden. Luckily, there was no shortage of water. Although the mill's central water-system had collapsed, the mill-race still rushed down from a reservoir in the Sierra Almijara, through a channel on top of an old Moorish wall, straight into a pool mid-way between the Panificadora and the large building at the heart of the complex.

ABOVE Tucked in the space previously occupied by the mill-wheel, the main bathroom has a bambo-and-pine ceiling and Granada tiles.
OPPOSITE In the main bedroom, doors with shutters made to a typical local design open on to a terrace. The hanging lantern is Syrian.

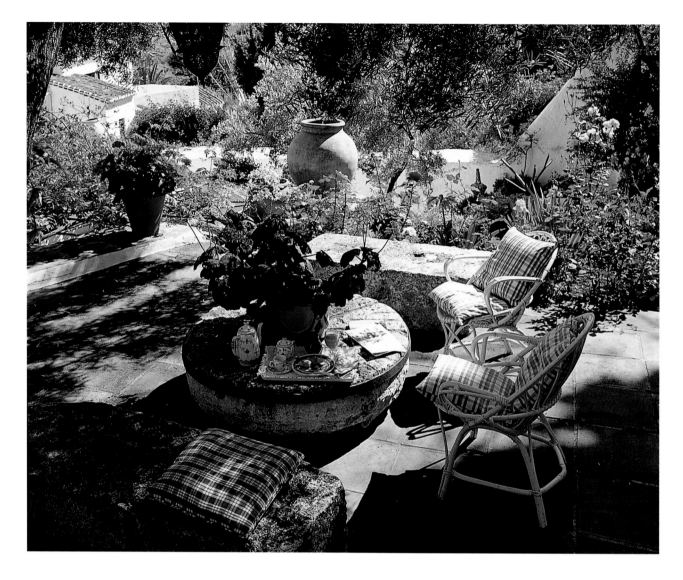

ABOVE The perfect place for breakfast at any time of the year, this hidden terrace is immediately outside the main bedroom.

When the moment came to tackle this structure – which was to become the main house – the Wakefields were determined to take their time. 'We started by doing the Big Room. It was better not to rush because we didn't know what to do. Nobody knew what to do. Everybody had ideas about putting in a gallery, dividing the space horizontally, putting in extra bedrooms upstairs. We could have doubled the accommodation we have now. And then one day our friend Tanis, who was married to Gloria Lorca, said, "You know, you don't have to do anything to this room, you can just leave it," and we thought, well, he's right, that's a good idea.' The roof was mended; the floor was raised to the level of the courtyard outside, then decorated with local, handmade tiles; the front windows were enlarged; an opening was made into the courtyard; and the walls were given several coats of whitewash. But none of the majestic proportions, nor the basic character, were lost.

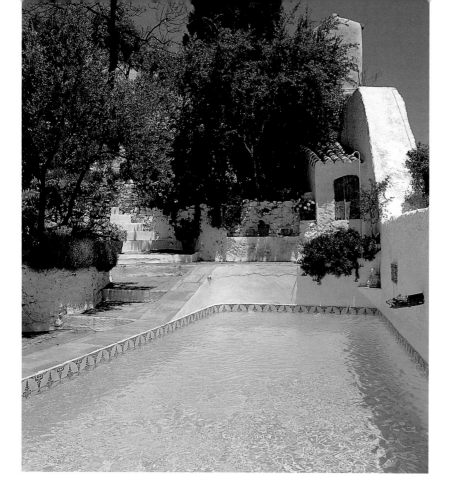

Today you enter a vast, airy space, with a tremendous, crinkly, tiled ceiling. The room is furnished with the sturdy, olive-wood, country furniture which has been traditional in the region for hundreds of years, and filled with treasures brought back from tours of duty in Japan and the Middle East. The Wakefields were *en poste* in Beirut during the civil war and, escaping at the weekends, spent many rewarding hours scouring the souks of Damascus and Aleppo. Peter Wakefield is a passionate collector of rare and beautiful pots and they are everywhere in the house, their rounded shapes wonderfully satisfying against the chalky walls. Outside, a wide terrace, shaded by a pergola smothered in a pink trumpet vine, leads through original, seventeenth-century arches into a courtyard; here a swimming pool glitters where the mill-pool used to be.

In the clear, blue heat of an Andalusian spring, you might be forgiven for thinking that the great, cool room, the shady terrace and the inviting pool beyond are all that you could possibly want for a life of bliss and Moorish delight. However, mention must also be made of the chastely pretty bedrooms, a cosy sitting room and a big, comfortable kitchen. The main bedroom, situated in the space previously occupied by the mill-wheel, has its own idyllic courtyard in which to hide away. As for the sitting room, which Mayté, the Wakefield's Franco-Spanish housekeeper, has elegantly christened *le salon d'hiver* – it is the first room you enter and used to be where you kept your mule.

LEFT From the secluded swimming pool, edged with traditional Granada tiles, pristine white steps lead to a further area of lush, terraced garden and enchanted, outdoor living-space.

The quintessential English cottage

A barrister and parliamentary counsel, Roger Jones had always been fascinated by architecture and antiques and, on several occasions, had bought pieces of furniture or a painting from the Brook Street showrooms of Sibyl Colefax and John Fowler, the legendary decorating firm housed in the early nineteenth-century town mansion of one of its founders, Nancy Lancaster. Six years ago, a serendipitous visit to the shop caused Roger Jones dramatically to change career. 'The company was looking for someone to run the antiques side of the business – would I be interested?'

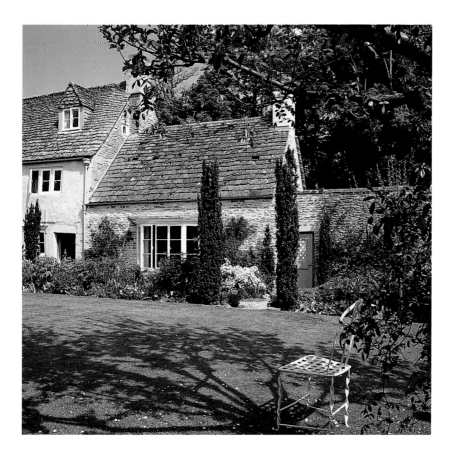

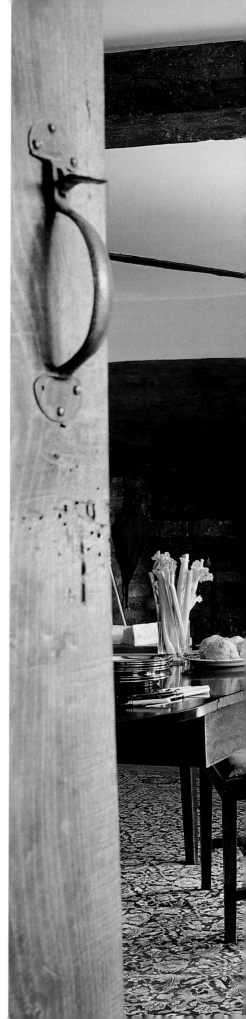

ABOVE The cottage, seen from the garden, with the new extension at right.
RIGHT The flag-stoned hall-cum-dining-room is dominated by a huge fireplace. The buttery note of the paintwork on the walls is echoed by the soft, cream ground of the curtain fabric – a herringbone linen weave printed to resemble crewelwork.

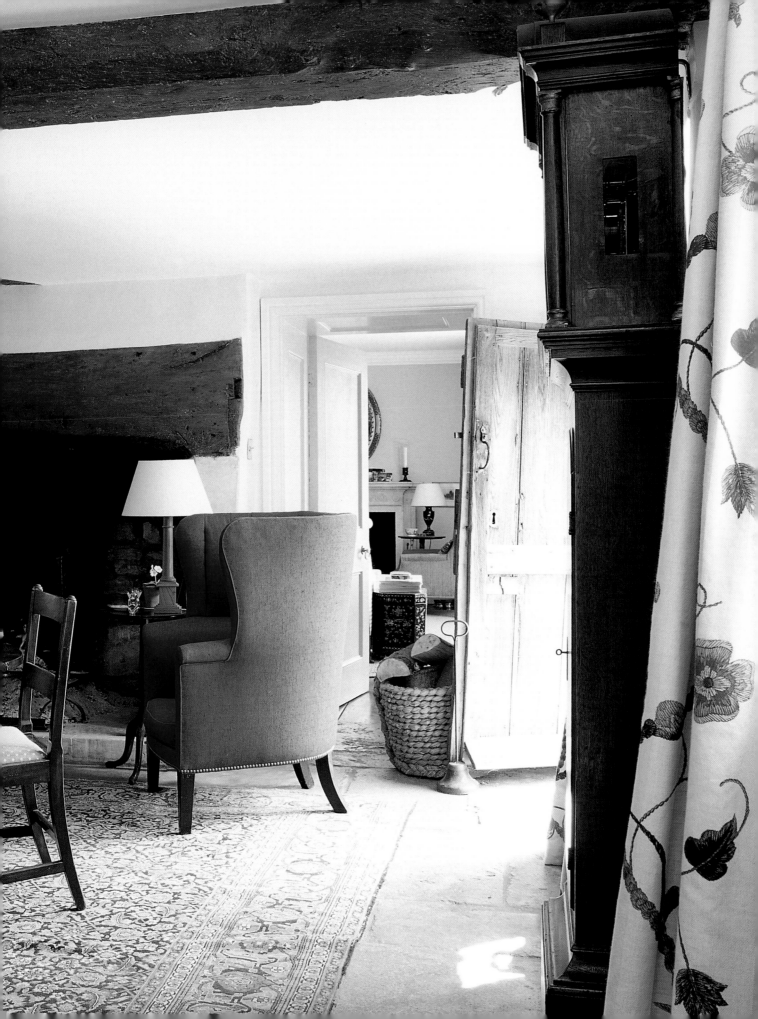

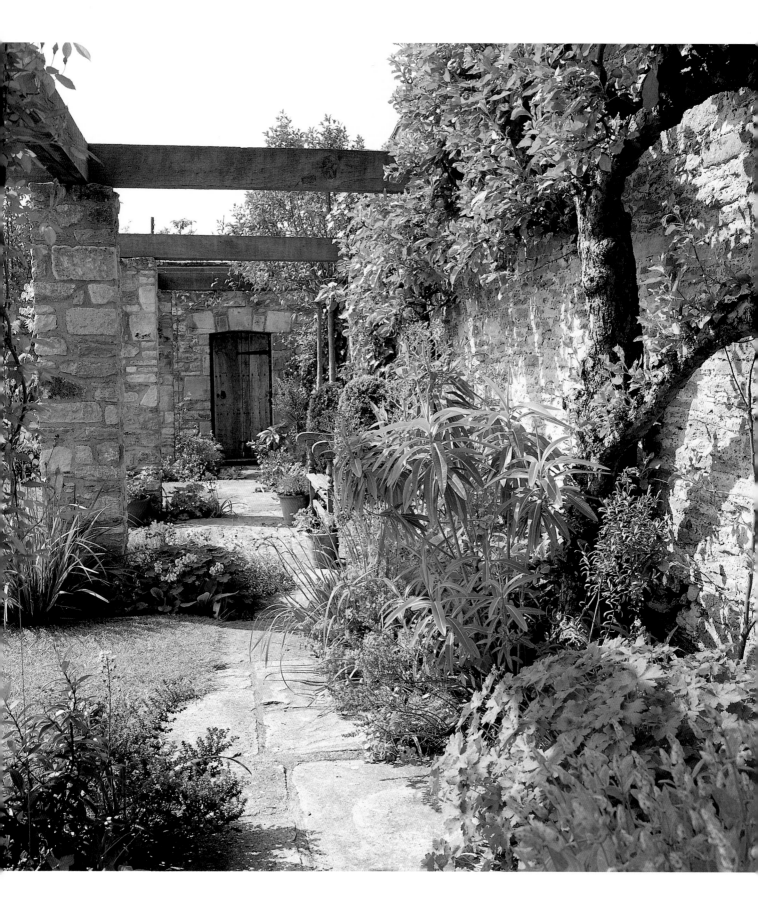

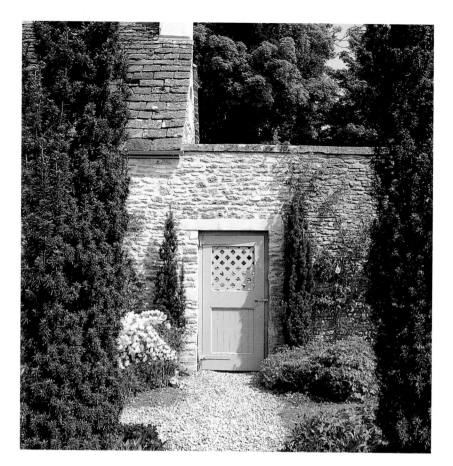

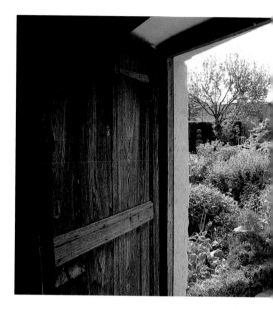

This was no casual inquiry: it had long been obvious to those who knew him and his weekend retreat, that Roger Jones exercised an exact, unerring eye when selecting his own pieces. Today he is a director of the firm and has built up considerably the antiques department.

The scope and scale of the seven antiques-filled rooms in Brook Street – which include Nancy Lancaster's famous 'butta yella' drawing room – are obviously far greater than in the seventeenth-century, Cotswolds cottage that is Roger Jones's weekend home, but his care for detail is equally apparent in both places. Bought fourteen years ago, the cottage was the first house Roger saw and he was the first person to see it when it came up for sale. One of several estate cottages, it is stone built, with a walled garden which was once part of a complex of kitchen gardens surrounding the 'big house'. 'I knew immediately that it was for me,' he says. 'Although small' – the present drawing room and dressing room above are new additions – 'I liked the atmosphere. I think it was the two fireplaces – the one with a wooden bressummer in the main room and the seventeenth-century one upstairs – that encouraged me.'

Having bought the cottage, the first thing he did was to put in central heating; then all the windows had to be replaced and original, blocked-

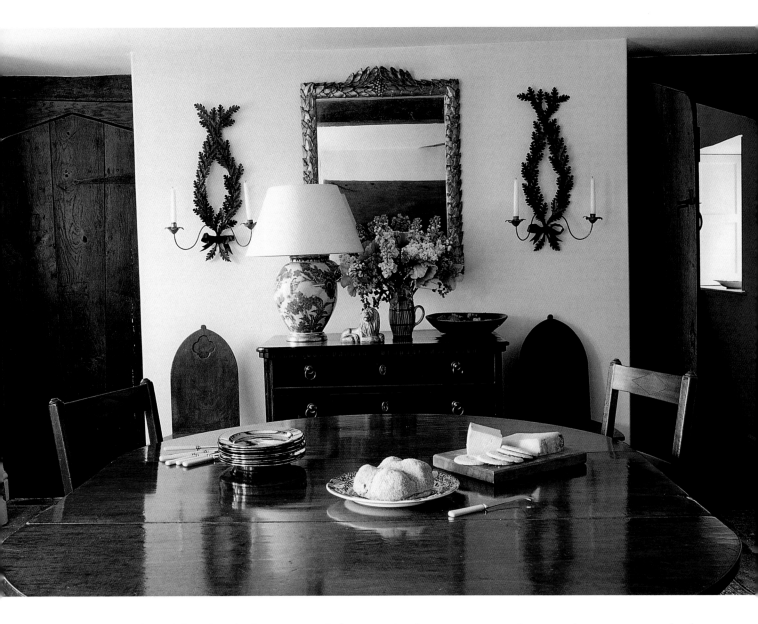

ABOVE Gothick hall chairs and a pair of wall sconces flank a chest of drawers and a mirror in the hall-cum-dining-room.

up windows on the front were opened up, so that every room in the house has a double aspect. A wood-burning stove in the main room was taken out and the surviving fireplace restored to working order, with Roger embarking on a series of remedies to solve the familiar problem of a smoking fire. Nothing worked until a specialist firm came along and widened the stack at the top.

A small lobby that replaced the original larger one has been done away with entirely, and the flagstoned hall you enter now doubles as a dining room. Upstairs, two small rooms were knocked into one to make the main bedroom, and new bathrooms were installed. 'For the first year or so it was wonderful, new details continually suggested themselves, and each weekend there was something different to consider.'

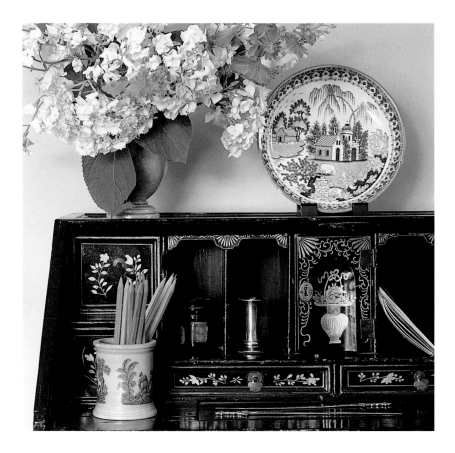

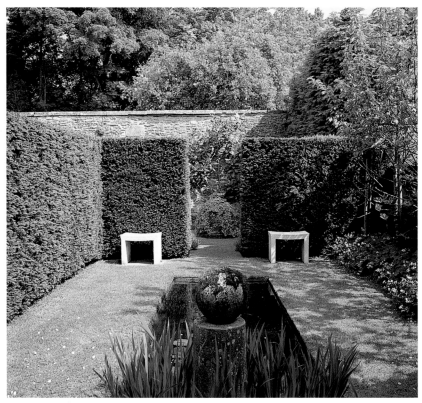

*ABOVE LEFT An early-nineteenth-century,
transfer-printed plate stands on a
japanned secretaire in the drawing room.
LEFT The rectangular lily pond replaced
a potato patch and is now the main
feature in one of the garden's formal
'rooms'. Stone stools are placed to either
side of the opening in the tall yew hedge.*

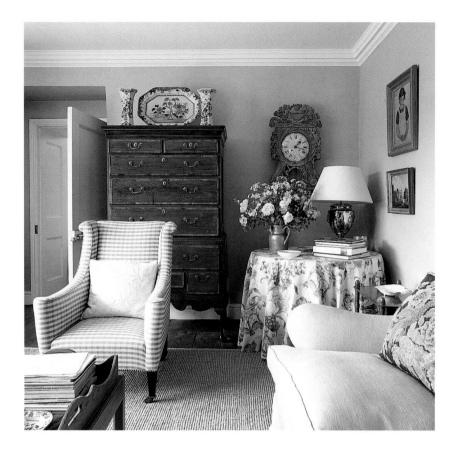

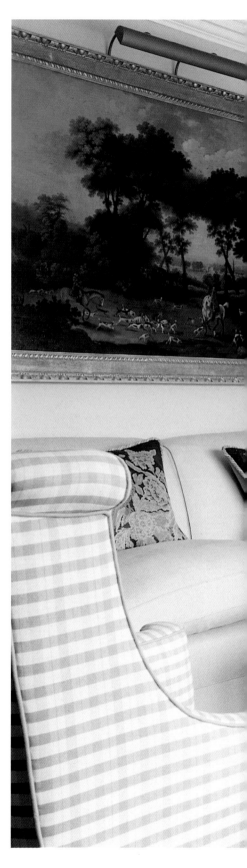

The present sitting room and dressing room were built in 1994. 'I had very firm ideas about what to do,' explains Roger. 'I wanted to build something slightly grander than the original house – I felt I had been given leave to do this by the more sophisticated style of the chimney-piece in the main bedroom.' He was helped by architect Peter Carey, whose work for the National Trust Roger knew, and he was fortunate at the time in being able to use reclaimed roof tiles, so that these lichen-encrusted stones give the appearance of centuries-old permanence.

Inside the cottage, wide, elm floorboards and a handsome chimney-piece from an architectural salvage company continue the illusion of something ancient which has been preserved. The fireplace opening in what is now the drawing room was so wide that, to make it draw properly, a double flue had to be devised: now, twin arms wind around the oval window upstairs, before rejoining.

ABOVE AND RIGHT Grey-blue walls in the sitting room are a classic foil for the wide-ranging collection of furniture, paintings and objects. Above the linen-covered sofa hangs a large hunting scene in oils. A check-covered armchair stands in front of a fruitwood tallboy supporting a garniture of blue-and-white Delftware.

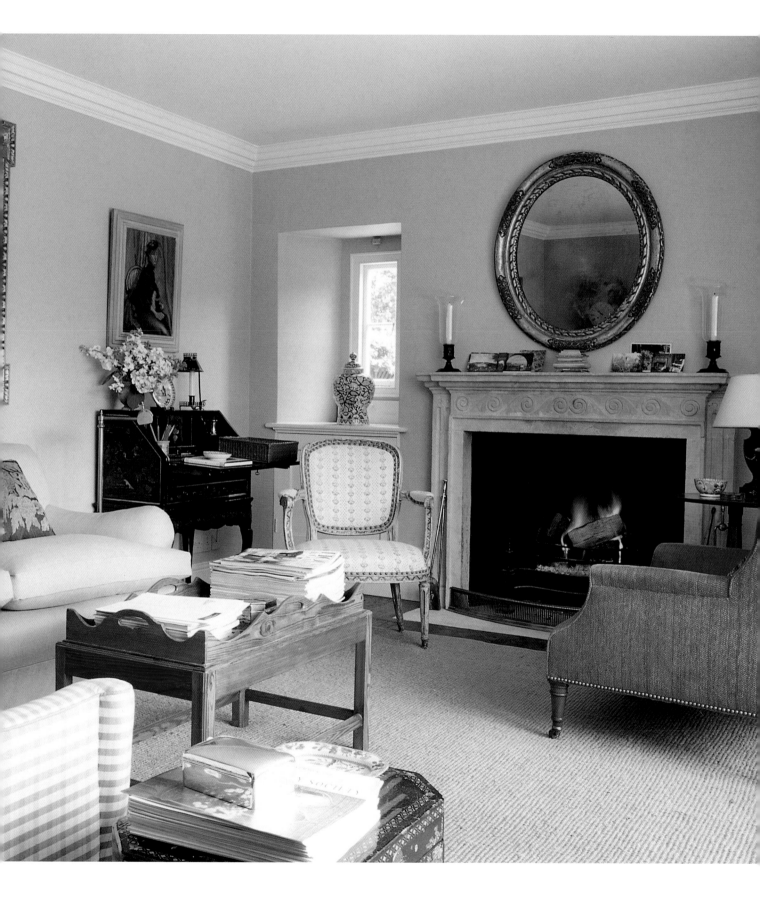

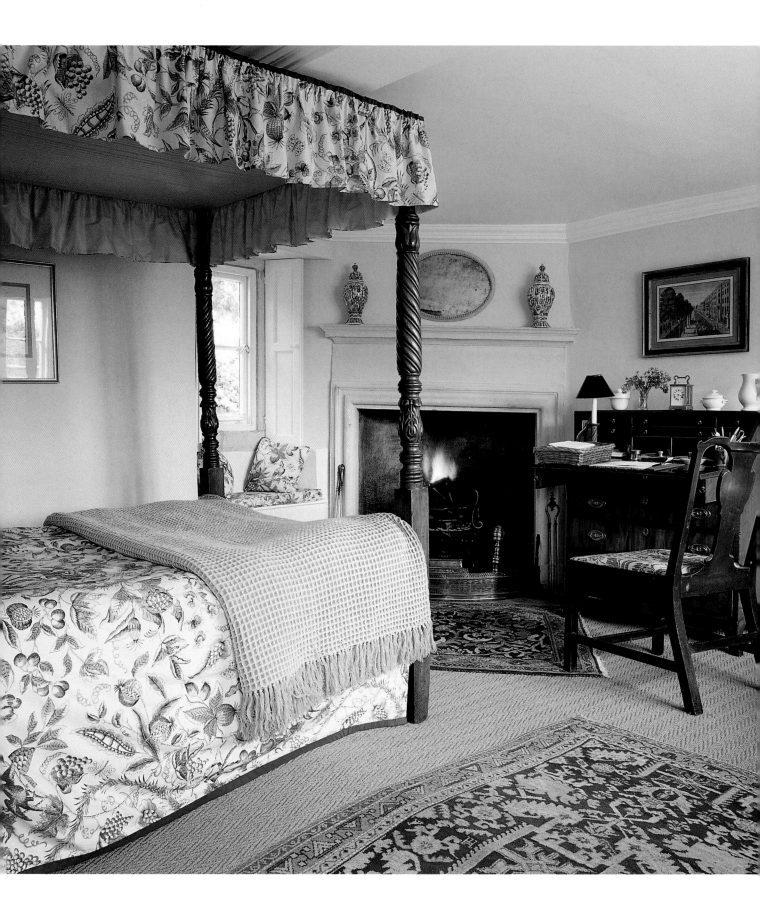

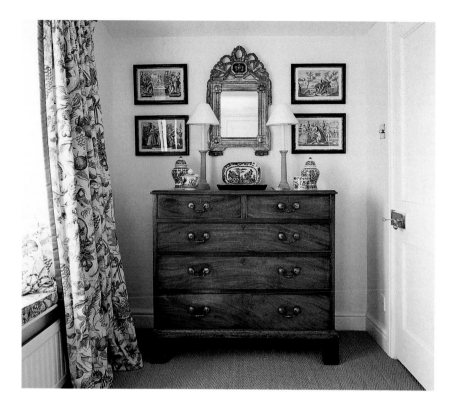

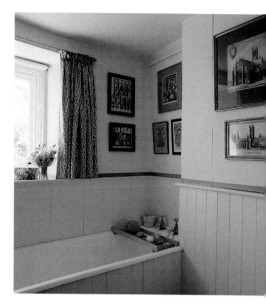

The garden, an exact rectangle, comprised a lawn and vegetable plot when Roger arrived. 'I knew I did not have time to weed, so the lily pond is now where once was a potato patch.' To the east, a large barn with a corrugated-iron roof extends the length of the garden; to screen it from view, Roger planted a row of hornbeam and crab apple. 'I have rather formal tastes,' he explains, 'but I also had to bear in mind that this is a cottage.' To this end he created a series of 'rooms' enclosed within yew hedges; a small loggia is the focal point for the path running the length of the house; more yew hedges surround the lily pond which reflects the pattern of the gate through which can be seen the countryside beyond.

With the encouragement of garden designer Christopher Masson, Roger has built a pergola along the far wall beside the kitchen – a delightfully shady spot for lunch when the sun becomes too strong. In addition, he broke up the expanse of lawn by planting five trees: three medlars, a catalpa and a mulberry. The long bed along the wall opposite the pergola has been subdivided using buttresses of yew.

What Roger now has represents the perfect weekend cottage – but, to its owner, things are not yet ideal. 'That's just marking the spot,' he will say, as he points to a painting, or a piece of furniture you have just admired. 'I'm always changing things and moving them around in order to improve them; but, once I'm happy, things stay.' Knowing his exacting standards, it would be unwise for anyone to bet on it.

OPPOSITE AND ABOVE LEFT In the main bedroom, a blue-and-white toile is a fresh complement to the yellow walls. The handsome chimneypiece, canted across a corner, was there when Roger Jones bought the house.
ABOVE RIGHT Eighteenth-century prints are hung formally in the bathroom.

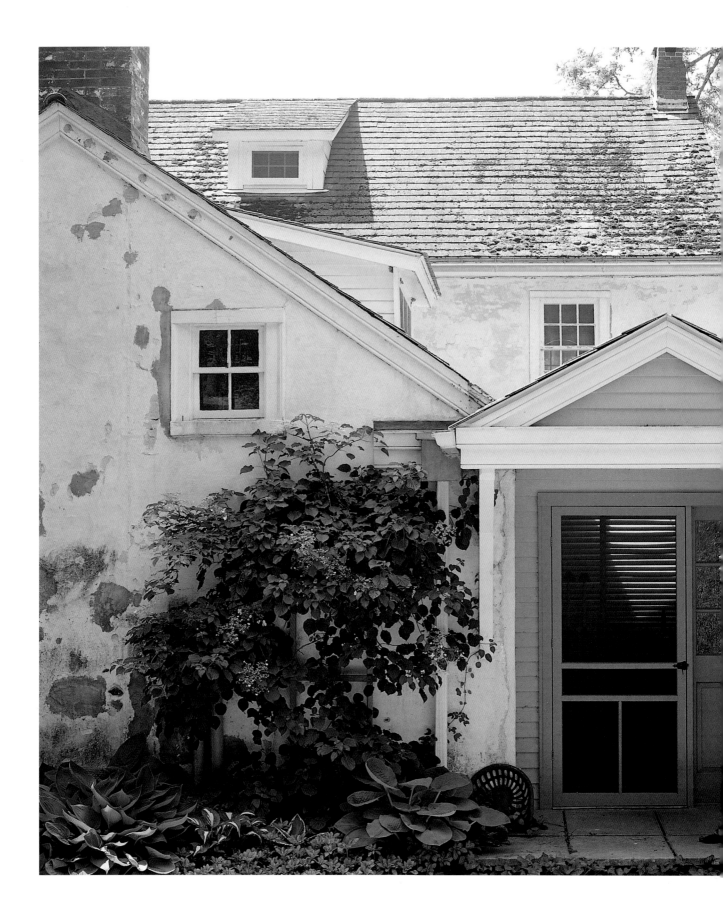

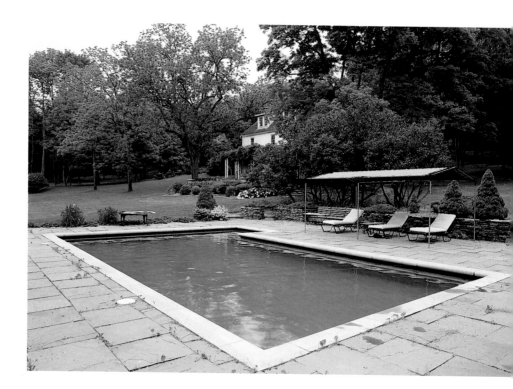

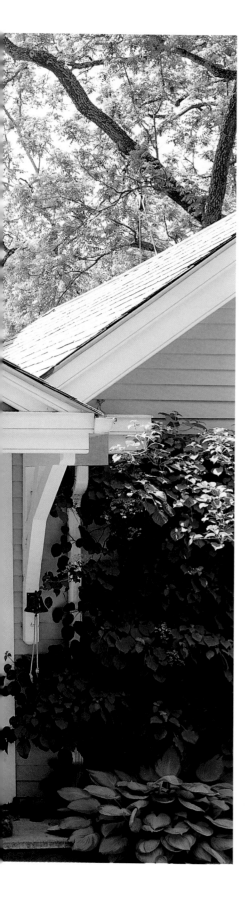

Classic rural style updated

Bucks County in eastern Pennsylvania is noted for its old stone farm-houses and picturesque wooded landscape. In the Thirties the area was discovered by well-known New York literary figures, such as Nathanael West, Dorothy Parker and S. J. Perelman, seeking an escape from the pressures of the city. Among the coterie was film producer Joseph Shrank, who found a small, mid-eighteenth-century house tucked away in a valley close to the Delaware River in Erwinna. This is the same house that, fifty years later, interior designer Laura Bohn and her husband, builder Richard Fiore, transformed into a serene, livable and thoroughly modern rural retreat.

ABOVE Looking across the swimming pool to the sloping garden and the house.
LEFT A pedimented porch shelters the entrance door. The exterior plaster has been patched where necessary and left to age naturally – typical of Laura Bohn's enjoyment of mingling history and modernity, both within the house and outside.

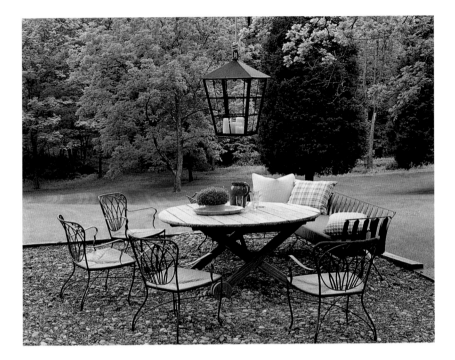

RIGHT Wrought-iron chairs and a weathered, wooden table stand on the pebbled terrace.
BELOW The south- and west-facing pergola supports mature wisteria.
OPPOSITE The kitchen, with its boarded ceiling and stone floor, is entirely new. An iron charcoal grill is inset in the central island.

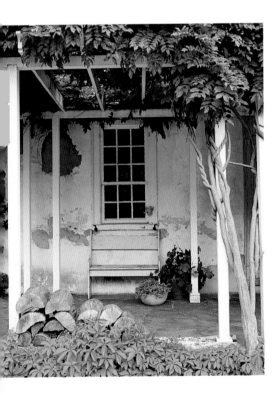

This simple colonial house, of a type known in New England as a 'saltbox', consisted originally of one room, with a small staircase up to an attic under the gabled roof.

Original interior features remain intact: the huge dining-room fireplace, complete with ironwork, where the family cooked and kept warm; the beamed ceiling and pumpkin-pine floorboards; the pine panelling on the door to the left of the fireplace. This opens on to a narrow staircase leading up to what is now an attic bedroom. Here, a steeply pitched ceiling and wide floorboards give the room a feeling of cosiness.

The rest of the house, a two-storey addition, was built in the 1830s. This extension provided two reception rooms off the original parlour and a new central staircase, leading to two more bedrooms upstairs and onwards to the attic in which Laura now has her office.

The house nestles on the side of a gentle incline running down to a stream, with a large old barn nearby; it is surrounded by sixty-five acres of woods and a pine forest planted in the Thirties. Laura and Richard have introduced cows, sheep, horses and a noisy group of chickens, that wander over the tree-dotted slope above the stream. There was never any doubt about the seductive charms of the landscape; however, it was no easy task to realize the simple glory of the house and make it work as an idyll for the twenty-first century. 'Everything was dark, painted forest green or brown,' Laura remembers. 'The ceilings were covered in red cabbage-rose paper. You could hardly see a thing. Nobody wanted to buy it.' Yet this was exactly the challenge Laura wanted. 'I love starting from

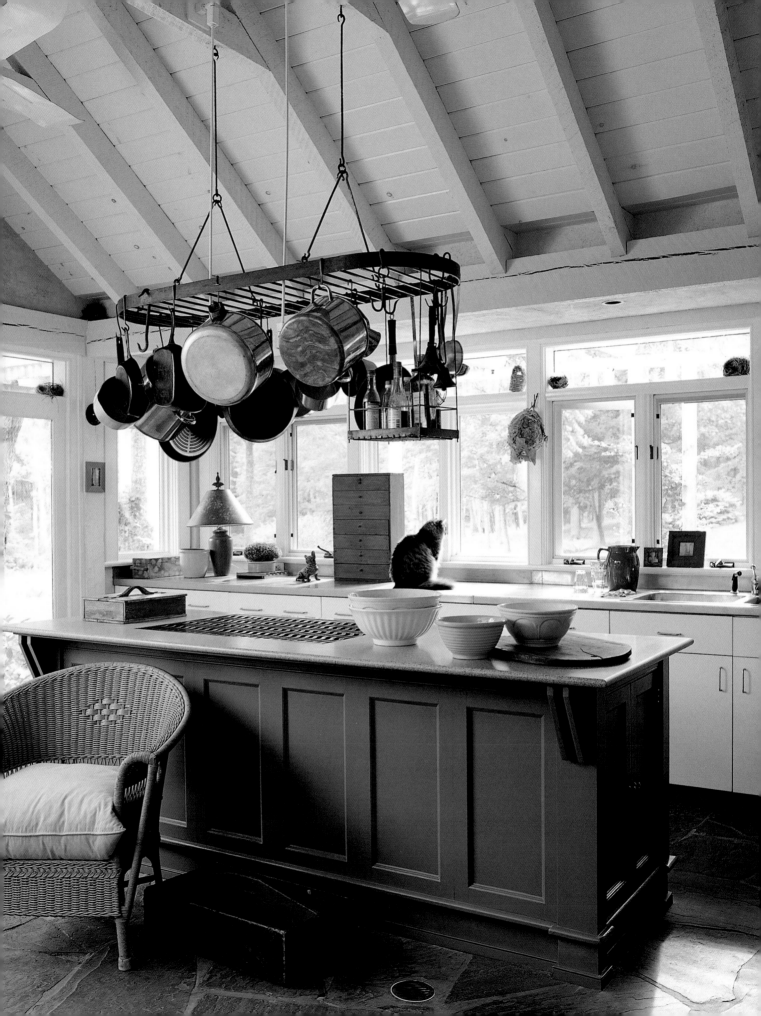

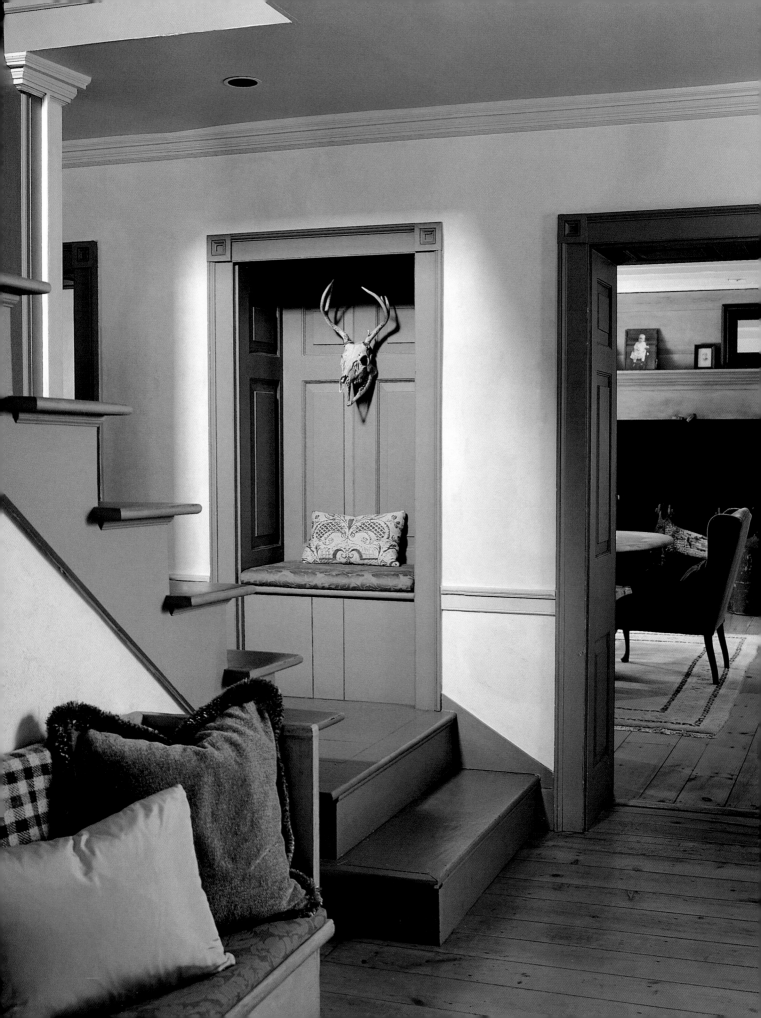

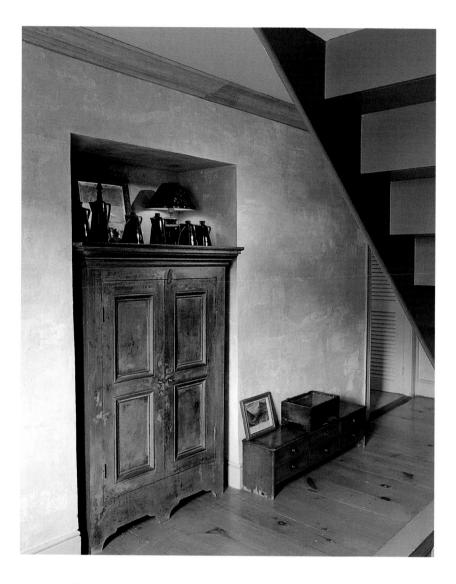

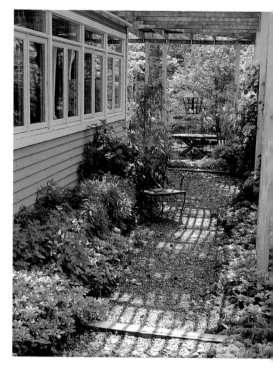

scratch. I'm not interested in a house somebody else has already decorated.' Fortunately, there were few structural problems: 'Every window and door was sound, and the walls were solid.' Laura began by working on the oldest room in the house, now the dining room. Apart from stripping the paint and bleaching the panelling, she also modernized the windows, and added mouldings to the ceiling. In the little bedroom upstairs, she added skylights and windows behind the bed.

Two doors lead from the dining room into two rooms of equal size, part of the 1830s addition to the house. Both have identical chimney-pieces and French windows opening on to a large stone terrace. These rooms were evidently designed according to Quaker doctrine, which required men and women to enter a house by separate doorways. 'I imagine a number of people lived here,' Laura reflects, indicating what were once two parallel sitting rooms, each with its own entrance; these

OPPOSITE AND ABOVE LEFT Removing the soffit from the staircase has opened up interesting, self-contained spaces. ABOVE RIGHT Although the garden gives the impression of being casual, the effect is the result of careful nurturing.

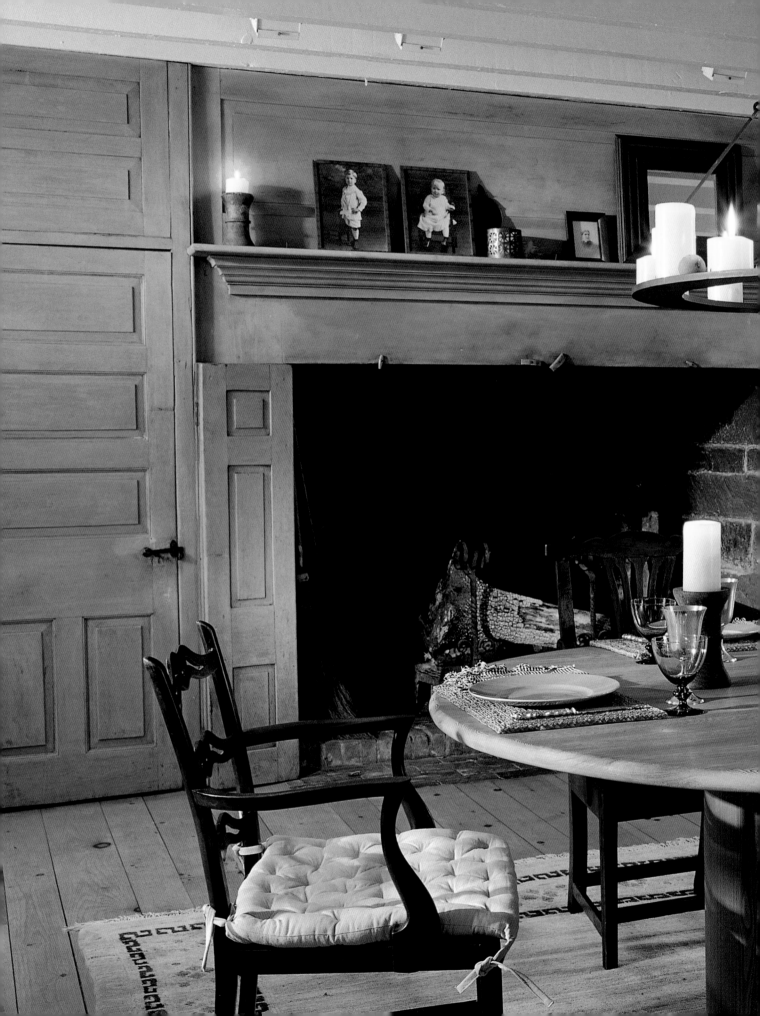

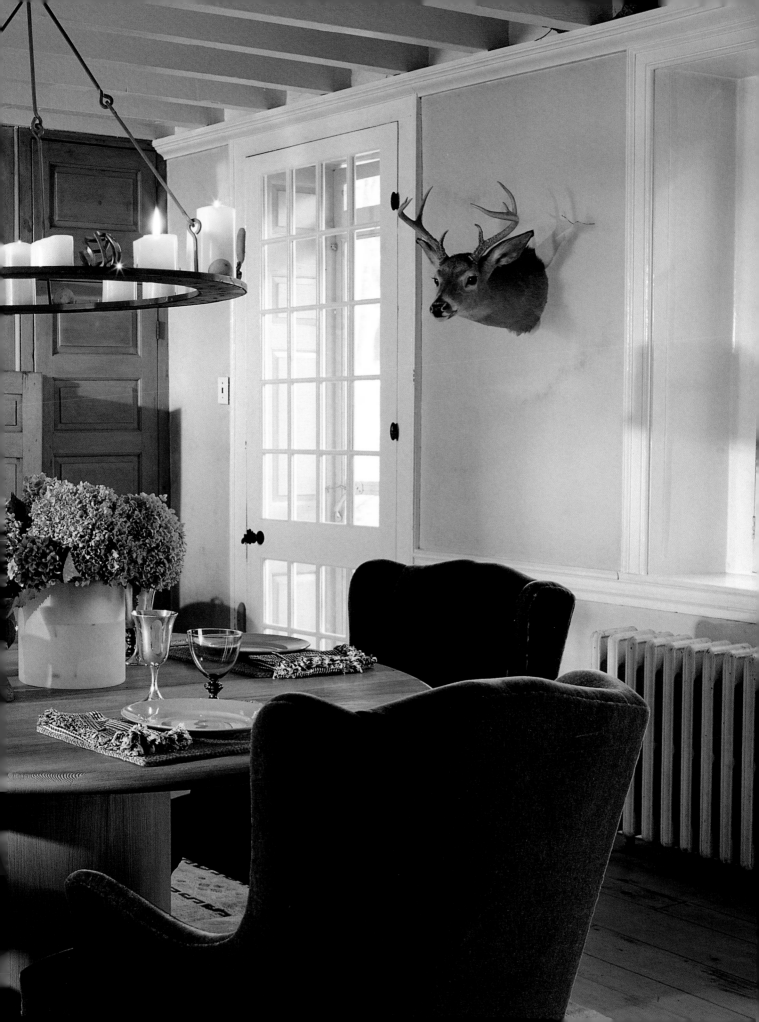

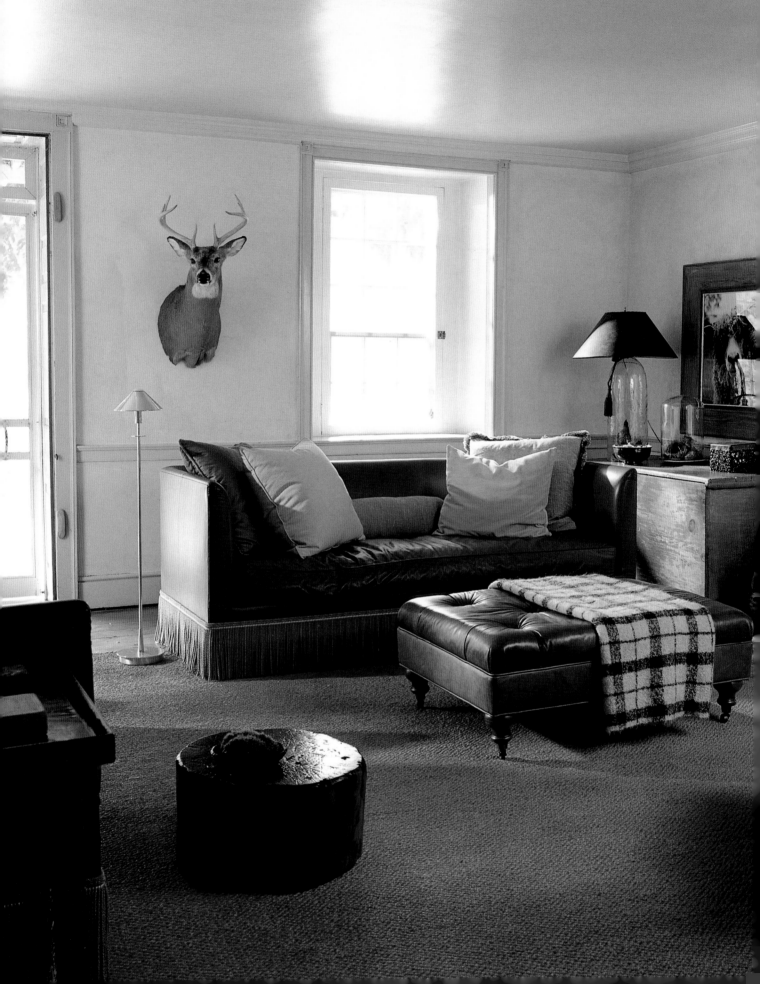

now serve as a sitting room and billiard room. Laura and Richard removed a wall separating the sitting room from the hall to open up the central 'spine' of the house; in addition they created an upstairs landing. Again, a wall was removed between two smaller rooms to create the main bedroom. Now the principal feature of the room is a series of panelled cupboards. A second spare bedroom has a built-in wardrobe and a bed framed in matchboarding. Throughout the house, Laura's preferred colour scheme of mossy greys and greens, with accents of soft brown and chartreuse, gives a feeling of continuity of space.

The house lacked one essential – a kitchen. Laura and her husband added a large kitchen wing to one side of the house. The kitchen has a slate roof and skylights, a vaulted ceiling with exposed rafters and a

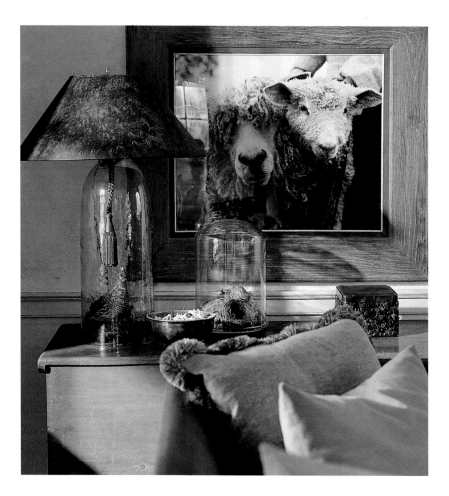

LEFT AND ABOVE Tactile materials, a natural palette and stuffed specimens set the tone in the sitting room, which is an updated version of classic East Coast rural style. The furniture is arranged around an earth-coloured sisal rug facing the original 1830s chimneypiece. PREVIOUS PAGE Beech panelling in the dining room complements the cedar table and nineteenth-century chairs. The chandelier was made locally to Laura Bohn's design.

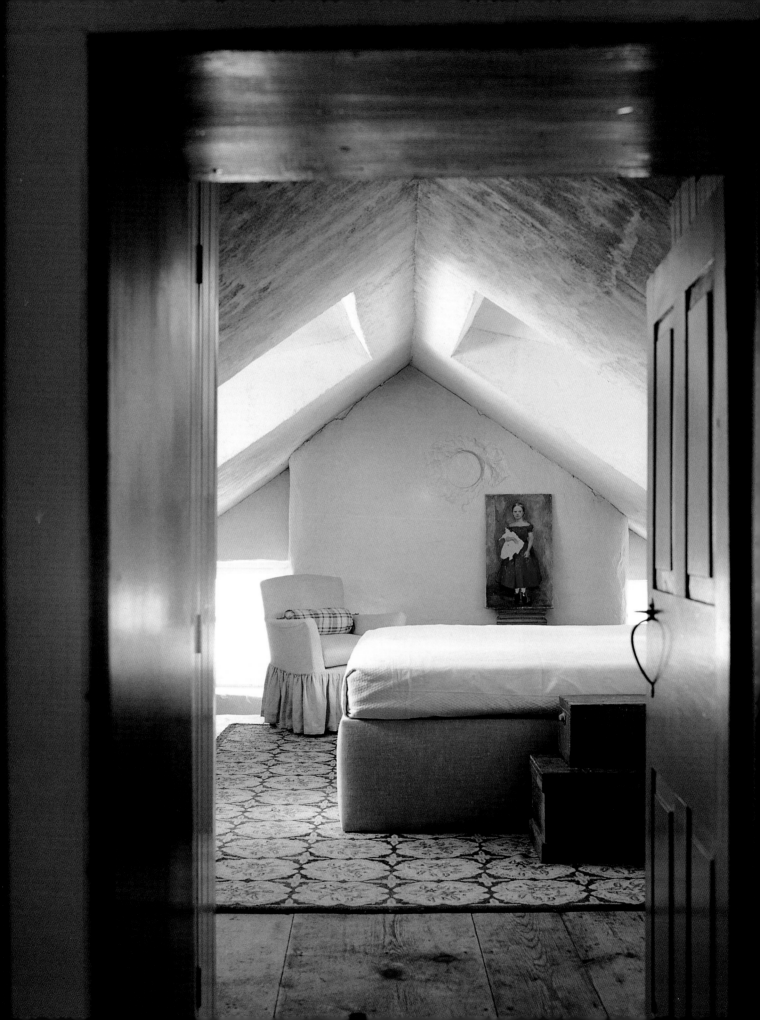

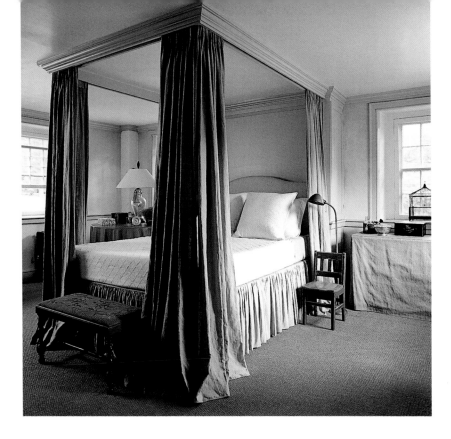

central island unit. In the extra space this extension produced, Laura and Richard created a new entrance to the house, with a second hall and pedimented porch, both with a gabled roof to complement the eighteenth-century façade. A pergola and brick path were added to the south and west sides of the house. Throughout the renovations, Laura and her husband were concerned with respecting the eighteenth- and nineteenth-century details, and the juxtaposition of old and new has been worked out with care. Thus the windows, with their original mouth-blown glass, have been given new frames and weather-screens, built into the wall with no ugly fittings showing. New plumbing and wiring were also installed.

'I like to combine modern elements with period styles,' Laura says. 'People told me that bleaching the pine panelling in the dining room would be too modern, but I did it anyway. In fact, the house is completely modern. The Shaker furniture we collected is modern in design, as is the plain look of the furnishings, with no patterns, only soft colours and textures.' Perhaps the best example of this combination of modernity and history is in the treatment of the interior and exterior walls. Mostly rough-plastered, the surfaces of the interior walls are textured and natural-looking. In the main bedroom, where Laura has given a pale paint wash to unsealed walls, she has allowed old damp staining to mottle the plaster: 'I like the subtle coloration it creates.' As for the exterior, she has left the plaster to age, patching where necessary. The result, like everything about this house, is appropriate to the architectural period and pleasing to the modern eye.

ABOVE The bed hangings in the main bedroom are made from raw linen. OPPOSITE The original attic bedroom, flooded with natural light, has a hooked carpet and a colourful naive painting.

A serene, modern elegance

On a pine-thick hilltop above Grimaud in the south of France, with sweeping views of the Gulf of Saint-Tropez, Belgian designers Claire Bataille and Paul Ibens have arranged a serene marriage of traditional Provençal architecture and spare, elegant, modern style. From the two small villas previously occupying the site has emerged a house of great simplicity, but rich in detail and witty, problem-solving ideas.

Because the village of Grimaud and the surrounding countryside are in a conservation zone, the designers were obliged to retain the outer walls and forms of the original houses and to replace the traditionally

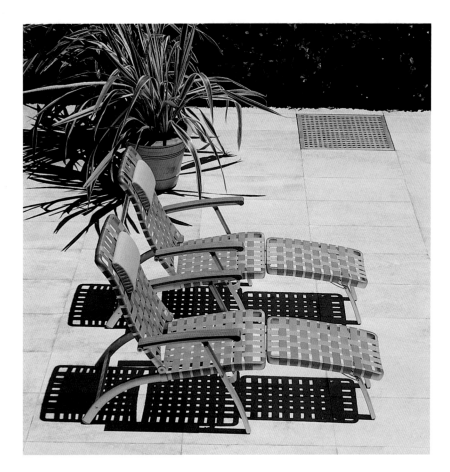

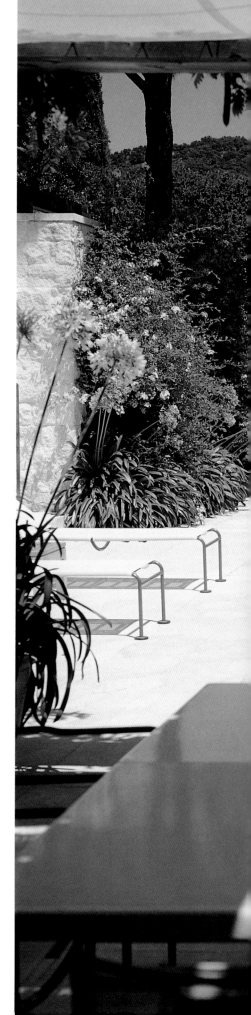

ABOVE Strikingly modern chairs are lined up by the swimming pool.
RIGHT The grey-tiled pool is surrounded by simple stone paving and enclosed by evergreen 'walls', creating an architectural space with the feeling of a room.

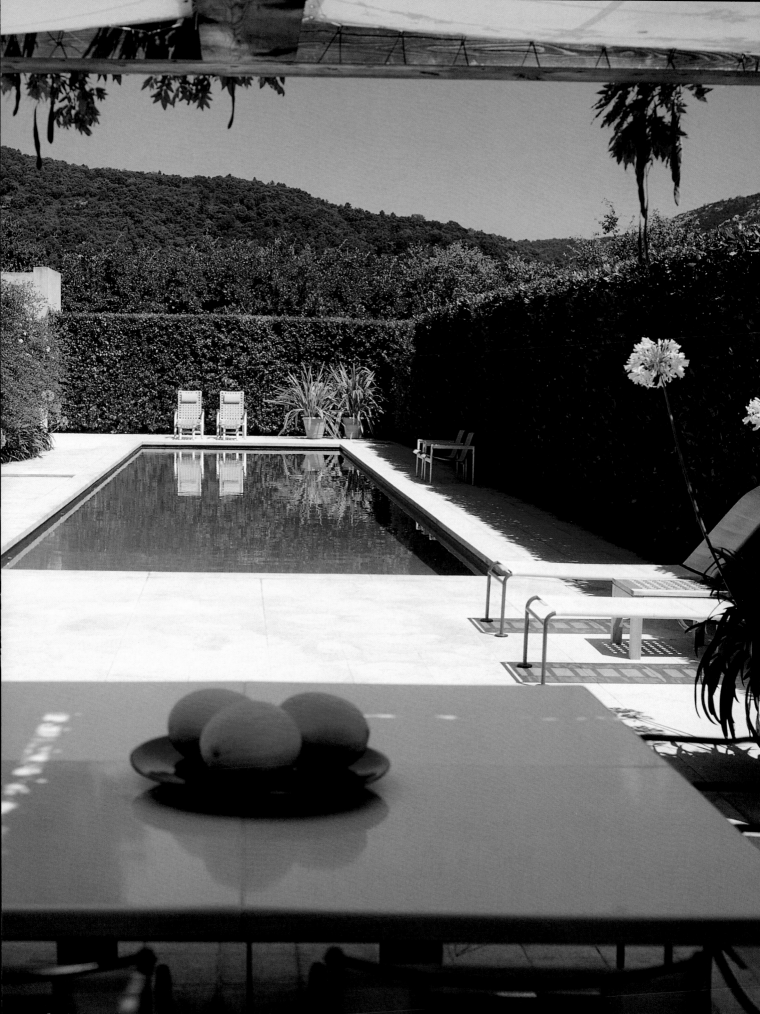

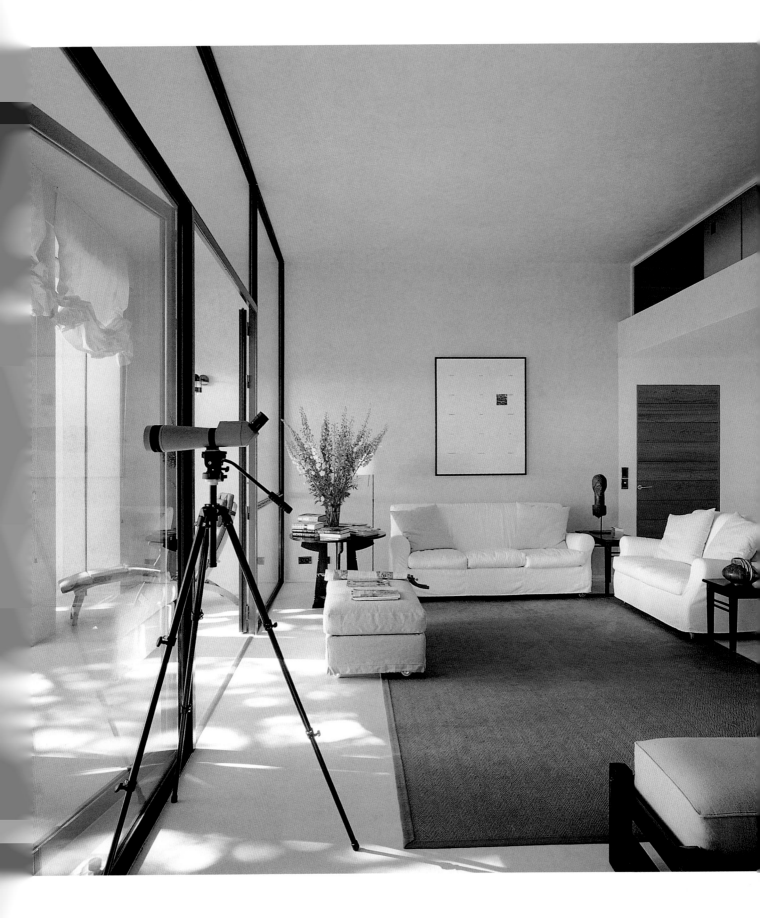

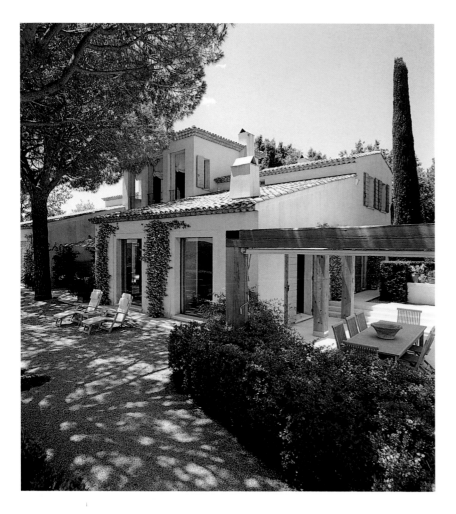

tiled roof. But, within this shell, they were at liberty to remake every-thing: the interior is now perfectly attuned to its new role as a peaceful holiday retreat for their busy clients.

The site itself posed some structural challenges, and a ninety-five-foot-long retaining wall had to be built to hold back the hillside behind the house. Now painted a dark terracotta red, this is a happy feature of the entrance, providing a sense of fortified privacy.

Walking through the solid, cedar front door into the main sitting room, the visitor is bathed in Mediterranean light and drawn through high, glass doors towards the terraced garden and the sight of the sea beyond. This central room soars upwards; above it is the main guest bed-room, with lofty windows and its own balcony. Both are part of the almost tower-like construction – for which planning permission was granted – between the two original buildings. Access to the upper floor is via a separate, exterior staircase.

The height of the triple windows on both floors is softened by ecru, ruched blinds. The walls of the sitting room are pale stucco, while the

ABOVE Formed within the shell of two villas, the house has a wide, shady terrace overlooking the swimming pool and sea. OPPOSITE The main sitting room is an airy, white space, the only colour coming from the linen rug and wooden door. A telescope focuses on the view of the sea.

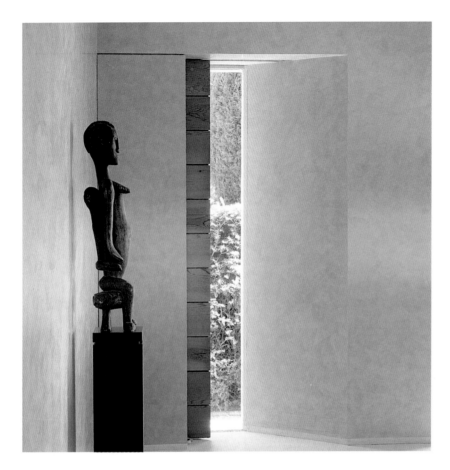

floor – like the majority of floors and terraces both inside and outside the house – is tiled with the local *pierre d'Estaillade*.

The renowned Belgian garden designer Jacques Wirtz worked with Claire and Paul and the owners to create a garden with a strong Mediterranean flavour; Wirtz's genius for hedges and green-on-green planting is much in evidence. The site is not large, but a sense of grandeur and space comes from the great pine trees in front and from the superb outlook. Each corner has been planned and planted with a designated use. A terrace at the south side, flanked by a lavender bed and an ancient olive tree and overhung by a tangle of pittosporum, is perfect for breakfast. At the north end of the house, a larger terrace shaded by a pergola is used for dinner. The central, mosaic-tiled terrace is sheltered and perfumed by jasmine-covered walls.

ABOVE A female figure from Zaire is seen against clear-blue walls in the dining room. RIGHT Looking from the main sitting room to the dining room; the frameless doors are hallmarks of Claire Bataille's work. The stool in the foreground is by early-twentieth-century American designer Gustave Stickley.

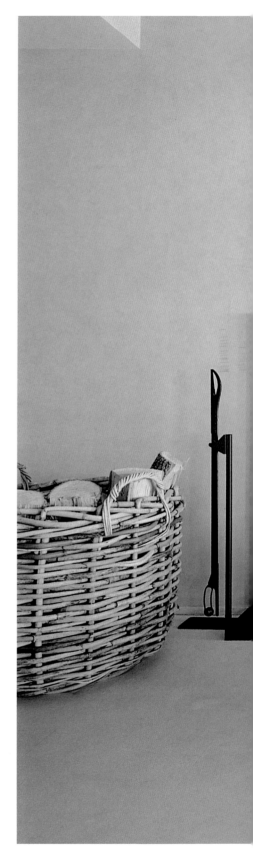

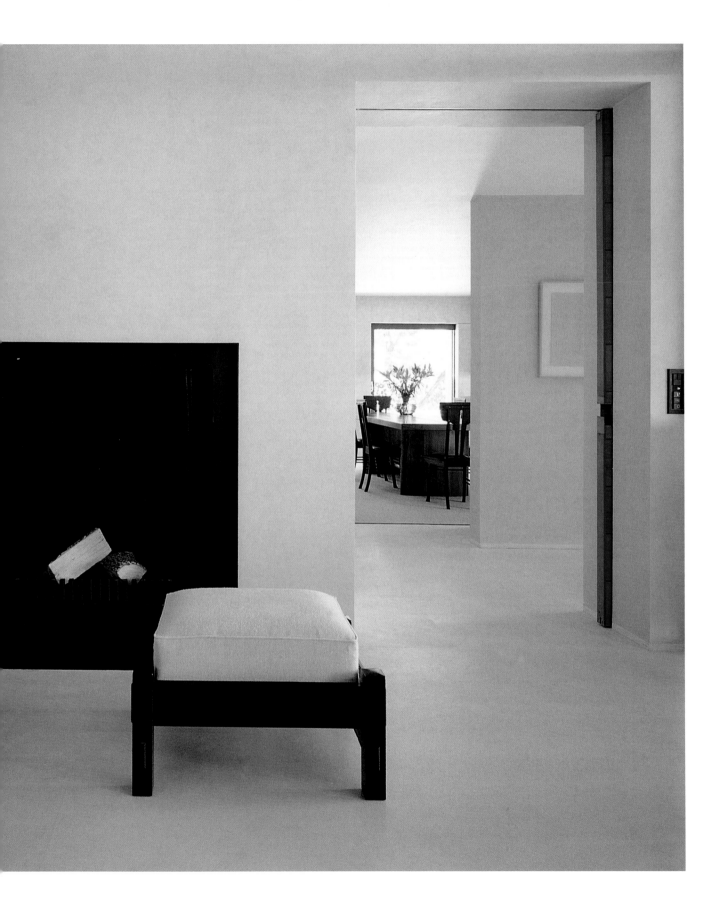

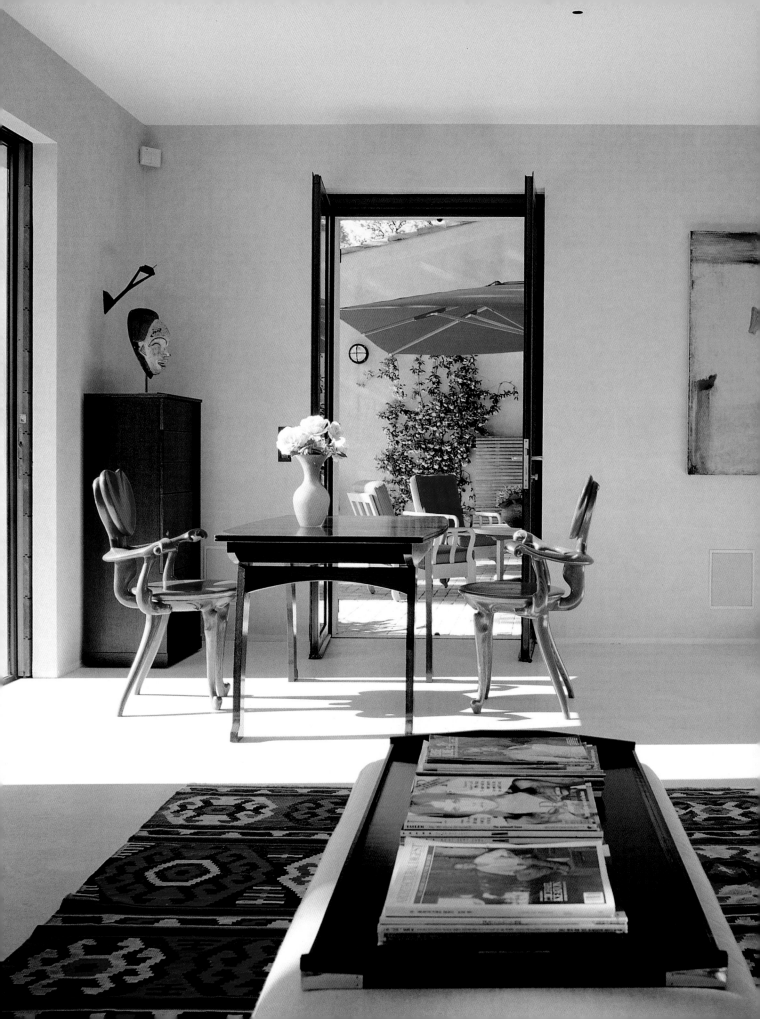

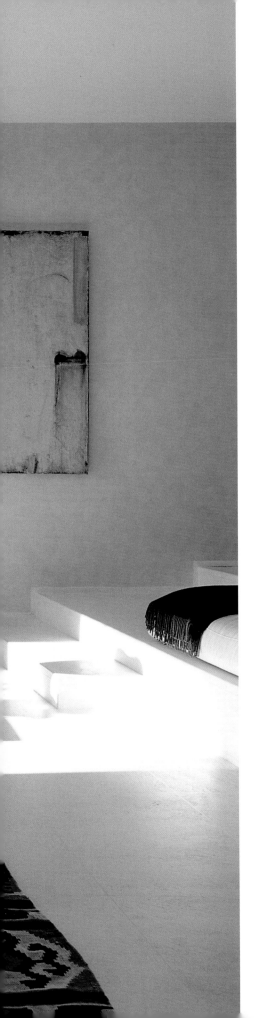

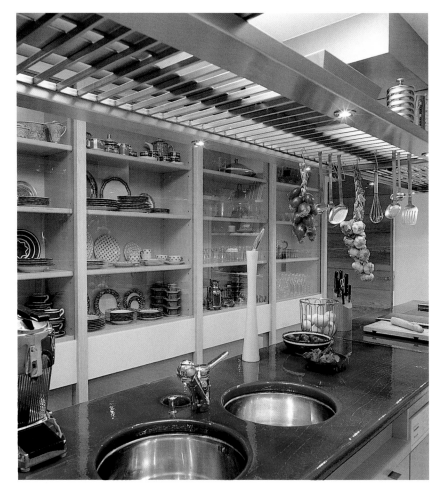

The swimming pool is tiled in grey mosaic, thus avoiding the usual turquoise glare. At one end is a pergola covered in white wisteria. (All the flowers in the garden, apart from the roses, are blue or white. Wirtz even imported white lavender, unknown locally.) A large, square table made from squares of pale lava, a summer kitchen and a minimalist barbecue tucked in the corner make this the ideal place for lunch.

Back inside the house, three long rooms abut the central sitting room at right angles: the kitchen at the back, the dining room in the centre and the library at the front, looking on to the terrace and towards the sea.

The kitchen has a glass wall at one end, which seems to bring the thick greenery of this part of the garden indoors. One side wall is lined

ABOVE Patterned tableware is ranged on shelves along one wall of the kitchen. The long, island worktop has inset, stainless-steel sinks.

LEFT In the library hangs a painting by French artist André Debono. Oak chairs by Antonio Gaudi face each other across a table by Art-Nouveau designer Gustave Serrurier-Bovy.

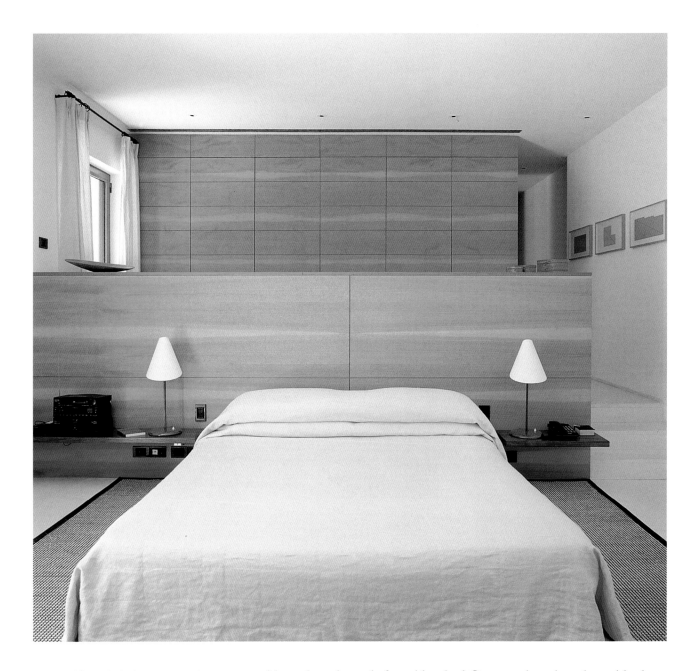

ABOVE The main bedroom, arranged on two levels, has cedar units providing plenty of storage space for clothes. The lower unit forms a bedhead on one side and, on the other, incorporates cupboards. Facing these are ceiling-high wardrobes.

with cupboards made from bleached Oregon pine; the other with glass-fronted cabinets containing colourful china, glasses and other accoutrements, all beautifully displayed.

The narrow dining room exudes an atmosphere of cool quiet, thanks to blue stucco walls which, like those in the main salon, were executed by Italian craftsmen. Again, there are floor-to-ceiling windows at one end. Claire and Paul increased the sense of light and space by opening, at seated eye-level, a horizontal slot which runs the length of the room and gives on to the library.

One of the hallmarks of the designers' style evident in this house is

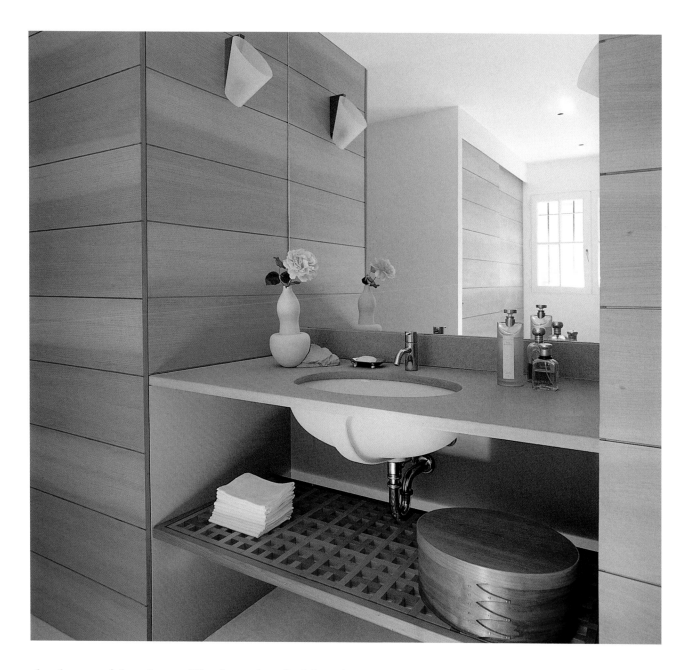

the absence of door frames. The doors close flush into the walls, enhanc-
ing the clear geometry of the place, and are made of red cedar, with
horizontal grooves, a style that reflects ancient, local door designs. Wood,
old and new, provides density and warmth throughout the house. The
heavy cherrywood dining table is a masterpiece by a member of the
Compagnons, an elite guild of French artisans, while the chairs and a
small buffet are by the Art-Nouveau furniture-maker Gustave Serrurier-
Bovy. Many other pieces by him, including a larger sideboard in the
sitting room, are dotted round the house, enhanced by the calm mod-
ernism of the interior architecture.

*ABOVE Cedar panelling, used throughout
the house, injects warm colour into the
downstairs cloakroom. The sculptural,
alabaster vase is by Anish Kapoor.*

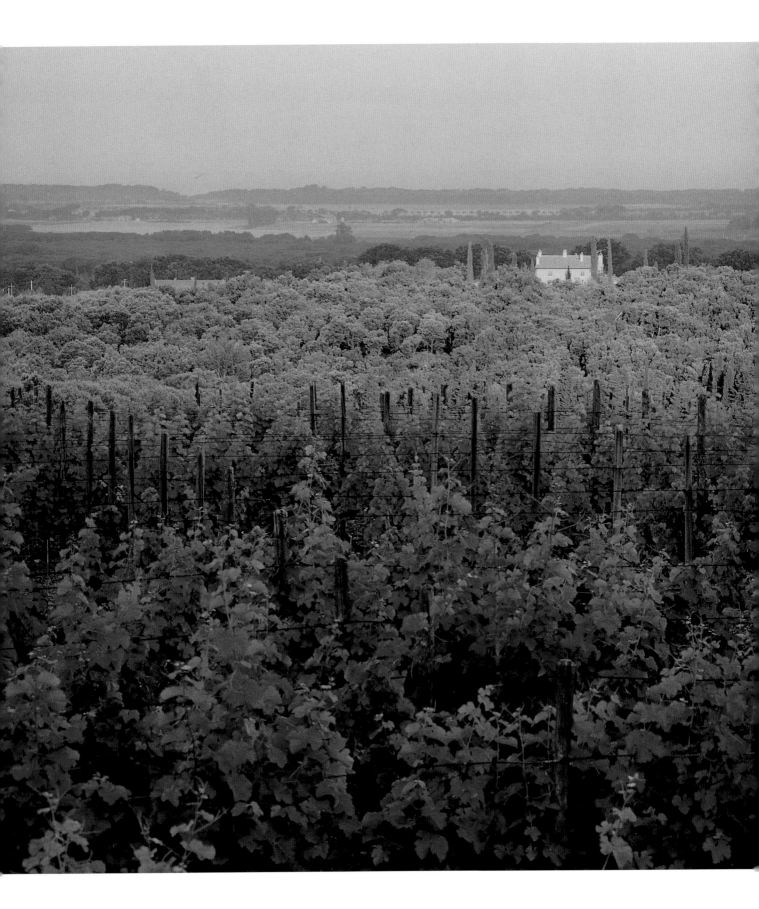

Tuscan hospitality

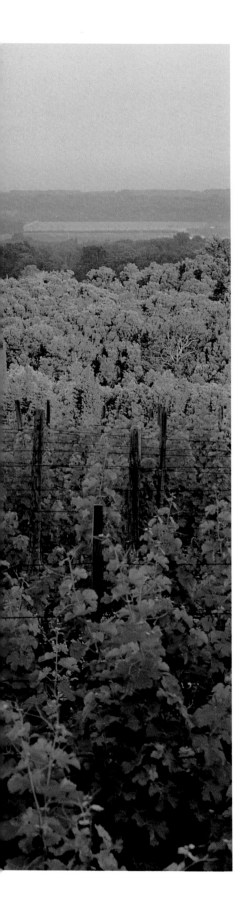

Part of the Via Aurelia, the ancient road from Rome to Gaul, runs through the flat Maremma plain between the Mediterranean and the Castagneto Carducci hills in Tuscany. Tourists speeding north or south along the motorway which runs next to it will miss the quiet charm of the area's landscape and villages. If they look inland, they may be tempted to explore the rolling, wooded countryside which gives way to the locally named Colline Metallifere (the metal-bearing hills) and the village of Bolgheri beyond. If they turn off, they will find themselves among ancient villages crested with castles, old orchards of peach and

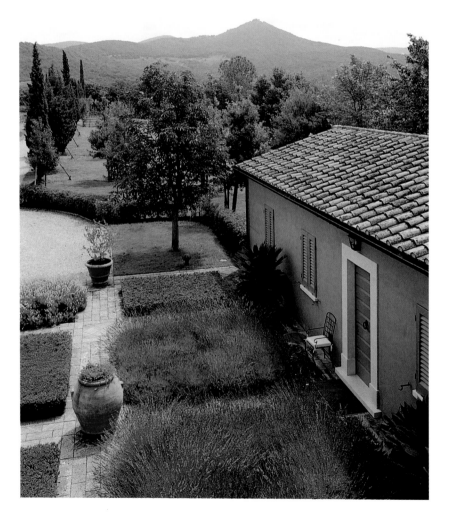

ABOVE The view from upstairs in the main house, showing part of the geometric parterre; the beds are planted with lavender and neatly clipped box.
LEFT The house is set within densely forested hills. In the far distance is the sea.

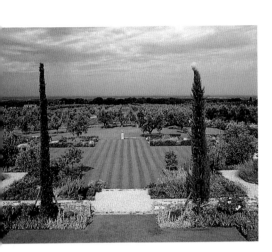

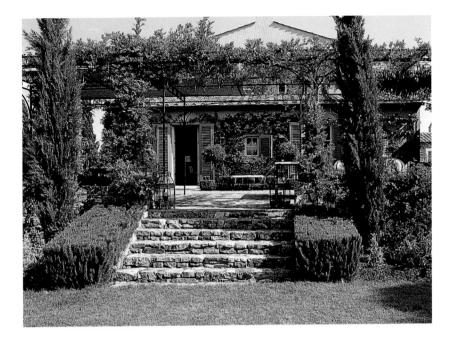

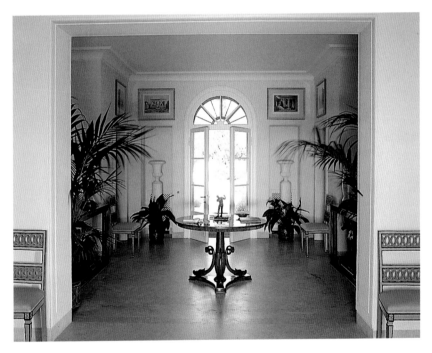

ABOVE Arabella Lennox-Boyd's garden design leads the eye outwards to the sea.
ABOVE RIGHT The guest wing, seen from across the garden.
RIGHT The pietra dorata di Vicenza floor and coarse-grained plaster walls in the hall are a pleasant foil for painted neoclassical chairs and framed, nineteenth-century prints of Egypt by David Roberts.
OPPOSITE The coat room contains massed arrangements of capriolo trophies. The capriolo is a roebuck whch abounds in the Bolgheri plains.

apricot, and vineyards. For here, the climatic and geological conditions are near ideal for making some of the best wine to be found anywhere in Italy and, arguably, the world.

The land at Ornellaia has belonged to the della Gherardesca family for 1,000 years. In the fifteenth century, their land holdings stretched from Piombino to Pisa, so that the area, which is surrounded by the famed vineyards of Sassicaia, was known as La Gherardesca.

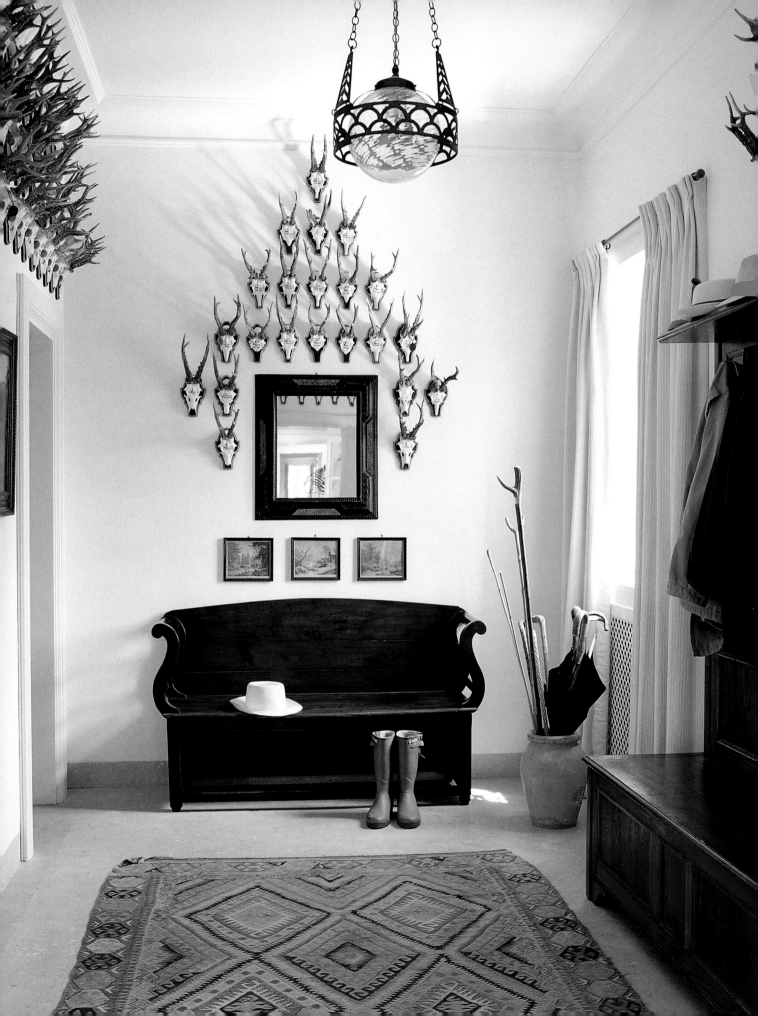

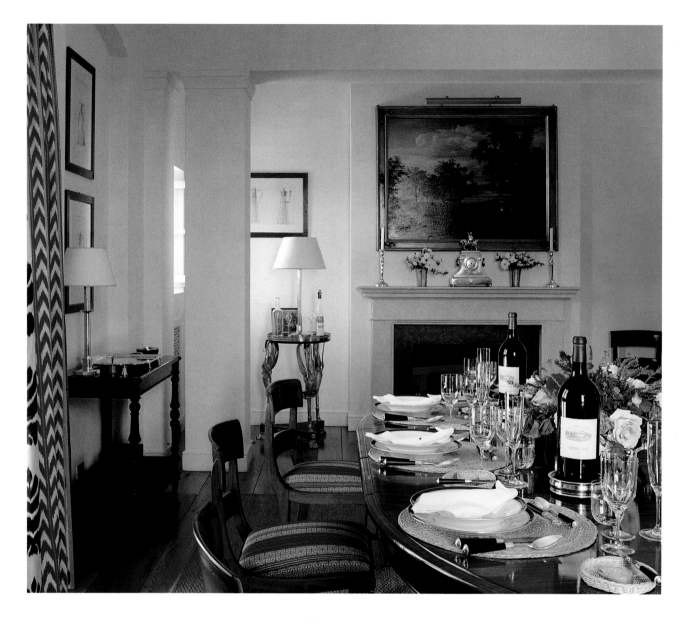

ABOVE *The dining room, with neoclassical Italian furniture, is hung with a series of framed designs for wine decanters by Bolin for Fabergé.*

When David Mlinaric of Mlinaric, Henry & Zervudachi was first invited by Marchese Ludovico Antinori to visit Ornellaia with a view to overseeing its conversion, an empty farmhouse stood on the site. It was not very old and was one of many on the estate, all of the same design. Set among the foothills of the Colline Metallifere, it looked over the vineyards to the sea and, beyond, to Elba. Called 'La Bandiera' (The Flag), the house at Ornellaia was a plain central block with two lean-to extensions, in the familiar form of ancient Roman farm buildings. Its name was incised in the façade with, above it, a ceramic coat of arms set into the stucco. This was the only ornament. Inside, the rooms were totally plain, but nobly proportioned. 'Initially, we intended to repair and convert the building as it was,' says David Mlinaric, 'but it turned out to

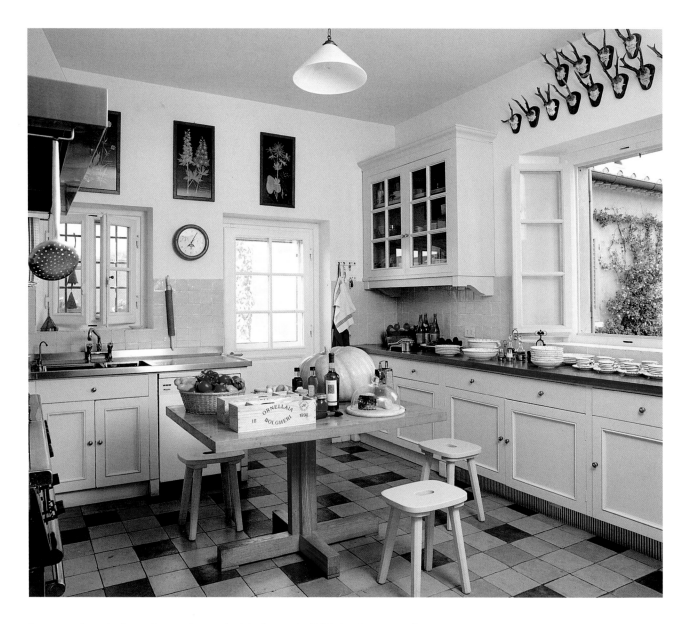

have no foundations. Instead, we decided to rebuild it in the same form but with garages and service spaces underneath, and a further two wings on the north side, one for guests and one for the caretaker.' Thus instead of a typical Tuscan farmhouse conversion, the brief had become one for a small villa – simple, unpretentious and in keeping with its surroundings.

The design was distinguished by its restrained use of details for the windows, doors, shutters, cornices, fireplaces and so on. 'We decided to use only local materials,' explains David Mlinaric. 'The effect was to be light, fresh and apparently artless: an envelope which would allow for additions and changes, as the owner's requirements changed over time. The house was to be surrounded by a garden – to link the building to the vineyards around it and to the landscape beyond.'

ABOVE The restrained style of the kitchen cupboards contrtasts with the chequerboard floor of Neapolitan tiles and the framed, pressed flowers on the far wall.

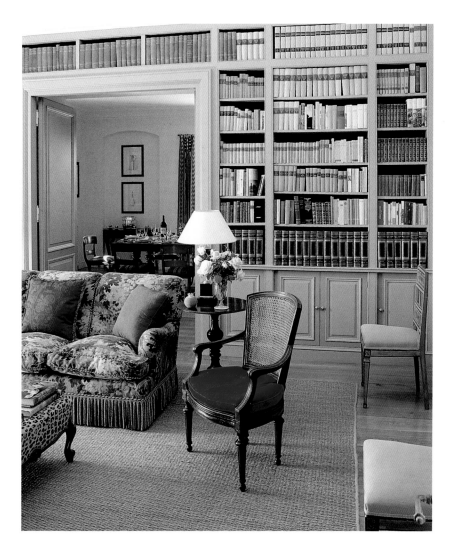

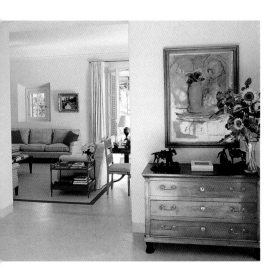

ABOVE Looking from the hall to a sitting room. The furniture, whether contemporary sofas or a neoclassical chest-of-drawers, has been chosen for its unfussy, timeless lines.
ABOVE RIGHT AND OPPOSITE The pale-green-painted library, intended as a winter sitting room, has seagrass matting and predominantly eighteenth-century furniture. The large painting by Muller, c.1915, is of the owner's aunt, Principessa Cora Caetani. The sofa is covered in tapestry.

In the interwar years, Cecil Pinsent – the English architect and garden designer who, though he worked largely in Tuscany, also designed Beli Dvor, outside Belgrade, for Prince Paul of Yugoslavia – built an elegant house by the sea for the owner's family. At Ornellaia, the present owner wanted to continue this Anglo/Tuscan tradition of building. He chose Arabella Lennox-Boyd for the garden and landscaping, while David Mlinaric was asked to design the house. 'Not being architects, my partner Tino Zervudachi and I worked with Andrea Taverna in Italy and Timothy Hatton in London,' says Mlinaric. 'Andrea Taverna, who lived nearby, organized the entire project; Timothy's architectural skills assured the precision we all wanted. As a result, there are no cover mouldings, pipe boxings or other such imbalances in the house.'

The plainness of the interior, which survives from the first buildings, was accentuated as the designers opened up rooms which, in the previous house, had been separated by walls. There are no passages; one

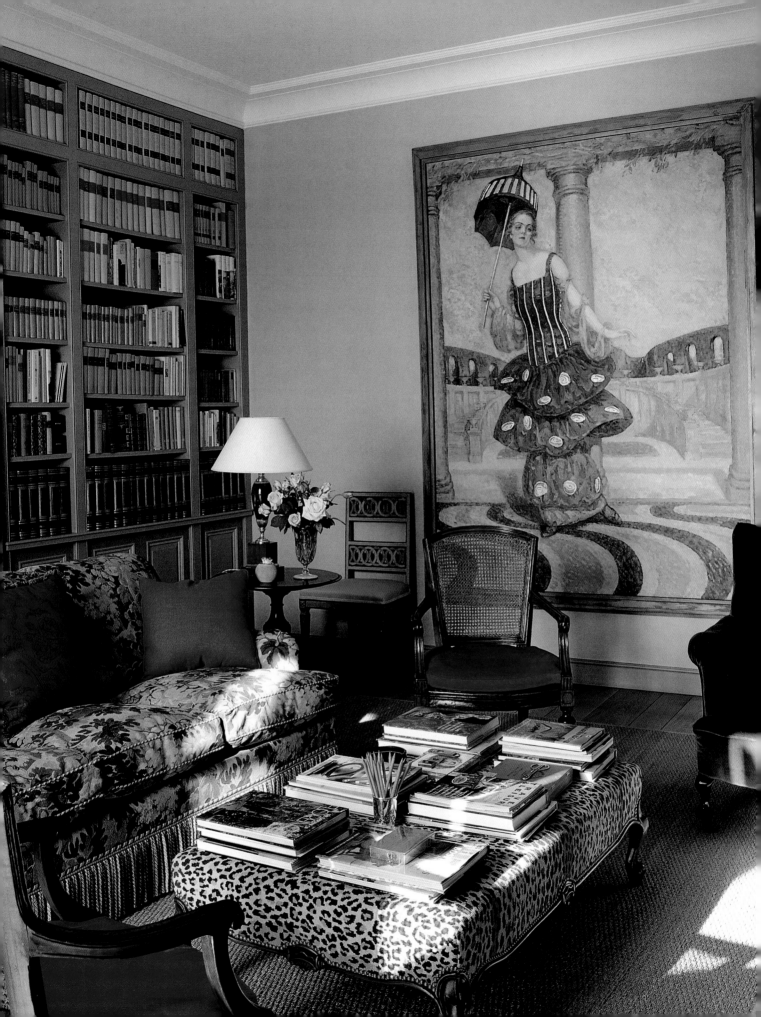

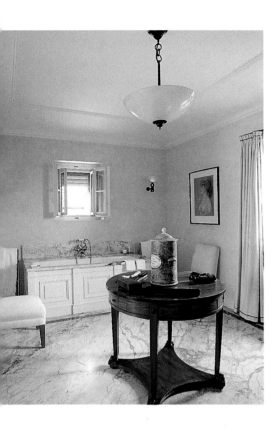

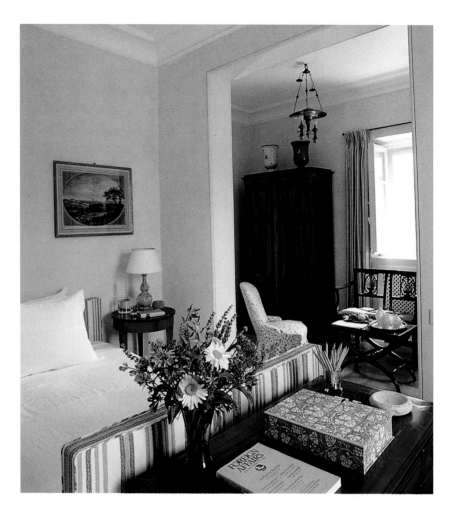

ABOVE An early-nineteenth-century table is the central feature in the main bathroom. ABOVE RIGHT A spare bedroom, with adjoining sitting area, has dark-wood furniture against soft-coloured walls.

room leads into another, sometimes in *enfilade*. The staircase is set between walls, as is usual in Tuscany. All bedrooms have separate bathrooms and terraces. The decoration, in keeping with the architectural detail, is simple: ivory, pale pink or pale green paint, cream cotton, few patterns, not too much furniture and most of it inherited. It is one of the simplest sets of rooms David Mlinaric has designed but, like all apparently simple solutions, it was achieved only after a great deal of planning and pruning.

All the ground-floor windows give on to Arabella Lennox-Boyd's garden, as beautiful now in its youth as it will be in maturity. The garden, like the house, is arranged as a series of 'rooms'; in summer, one moves through it much as one moves through the house. There are beds filled with roses, lavender, rosemary and lilies. Topiary, pergolas and citrus trees in terracotta pots shade terraces close to the building. All the colours and shapes one expects to find in a Mediterranean garden are there and, as it is skilfully maintained by Donald Leevers of Volterra, many plants and flowers thriv here which are more familiar in the

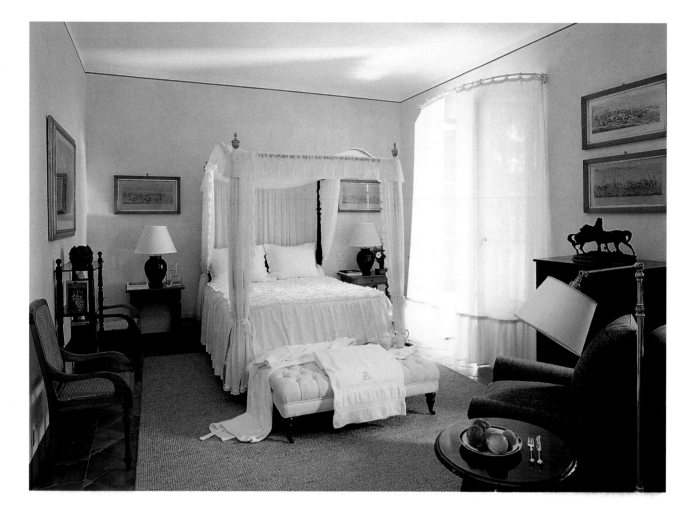

temperate climate of England. There are long beds of iris and espaliered fruit, a symmetrical herb garden, and dry-stone walls and steps border the English-style mown grass on the terraces. These lead to areas of orchard-length grass planted with the parasol pines familiar from Turner's paintings of Italy. These, in turn, lead to the vineyards and orchards, then to evergreen forests of holm oak and bay. Ludovico Antinori's vineyards were first planted at the estate in 1981 and now consist of approximately eighty hectares.

As the raison d'être of the house is the vineyard, it is not lived in continuously. When the owner is at home, it comes to life. There is always delicious food, the wine, of course, and the ease and comfort of Tuscan hospitality. The standard of living at Ornellaia is very high, but this is nothing to do with luxury. The age-old but simple rituals between host and guest occur happily and naturally. It is an ancient place given twentieth-century accent and point by the needs, imagination and expertise of Lodovico Antinori, continuing his long family tradition of Florentine merchant nobility.

ABOVE In this bedroom in the guest wing, the walls are decorated with hunting prints. An elegant four-poster bed has sheer, white hangings.

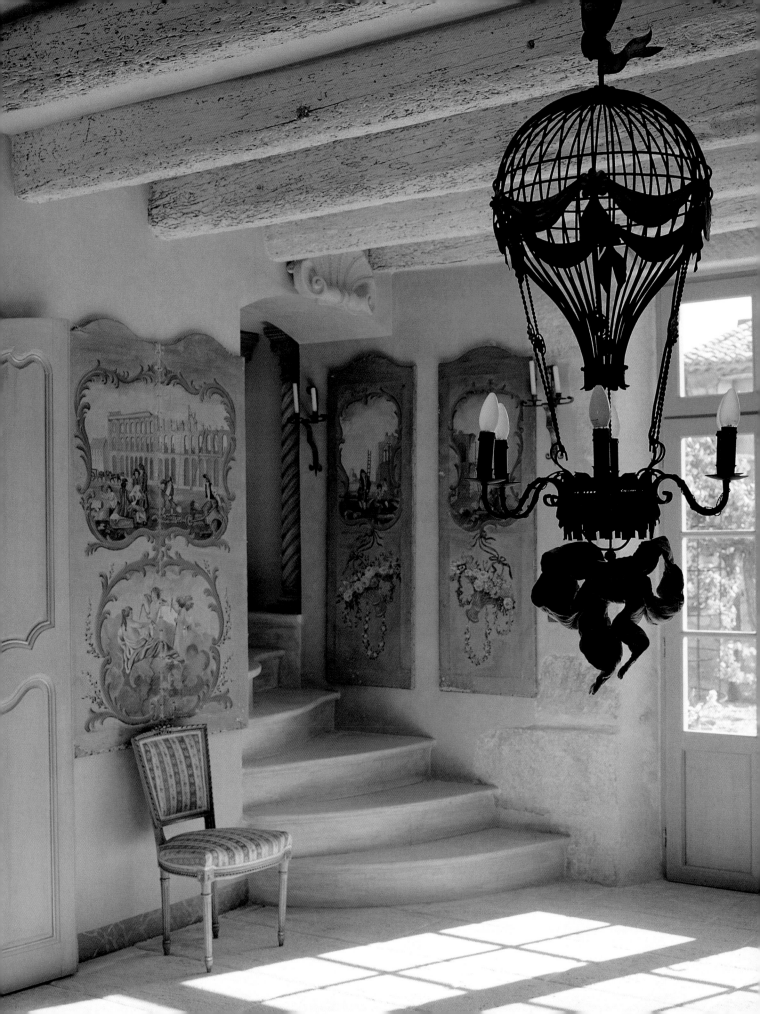

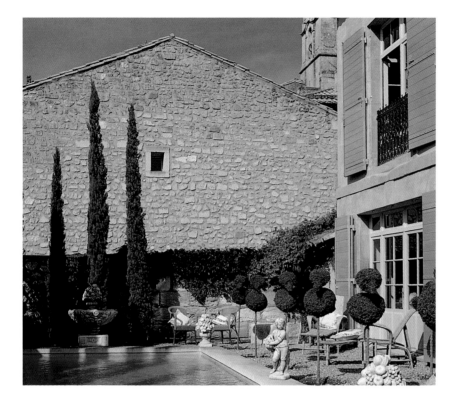

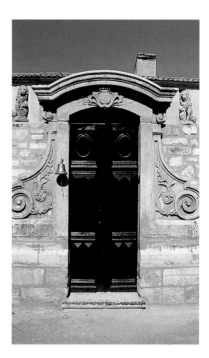

Theatrical fantasy in Provence

This house in southern Provence is unlike other houses. It is more like a theatre set, a magical fantasy that expresses its American owners' passion for traditional French cafés and bistros, with their tin ceilings, Edith Piaf music, crunchy paper tablecloths and waiters in long, starched aprons. In a tiny village next to St-Rémy-de-Provence, Tom and Diane Berger's house is a dreamland of Provençal hospitality and dramatic decoration.

By taking Diane to her favourite French restaurants in New York, Diane's mother instilled in her daughter a lifelong love for all things French. Tom Berger spent his childhood summers in France, making the crossing from the States on stately old ships like the SS France and the Queen Mary. Both upbringings fostered a sympathy with the French mentality which deepened when the couple, by then married and living in London, began to revisit France. After three summers spent in this way, they decided to search for the perfect house to rent: they intended to focus on one village or town, then find and buy their dream project.

ABOVE LEFT A note of playful formality surrounds the pool.
ABOVE RIGHT The door was salvaged from an eighteenth-century chateau.
OPPOSITE The Bergers' eclectic tastes and passion for collecting are exemplified in this staircase area where exquisite, eighteenth-century, painted panels are juxtaposed with a wrought-iron 'Montgolfier' chandelier.

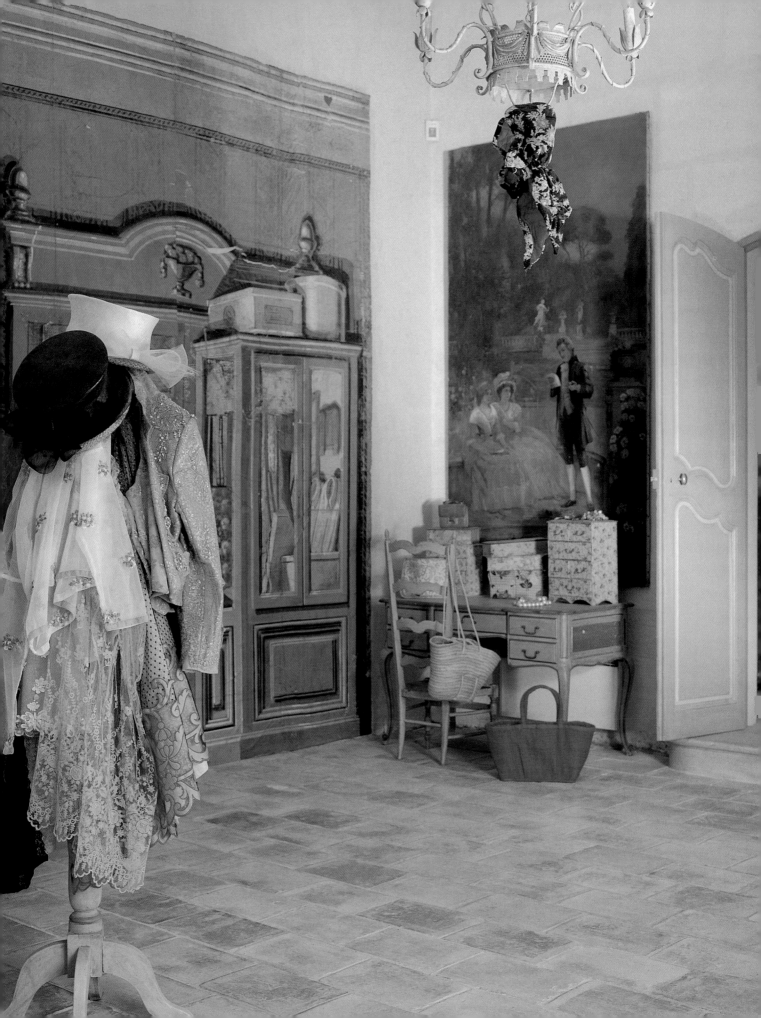

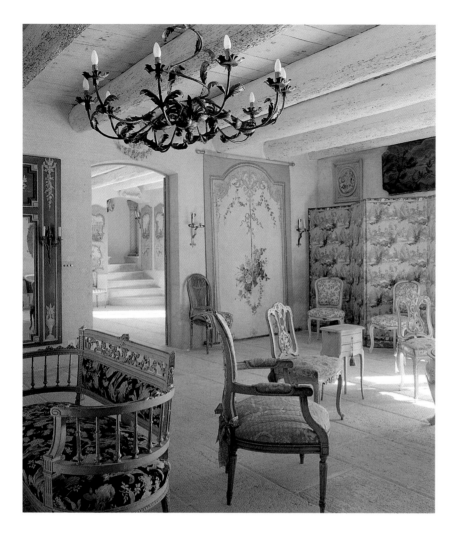

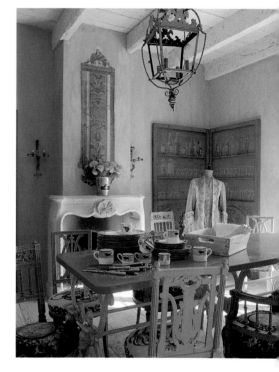

While they were trying out the lifestyle of home-owners in Provence, the Bergers realized that what they wanted most was to live in a small, 'authentic' village rather than a big town. 'What I hoped for was a village house with a chateau feel. I wanted enough room for a pool and a field of lavender, but only a walk away from the local market.' A fairly tall order, Diane recalls. However, a telephone call from the local estate agent produced an interesting prospect. Coming on to the market was a house that had been in the same family since it was built in the eighteenth century but had last been left to two elderly nuns who lived in the convent across the street and who had recently died. 'Its façade was listed Grade 1 by the Monuments Historiques, but inside was a wreck,' says Diane. 'In the room that is now the dining room, there was a cathedral-height ceiling with a ladder going up into a big black hole; that "hole" was to become our bedroom. We bought the house virtually there and then, without even seeing upstairs.'

Diane Berger is known both for the element of fantasy and for the

ABOVE LEFT An eighteenth-century wallpaper screen is placed against a wall in the heavily beamed salon.
ABOVE RIGHT In the dining room, a harlequin set of French chairs surrounds a pink-topped, wrought-iron, butcher's table. The screen came from a café.
OPPOSITE Terracotta floors and lofty ceilings are typical of Provençal interiors. The pale colour-wash on the walls makes a gentle backdrop for the Bergers' agglomeration of flea-market booty, which includes trompe l'œil wallpaper – depicting a shop front – and a stand of vibrant clothes.

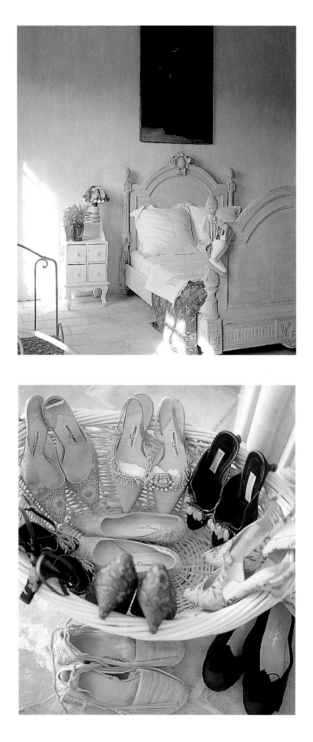

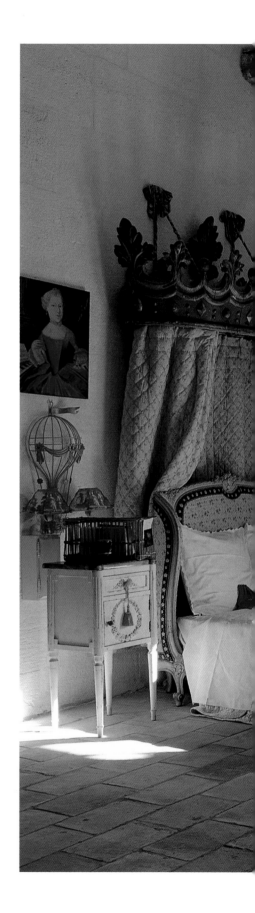

TOP *The cool, Van-Gogh-blue spare bedroom.*
ABOVE *Espadrilles and spangly Manolo Blahnik mules reflect the dichotomy of Diane Berger's Provençal life.*
RIGHT *In the main bedroom, a large wooden crown makes an exuberant, witty corona. Antique linen and quilts cover the eighteenth-century bed.*

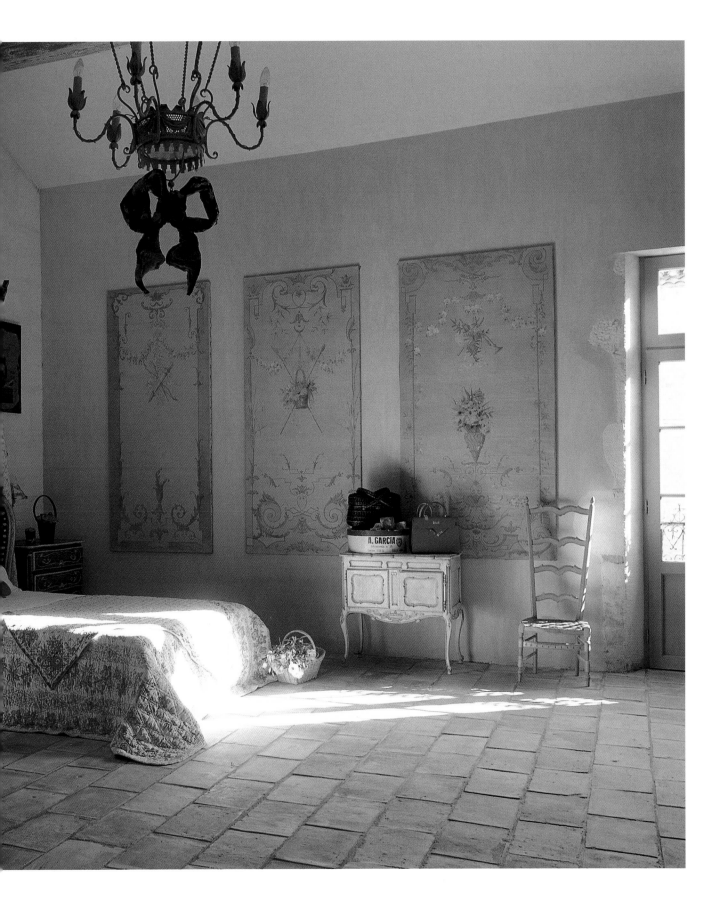

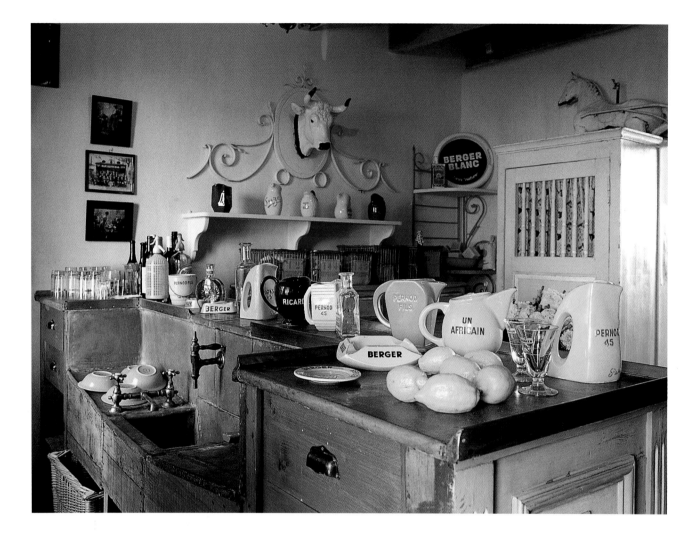

ABOVE Bull motifs, sunshine colours and vintage café wares characterize the cheerful kitchen.

historical detail she gives to her houses. The books she has written on interior decoration – *The Dining Room, The Bathroom, The Bedroom* and *The Kitchen* – mix art and design history with modern chic and function. But in this house she wanted to go further, to create something really fantastical. She wanted the house to reflect the love she and Tom share for Provence, the flea markets, the village fêtes, the café lifestyle, even the bullfights they both recognize as part of the region's heritage. So they started hunting for appropriate contents for their house, buying piece by piece as and where they could: scraps of vintage *bouties* (the local regional quilts), fragments of antique ribbons and, on one lucky day, seventeen doors from a chateau. When asked what her religion is, Diane always answers: Isle-sur-la-Sorgue – the location of a famous Sunday flea market which Tom and Diane visited every week.

The Bergers were very anxious to employ the traditional methods of building which give Provençal architecture its unique style. The work, which involved gutting the house, tearing down walls, replacing the mud

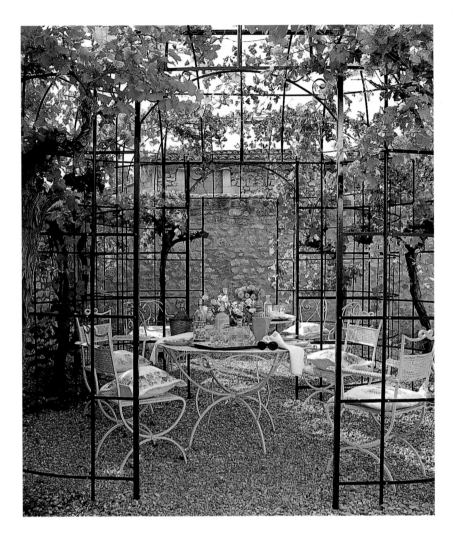

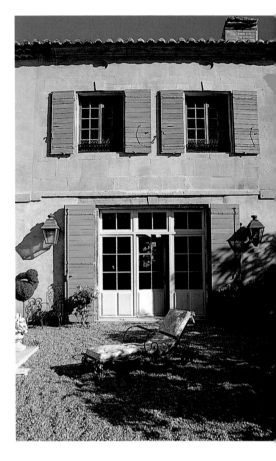

floor and installing wiring and plumbing, was undertaken by the local builder who was also the mayor.

Discovering the detail of the old building techniques required research. Diane made friends at the Souleiado Museum in Tarascon, the starting point for those interested in historical Provençal style. She then applied to the Monuments Historiques in Paris for permission to paint the exterior of the house pale pink: she enclosed a pale pink ballet slipper, a swatch of vintage fabric from the Souleiado Museum and a dab of original paint from the museum's vaults. Not normally known for speedy decisions, the Monuments Historiques sent its approval – and congratulations – by return post.

The Bergers have found their idyll and the love-affair continues. They see their women bullfighter friends and marvel at their femininity; Tom scours the markets for fresh basil or the perfect tomato; they relax in a place where, in many ways, time has stood still. For a couple living a hectic life in London, it is amazing how quickly they 'go local' on arriving.

ABOVE LEFT The nineteenth-century, wrought-iron furniture in a vine-covered arbour came from local flea markets. Diane Berger repainted it pink. ABOVE RIGHT The pale pink used for the exterior gained approval – and praise – from the Monuments Historiques.

EXOTIC
ESCAPES

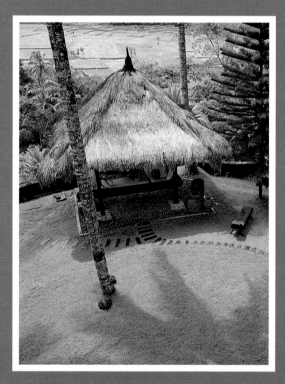

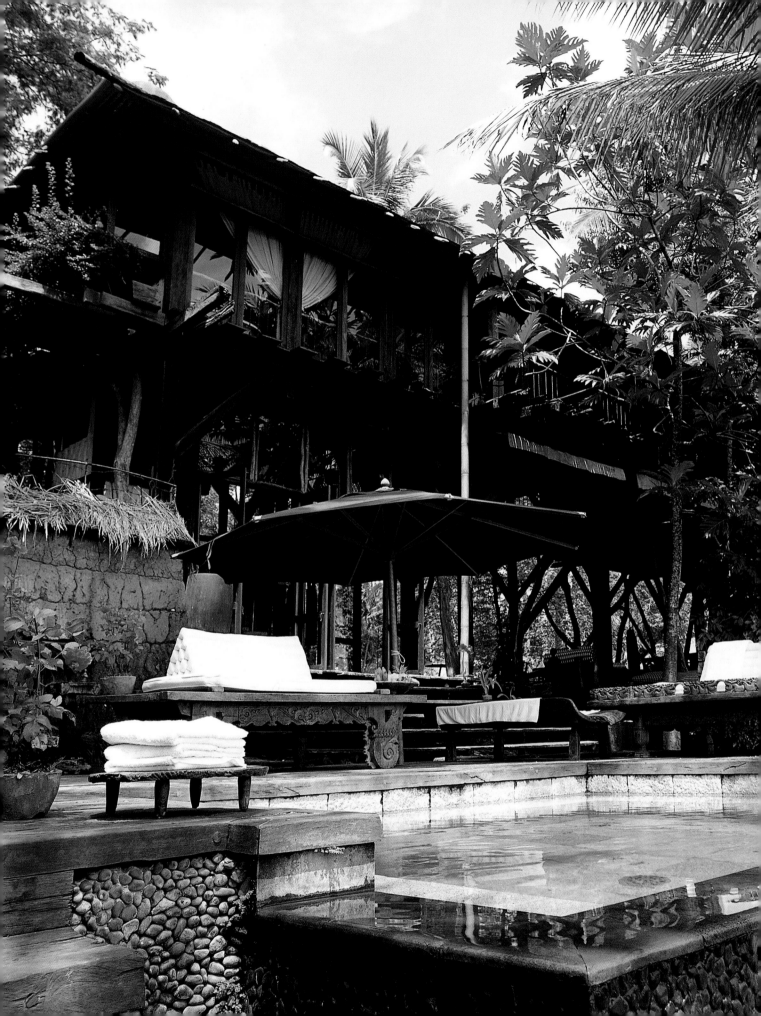

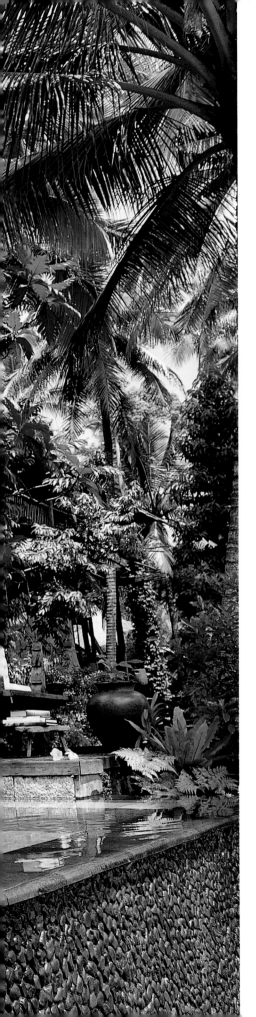

Design for the jungle

The jungle land overlooking the river Ayung is the most desirable real estate in Bali, offering staggering views over the rice fields and river to the volcanic mountain range beyond. Here, on a prime site, John and Cynthia Hardy have built a remarkable house which reflects their commitment to the island's culture and environment.

Bali has a rich, spiritual heritage and has retained its identity, despite a flourishing tourist trade. Nowhere is this more evident than in the nearby hill town of Ubud, first known to Westerners in the Thirties, when a circle of European artists settled there, their presence and enthusiasm an encouragement to traditional arts and crafts. In the surrounding villages are still many craftsmen whose ancestors originally made ceremonial artefacts and jewellery.

It was this skill that first aroused John Hardy's interest when, in 1975, he arrived in Bali on a travel bursary won for his work as an ice sculptor in Canada. Bali tends to engage visitors, sometimes even changing the

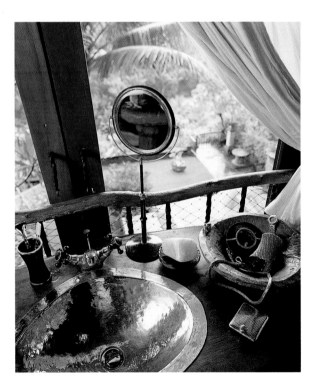

ABOVE Next to a hand-beaten, brass basin in the main bedroom are pieces from the John Hardy Collection, made from silver-inlaid, black palm wood.
LEFT Raised on ironwood posts, the house is light and attenuated; the geometric lines of the structure integrate with the dense, tropical vegetation.

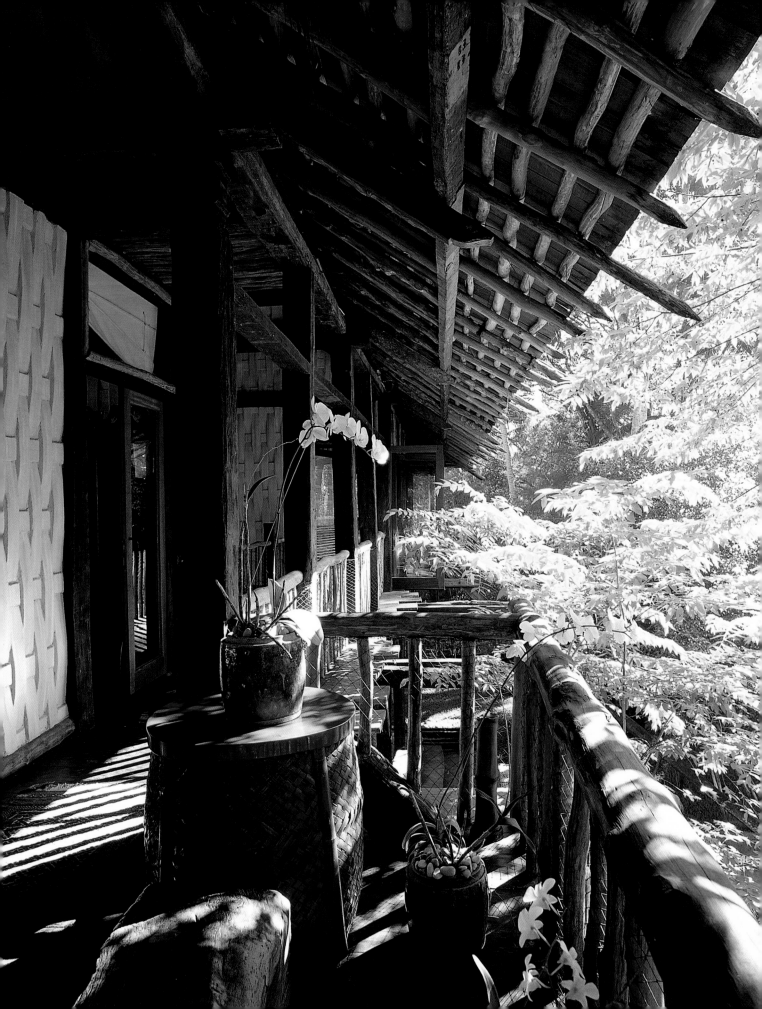

course of their lives. Cynthia abandoned her law studies when she arrived in Bali on the first leg of a round-the-world trip. When she and John met, John was already working with local craftsmen in a 'hippie' fashion, but the business really took off once their partnership was established. Their range of exquisite jewellery, initially in silver, now in a variety of materials, reinterprets traditional design in a chic, timeless way.

When they decided to build their house, they were conscious of the special qualities of the location. Surrounded by countryside of outstanding beauty, they wanted, above all, to create a home which 'looked light on the land', where they could live with their daughter and the children of John's previous marriage.

They chose Malaysian architect Cheong Yew Kuan to translate their desires into practical reality. The design of the resulting building is attenuated and insubstantial to the point of transparency, but while it is spare, it is surprisingly practical: satellite televisions are concealed within traditional furniture, and kitchen equipment is state of the art. This may be a simple lifestyle, but unsophisticated it is not.

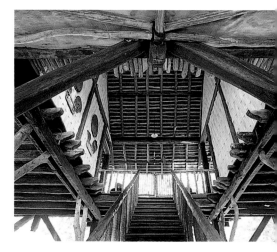

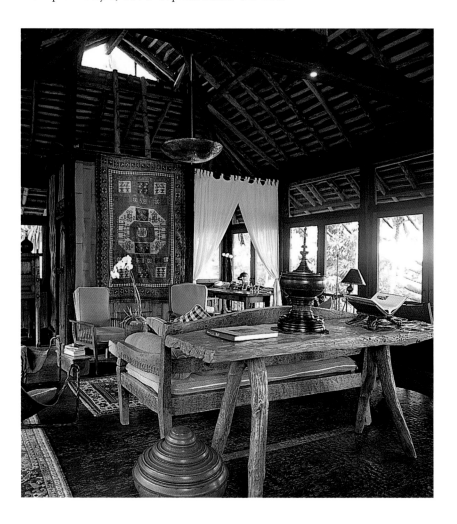

ABOVE The ironwood staircase leading up from the lower deck has lighting at low level 'to avoid treading on snakes at night.'
LEFT The study is furnished with antique Javanese furniture, Dutch colonial chairs and Caucasian rugs.
OPPOSITE On the upper floor, skirted by a balcony, walls are of plastered bamboo. Orchids flourish in the dappled light.

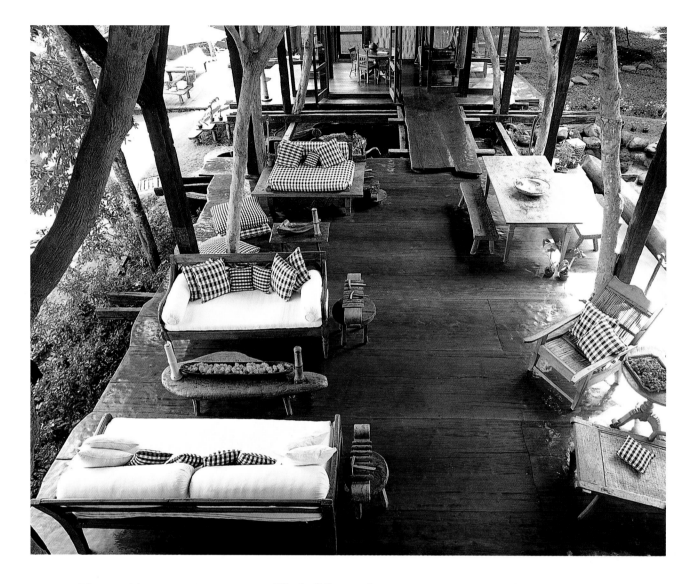

ABOVE The entertaining areas on the open, lower deck are connected by gangplanks. At night, sailcloth 'walls' can be lowered at the sides.

The building took some two years to complete, during which time the family lived on site in a tent. The fifty local carpenters used traditional construction techniques – hardly any screws or nails were employed – which accentuate its organic appearance.

Cheong Yew Kuan's inspiration was a print of a Borneo long-house. Bornean long-houses are built on poles, a system which allows domestic animals to live below, while keeping termites and ants out of the living quarters. The first floor of the Hardys' house is therefore left open, framing a view of the distant hills. The external walls – where they exist – are plastered bamboo, which blends into the surroundings, and the shingled roof reaches the level of the palm-tree tops. The frame is constructed from Y-shaped tree trunks and recycled ironwood telegraph poles. A colossal ironwood staircase at the core of the building is lit at low level with tiny stage lights – 'to avoid treading on snakes at night,' says John.

The main approach to the house is through the lush garden, via a thatched mud gateway and along a path of stones. Within the garden are other structures, including places for contemplation, the older children's garden house, and a pool made with stones, originally used as ballast in returning cargo ships. The family's private entrance, however, is through a dramatically winding mud tunnel which serves as a natural 'backstairs' to the kitchen and ends in a garage.

Linked by a series of gangplanks, the entertaining areas of the house are like floating islands. The lower deck is left open, although a vast sailcloth drops at night and during frequent downpours; there is a low central table in the main part, flanked by seating areas. For evening parties the table is laid with local delicacies – dishes of roast suckling pig, barbecued fish and smoked duck – while from overhead beams hang fragrant garlands of flowers.

The glassed-in second floor, sixteen feet above ground level, has French windows running its length. These let in the breeze between dawn and dusk, when the air-conditioning starts up and they are shut. The study, furnished by Cynthia with antique Javanese furniture, Dutch colonial chairs and Caucasian rugs, is surprisingly cosy for what other-wise resembles a glamorous tree house.

Beneath the rough rafters in the main bedroom is a colossal teak bed, swathed in muslin, and wardrobes made of bamboo. The door handles

BELOW The main entrance to the house winds through tall trees.

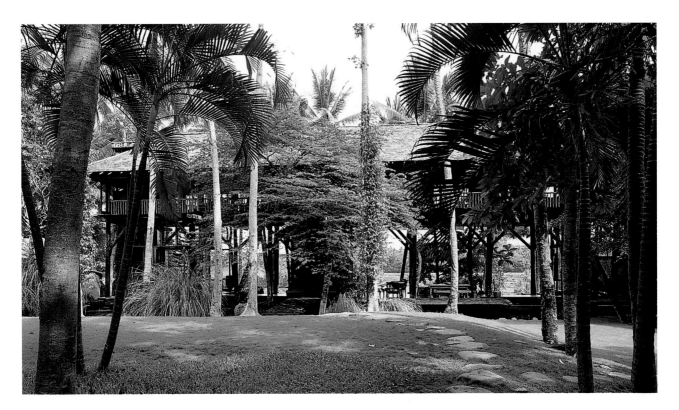

and wrought-iron balconies were made by a member of the Pande cast, whose people once forged knives using molten lava to soften the metal. The bathroom, open on all sides, has a heart-shaped basin, a shower head of hand-beaten brass and a shaving mirror framed in silver-inlaid, black palm. These, like all the light fittings, have been made in the John Hardy Design Studio. Throughout the house are idiosyncratic objects: fruit bowls, dishes, goblets, pens and canes – some copied from historic examples – embellished or filigreed by Hardy craftsmen. Set among paddy fields, the Hardys' factory employs some 400 people, many descendants of the goldsmiths who worked for the Balinese kings before the island came under Dutch control between 1894 and 1949.

John and Cynthia often work on a balcony overlooking the red plaster walls and green-tiled roofs of the workshops – a view enhanced by the flowering flame trees all around. The flowerbeds beneath the factory have been replaced with year-round fruit and vegetable cultivation, a project designed to make the workers' canteen self-sufficient, and which has also helped to draw local interest back from tourism to agriculture. This is another of the Hardys' enthusiasms: here, with a wealth of local skills, it has been possible to create beautiful, traditional objects in a working environment that simultaneously regenerates the economy.

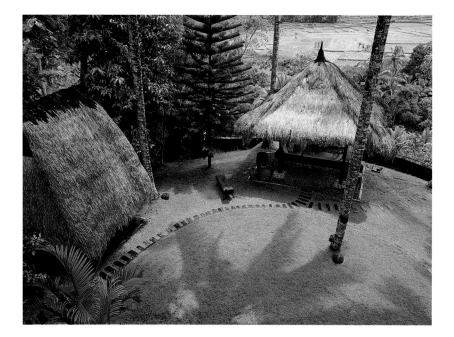

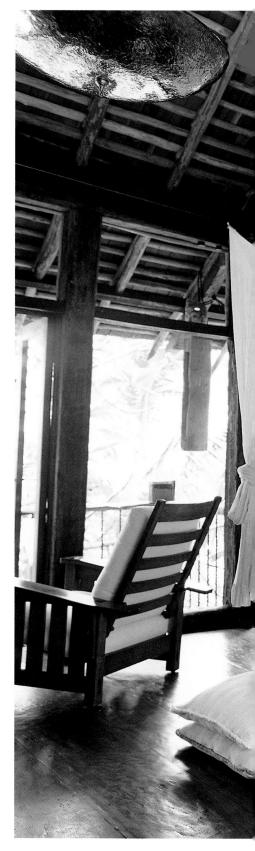

ABOVE Vernacular-style, thatched pavilions provide shelter in the garden.
RIGHT In the main bedroom, hangings of unbleached muslin – used in nearby Java for straining tofu – swathe the large teak bed. During the day, the hangings are tied back casually. Dark, polished wood and white fabric are natural and cool-looking.

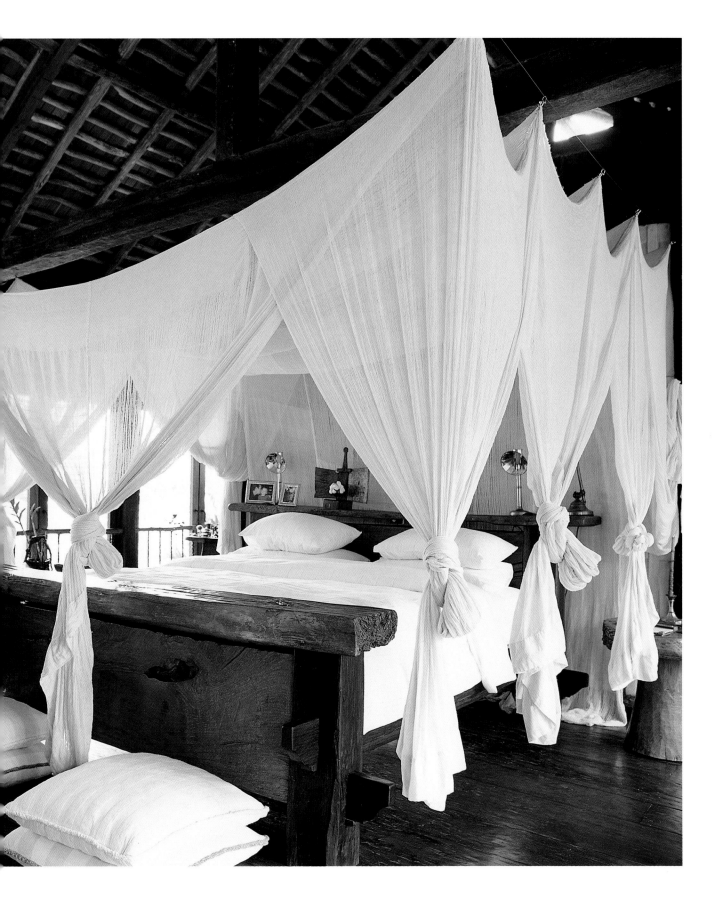

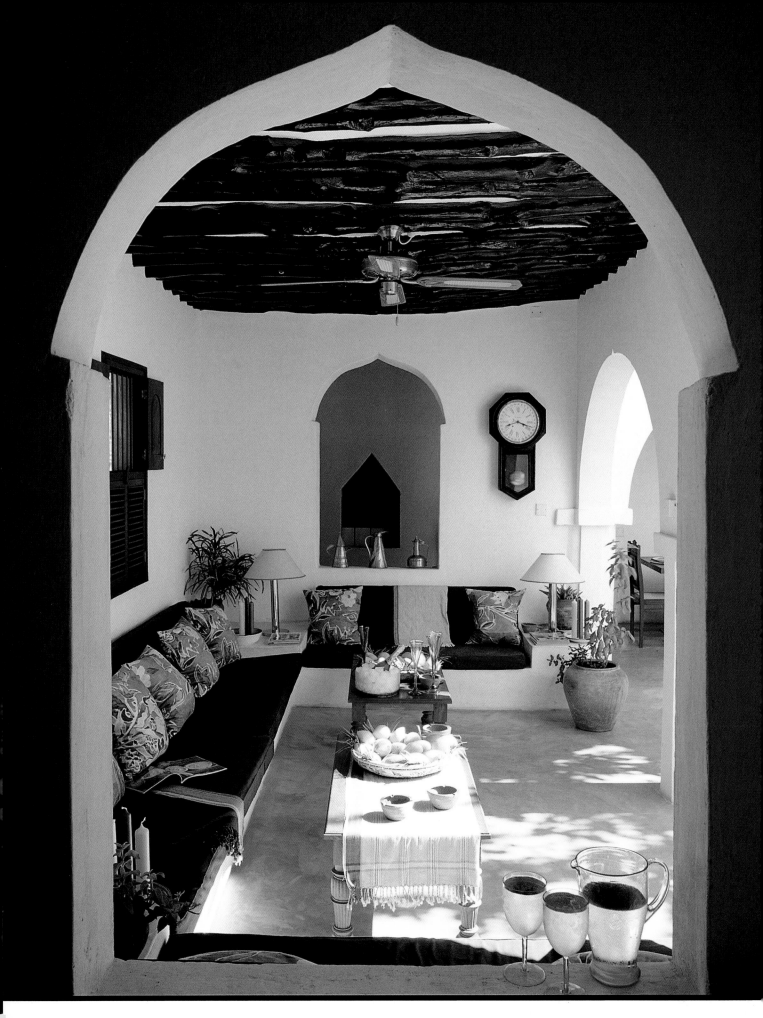

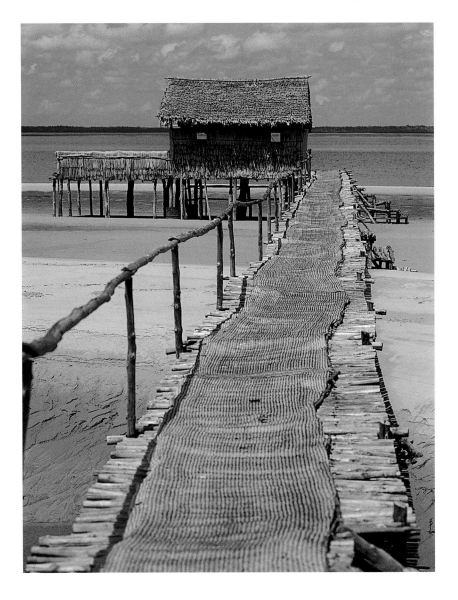

Magical Lamu

The streets of the village of Shela are narrow and secret, more private even than those of Lamu, the main town of the small island of the same name off the coast of Kenya. The Arab houses, with their splendid carved doors, rise tall and white, revealing nothing to the outside world.

Shela House, which lies some 300 yards up the steep hill from the landing stage, looks no different from the others – not that one can stand back to look at it, for the street is barely wide enough for a donkey laden on both sides – and certainly there is nothing to suggest that it was built by an Englishwoman in the Twenties.

ABOVE The landing jetty at Kipungani, a short boat trip from the house. OPPOSITE Off the main courtyard, concrete benches in the local style are covered with comfortable cushions.

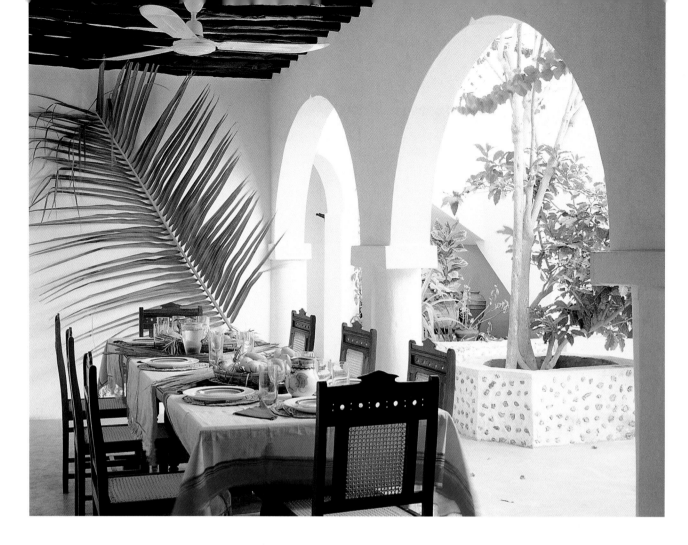

ABOVE *Seen from the dining area, the
view of the camellia tree in the courtyard
is framed by arches.*
OPPOSITE *The upstairs terrace, leading
off one of the bedrooms.*

Kay Wilson was a strange person, who came to be known as the witch
of Lamu. She built simply, in the local tradition, her house surrounding
a courtyard with a deep well in one corner. The villagers at first resent-
ed her, partly because her house blocked a pathway to the mosque. But,
more importantly, because she had enclosed the village well in her courtyard. They came, threatening her with spells and curses. But she was a
woman of presence and resource. She stood at the top of her stairway
and harangued the villagers.

'My magic,' she declared, 'is stronger than yours.' To emphasize the
point, she swept down the stairs in flowing robes, loudly singing *Onward,
Christian Soldiers*. More practically, she won them over with sacks of pres-
ents borne in by the donkey-load.

Yet who is to dispute her powers? There are many tales of the spells
and curses that she in her turn put upon people; some are believed to
have been fatal.

Kay Wilson died in 1981. Since then the house has had a chequered
history. For some time her lawyer used to let it out; that was how two of
the present owners, David Campbell, a media consultant, and his wife
Leslie Duckworth, a designer, came to know and love the place. They
had been regular visitors to Lamu since their undergraduate days.

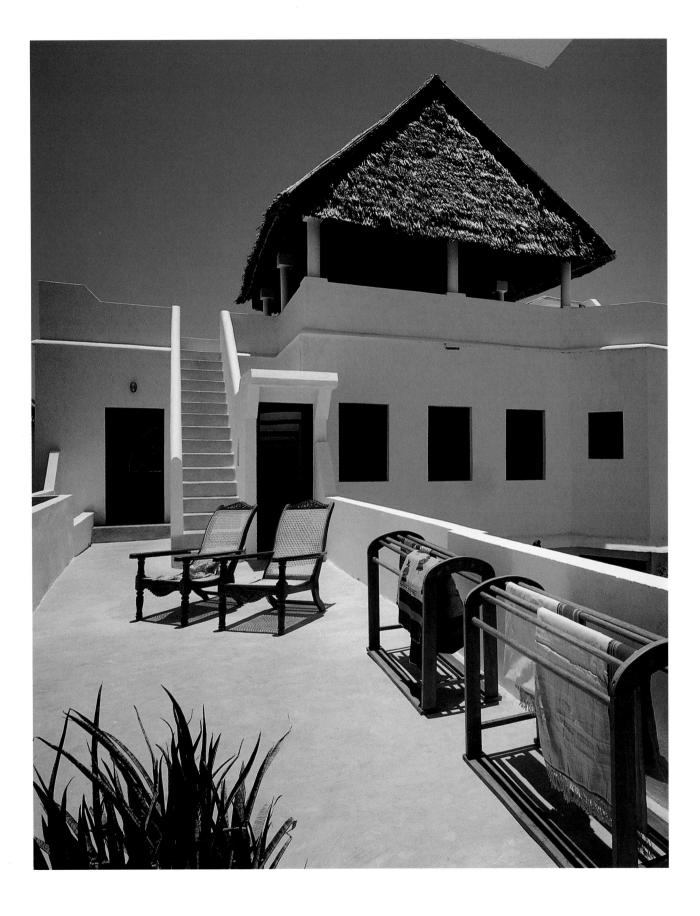

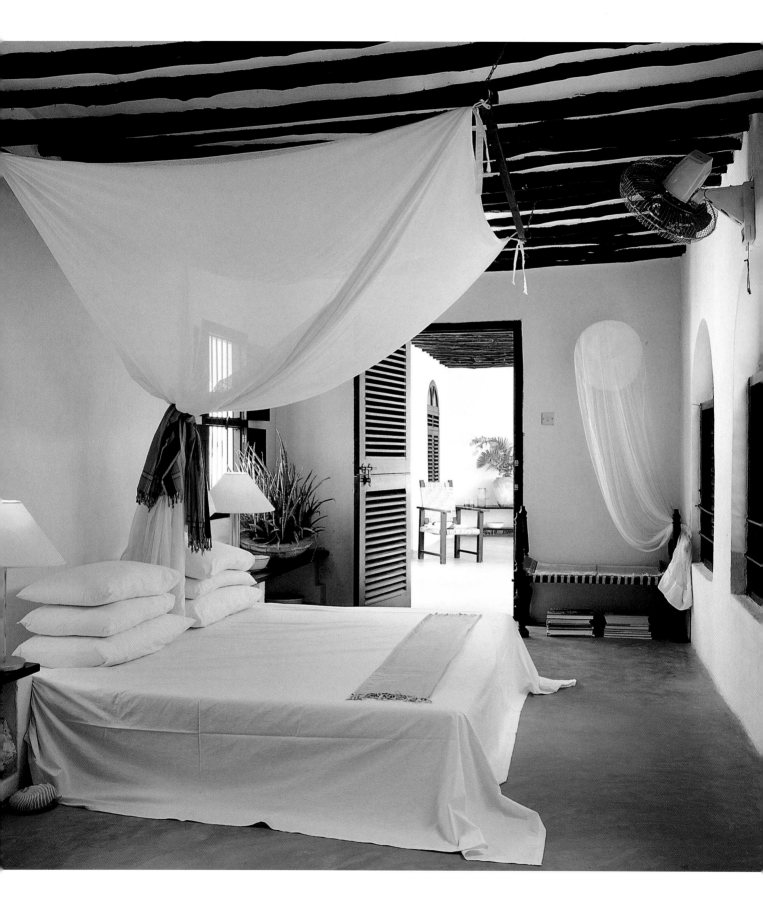

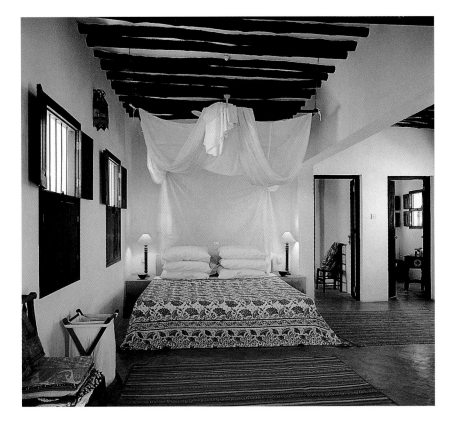

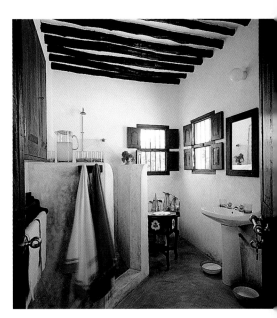

*OPPOSITE AND ABOVE LEFT The
bedrooms have shutters at the windows
and are coolly furnished. Billowy
mosquito netting is draped over the beds.
ABOVE RIGHT The bathrooms combine
modern fittings with local building
materials.*

They thought they had arranged to buy the house, but were gazumped by an Englishman whose reasons for getting it seem to have had little to do with the fine views of the sea or the peace and quiet of this remote village. It is true that the recorded call of the muezzin from the adjacent mosque is loud, especially when it cracks the calm of the dawn, but his alterations seem excessive. He spent his days in an enclosed room that he fitted with a fireplace more suited to an English manor-house, and a buzzing air-conditioner that drowned the calls to prayer.

When he died, the house was sold – but it came back on the market again a year or two later. Leslie and David Campbell had rented the house on several occasions in the past, and it had become famous up and down the beach for the wonderful oyster lunches that they served there. They decided to have another try at buying the house, and fortunately this time they were successful.

The property, by this stage, was in a rather sorry state. The well, which is seventy-five feet deep, had fallen in. The paint was peeling, the floors were cracked. But the new owners simply started to repair it. In doing so, however, they found that all sorts of irresistible possibilities presented themselves so that, in the end, after a long year's work, they were quite overwhelmed and engagingly embarrassed by the proportions of the final, finished house.

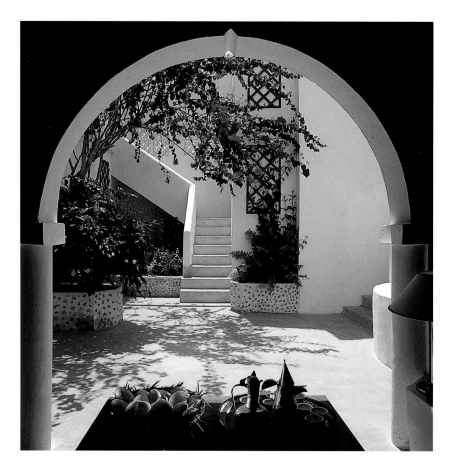

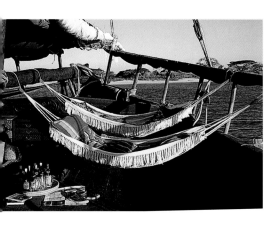

ABOVE Hammocks strung on a dhow encapsulate the escapist lifestyle. ABOVE RIGHT Magenta sprays of bougainvillaea decorate the courtyard.

With the help of Rob de Boer, a Dutch construction engineer, who is an old friend from university days and owns a house nearby, they cut new windows, opened up arches and moved staircases. The noisy and lively building team was composed of locals from Lamu town, overseen by a master builder from Pate island. The coral rock used to build the house came from Manda island, just across the water. Most of the other materials came from Mombasa, often by boat all the way, the road being rough and dangerous.

The mangrove-pole joists, *boriti*, which are very much in the local tradition and which, to a large extent, dictate the width of the rooms, were replaced throughout – 412 of them in all. The builders did, however, manage to widen some of the rooms a little.

David and Leslie built two apartments on the top floor, and two thatched eyries with superb views of the sea, the island, the town of Lamu, and lateen-sailed dhows. The end result has four double rooms, each with a shower and a veranda, and two single rooms, allowing the house to sleep ten in perfect comfort.

The overall impression the owners wanted was of whiteness and of wood. The huge, old bits of furniture left from Kay Wilson's day were

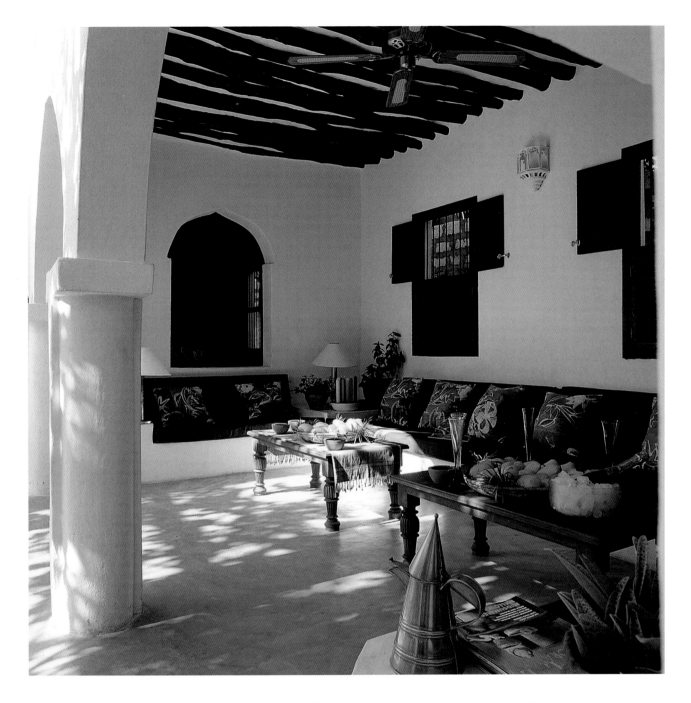

mostly disposed of, but the new owners kept or bought simpler, traditional pieces such as planters' chairs. What colour there is comes from the cushions, the rugs, the bedspreads and some painted beams.

The Campbells use the house as much as they can. They enjoy snorkelling, bird-watching, body-surfing, walking, sailing and fishing – and there is a marvellous Giriama cook, whose crab with coconut sauce is one of those dishes to remember on lonely nights. All this in a world with no cars. Heaven.

ABOVE The sitting area off the main courtyard has painted concrete seating built against the walls.

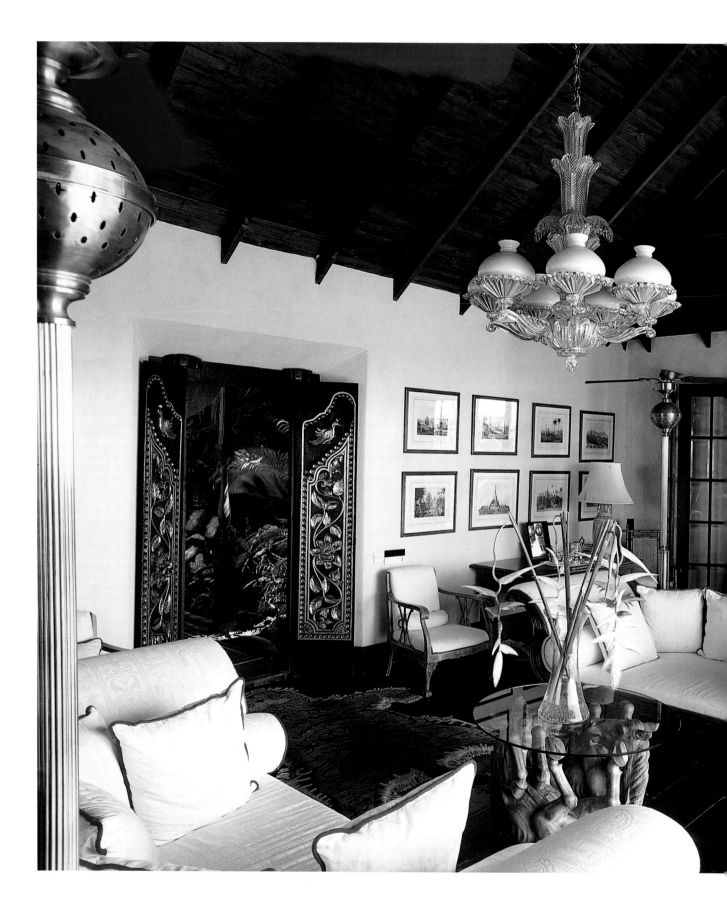

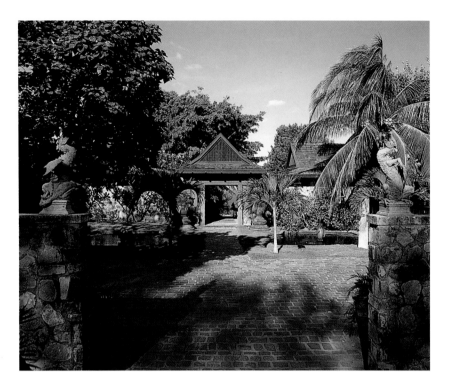

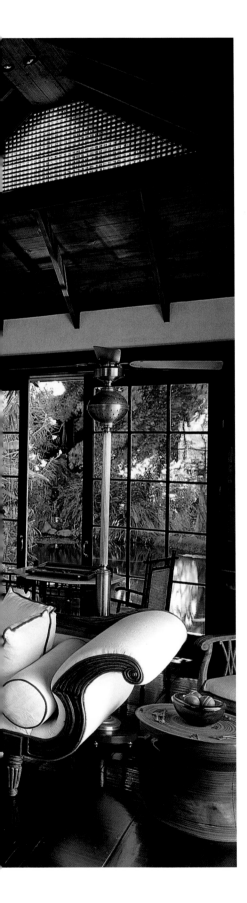

A house of many parts

It's unusual to find in a single house a Javanese dining room, an Italian bedroom, a colonial-style drawing room (complete with mid-nineteenth-century crystal chandelier), an English study and a state-of-the-art Johnny Grey kitchen. But these and other exotic, whimsical and surprising elements comprise Mandalay, the Caribbean holiday home of publishing mogul Felix Dennis.

Felix maintains that he had no intention of buying anything when – on some spurious pretext – his mother, Dorothy, and his companion, Marie-France Demolis, lured him to the island of Mustique and then persuaded him to look round David Bowie's hill-top estate which happened to be on the market. He told them he wasn't remotely interested, that he was 'quite cross actually' – and bought it on the spot. That was in 1995 and since then he has fulfilled his intention, voiced that day to

ABOVE The gate to Mandalay is guarded by griffins which, when evening comes, spew fire. They were made in Scotland by sculptor David A. Annand.
LEFT The colonial-style drawing room is lit by a handsome, mid-nineteenth-century chandelier. The plain white upholstery has a narrow edging of colour.

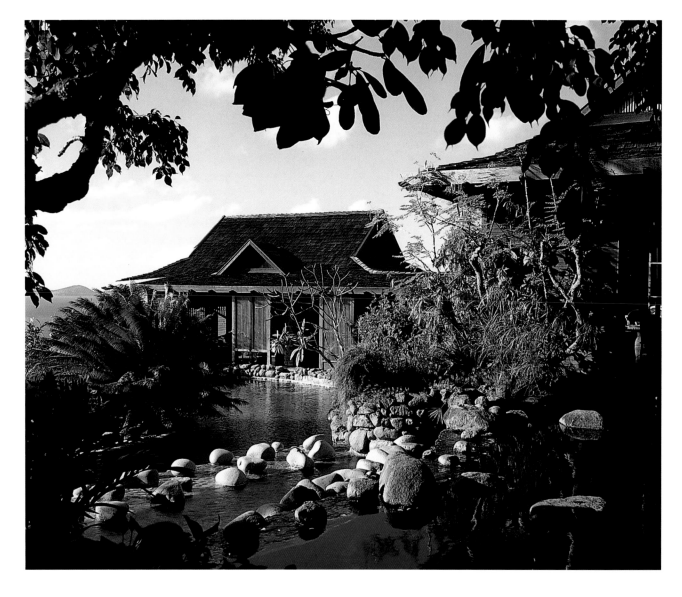

ABOVE The pavilion at left houses the main bedroom; the one at right is the drawing room.
OPPOSITE The balustrade around the dining pavilion is decorated with a carved dragon, the Indonesian god of music.

Marie-France, to turn the house into a free 'hotel'. Felix and Marie-France spend up to twelve weeks a year at Mandalay but virtually every other week of the year sees the house occupied by friends, relations, employees or simply people Felix thinks could do with a holiday. But then this one-time co-defendant on a charge of 'conspiracy to corrupt morals' in the *Oz* 'school kids issue' trial is famously and unconditionally generous. He is also unconventional and not over concerned with other people's good opinions.

He tells a characteristic story against himself: 'I arrived in Mustique full of piss and vinegar – full of ideas, I mean. I wanted to build this and that, landscape the whole place, construct a helipad. "Fine," said the chief executive of the Mustique Company, "let's look at the map. Here are six sites which would do nicely as helipads but unfortunately we don't

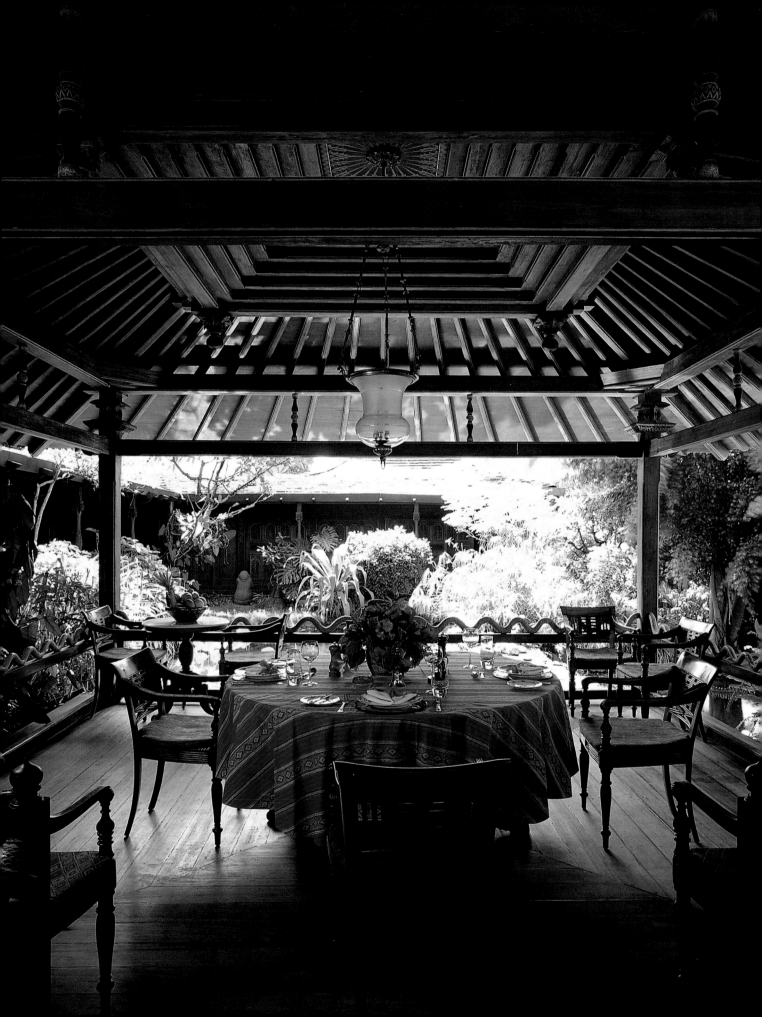

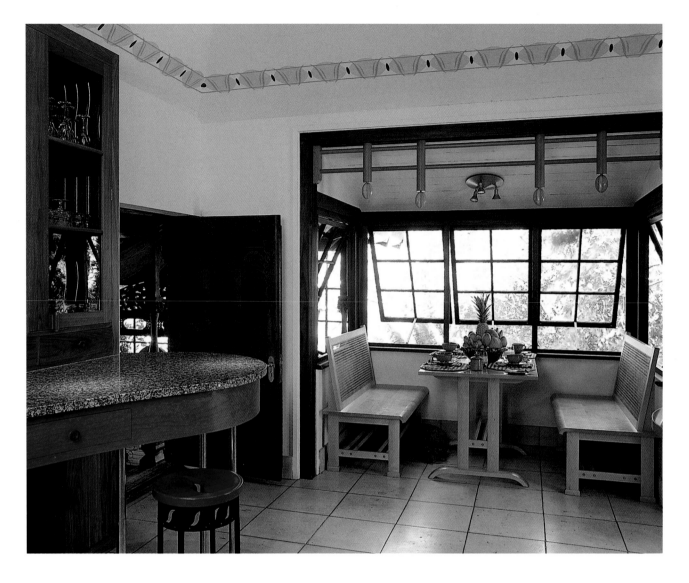

ABOVE The breakfast niche in the Johnny-Grey-designed kitchen has a table and benches made of sycamore.

allow helicopters on the island".' Felix laughs, 'It's socialism for the rich.' He did, however, build something – a library which he stocked as a gift to the tiny island's permanent population.

He also started a major regeneration programme at the house itself, which was being destroyed by termites. 'Despite all the money I've spent on Mandalay, it's still David Bowie's house,' Felix says of the mysterious, exotic complex of Indonesian-style pavilions built round three sides of descending terraces of ponds and pools. The complicated house originally took three years to build, constructed by Mustique-based architect Arne Hasselqvist in collaboration with New York-based designer Robert J. Litwiller, who in turn coordinated designer Linda Garland and landscape architect Michael White, both of whom are based in Bali. It also took more than fourteen container-loads brought from the four corners of the earth to furnish it.

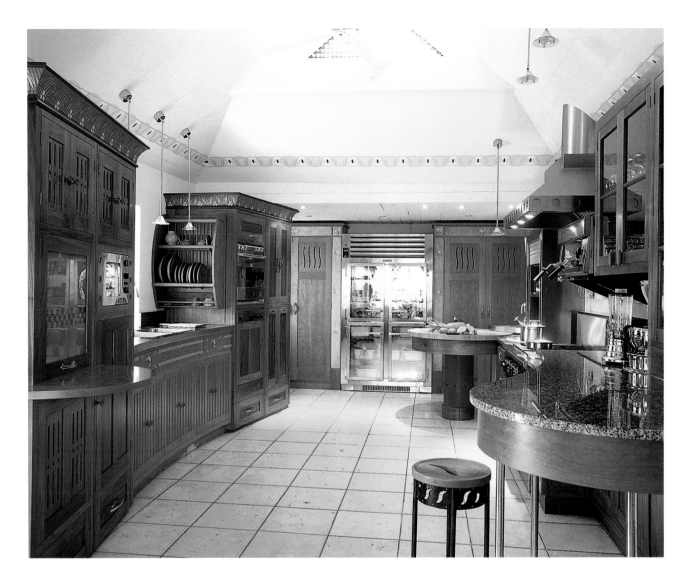

ABOVE The cabinets in the kitchen are made of walnut and cherrywood.

Felix wisely bought most of the contents of the house as well, which gives it a settled, timeless air; it's hard to tell which continent you are in or which century. That is, unless you investigate some of the back offices where technology rules. Larders of varying temperatures, a laundry and workshops have all been tucked under Balinese-style shingled roofs, and, elsewhere, air-conditioning, music systems, infinitely variable lighting and highly sophisticated communication systems remind you that the owner's fortune derives from his stable of computer magazines.

But it is books which are Felix Dennis's great love; and it was the need to house his several thousand volumes that led him to commission Peter Falkner to design a quintessential English study – the only hint that you are not in the Home Counties are the stylized griffins that adorn the otherwise classical pediment crowning the principal bookcase. There is, surprisingly, nothing incongruous about passing from the deep shade of

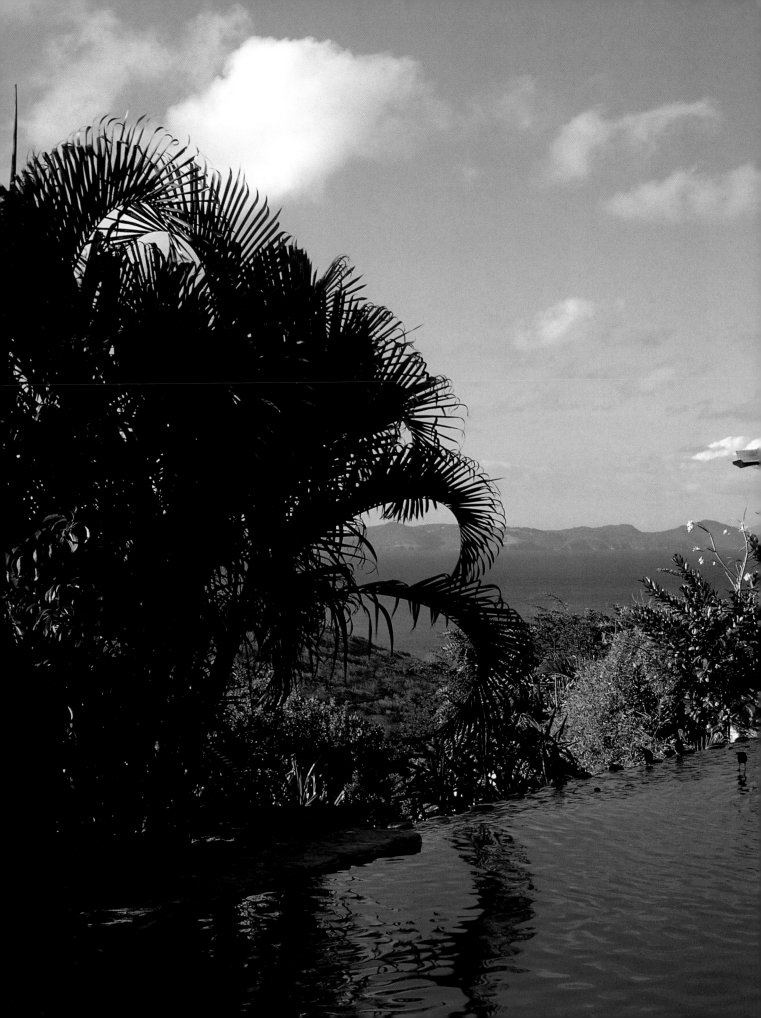

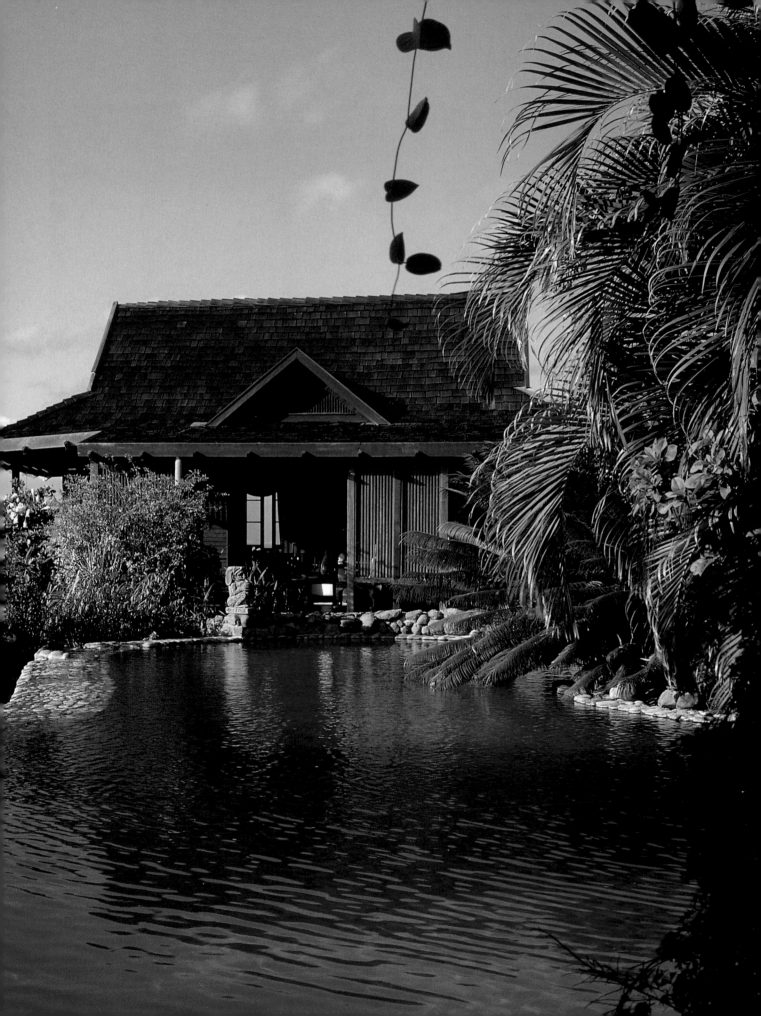

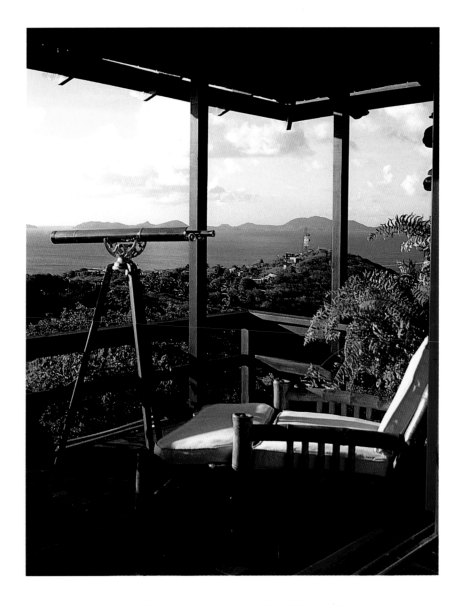

ABOVE The west-facing balcony of the main bedroom pavilion.
OPPOSITE The veranda was created from teak house-fronts from Java; the carved columns were inspired by originals on the Indonesian island of Sumbawa.
PREVIOUS PAGE Built as a complex of Indonesian-style pavilions, Mandalay surrounds on three sides a series of descending ponds and pools, facing west towards Britannia Bay far below.

the veranda created from intricately carved teak house fronts transported from Java, into the bleached-and-limed-oak study beautifully crafted in Wales by John Nethercott and his team.

At the other end of the veranda is a door leading to Felix's new kitchen – and a beautiful, practical, joyful kitchen it is. Designer Johnny Grey made it in England and oversaw its assembly on site. So inviting it is, and so stuffed with good things, that the chef is much visited by house guests, sometimes on the pretext of checking the time in New York or London on the battery of kitchen clocks, but in reality to raid the fridge or the bar or to discuss recipes.

By day the house is full of secrets. It is not designed to be seen as a whole and there are a dozen unexpected places to discover. In the evening the house is even more magical. With views west over Britannia

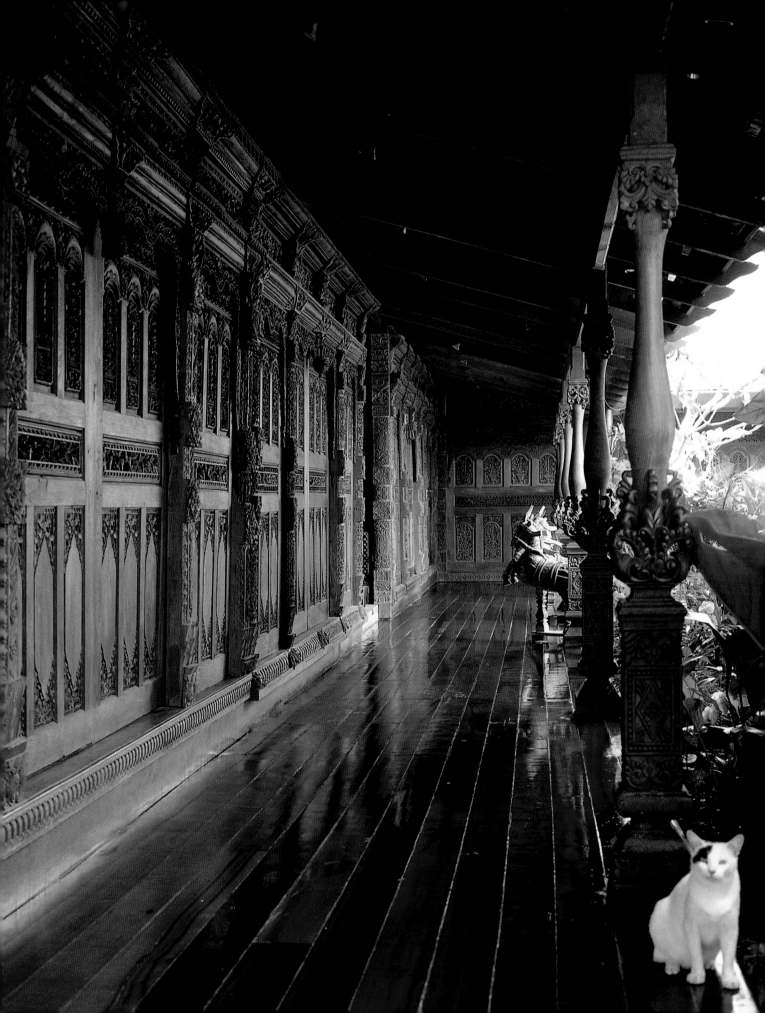

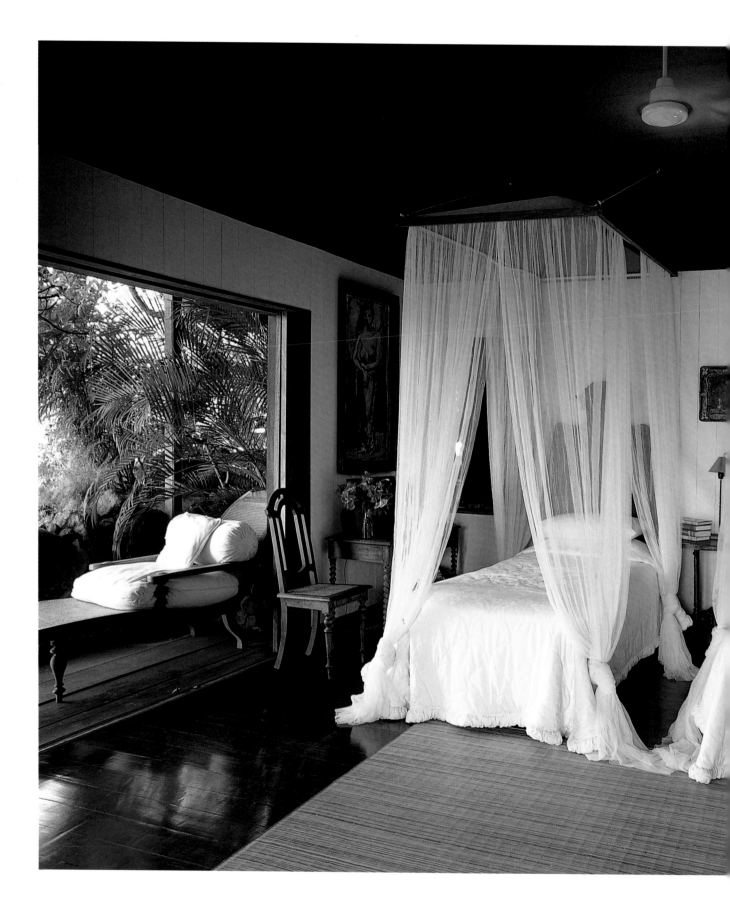

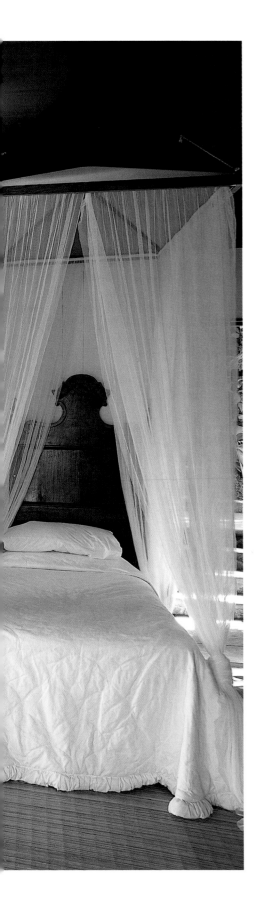

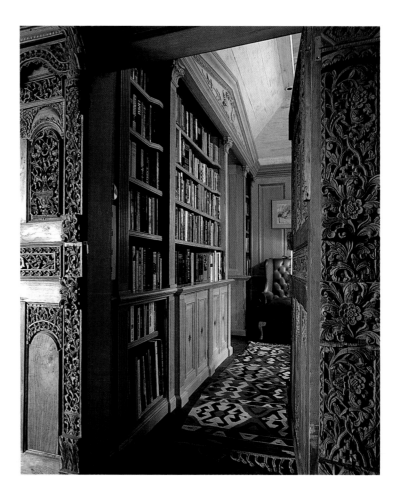

Bay far below, almost every window, veranda and terrace seems to afford a unique glimpse of the sunset. As the sun sinks into the sea, people become reflective, silenced by the beauty of a tropical evening: the night noises, the clumsy flight of disoriented moths, and the reedy sound of distant music from an anchored yacht.

Of all the houses on the island, Mandalay is one of the most contained and private. It crouches among luxuriant vegetation and water, following the contours of the hill side. It is also extraordinarily fragile: termites can and do burrow through concrete. Preserving a wooden building full of beautiful things in this climate is a full-time job, as is gardening on those baked hill sides. The house has been lucky to fall into the hands of an idiosyncratic enthusiast.

ABOVE The study, seen here from the veranda, has bleached-and-limed-oak bookcases and panelling made in Wales.
LEFT The 'Italian' bedroom, which is situated on one of the lower levels, has carved, wooden bedheads and a veranda which gives on to the swimming pool.

MOUNTAIN HIDEOUTS

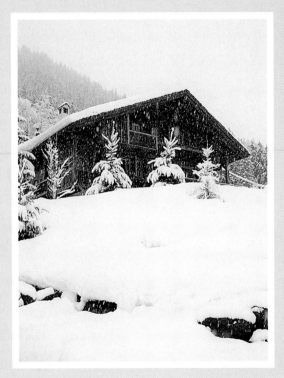

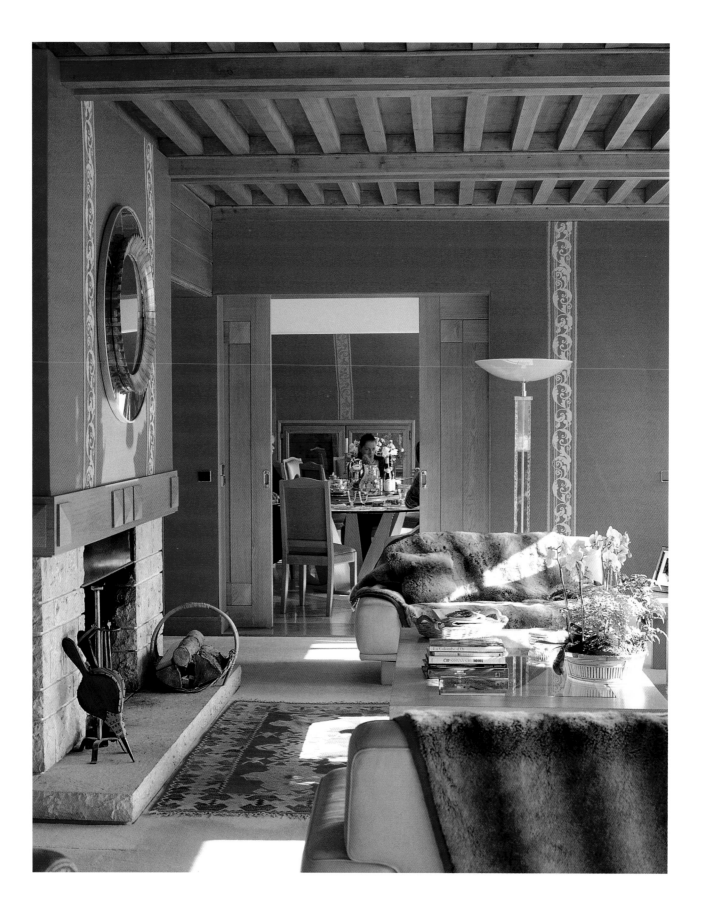

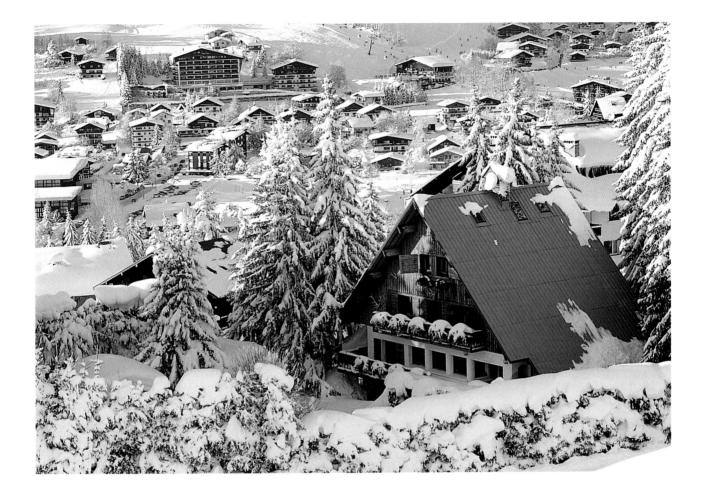

Back to the Forties

At the turn of the century, the French Alpine village of Mégève was overshadowed as a ski resort by its illustrious Swiss counterpart, St Moritz. The arrival in the Twenties of Baron Edmund de Rothschild and his wife, however, assured a significant upturn in its popularity. The Rothschilds fell in love with the beautiful Mont d'Arbois region and, choosing to spend winter holidays there, commissioned several chalets to be built for themselves and their family. The architect they used, Le Même, was a former student of Art-Deco designer Jacques-Emile Ruhlmann, renowned for his beautifully made furniture inlaid with exotic materials such as tortoise-shell, lapis lazuli and ivory.

A second generation Mégève/Le Même commission, Chalet le Sarto was built in 1942 for a wealthy textile family from the north of France; it remained in the same hands until 1983, when it was bought by its present owners, Philippe and Annick Charriol.

ABOVE The chalet is enfolded by the beautiful alpine scenery of the Mont d'Arbois region.
OPPOSITE Beyond the granite-and-oak chimneypiece, flanked by leather sofas, sliding doors open on to the dining room in the new extension.

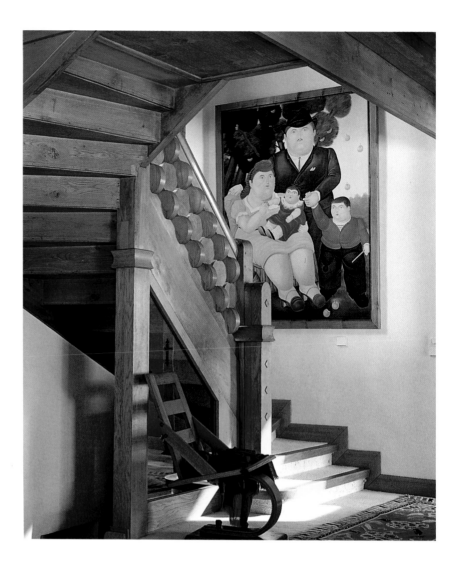

RIGHT At the foot of the weighty oak staircase is a painting by Columbian artist Botero.

Philippe Charriol, French watchmaker and jeweller, brought to the restoration and decoration of Chalet le Sarto the full force of his style and originality. He was ably assisted by his wife, who shares his love of colour, texture and design.

When, sixteen years ago, the couple first saw the chalet, its chief selling point was the fabulous location. Annick remembers thinking it stood head and shoulders above the other thirty-five chalets they had looked at in the Haute Savoie. 'It's surrounded by tall fir trees and nestles at the bottom of a hill called Le Chemin du Calvaire,' she explains. 'Fourteen tiny mid-nineteenth-century chapels and oratories lead to the summit, retracing the Passion of Christ and representing the stations of the Cross. We can ski down virtually to the front door of the chalet, and most of the bedrooms look out over the hill.'

In addition to its enviable position and proximity to Geneva, where Philippe has his head office, the chalet boasts wonderful original Forties

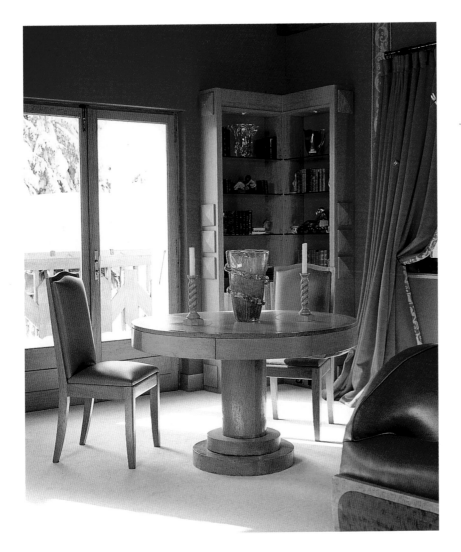

woodwork with which the Charriols fell in love. The panelling in the three main bedrooms is particularly striking, while the oak staircase has huge, chunky newel posts and 'balusters' composed of what look like giant wooden coins stacked drunkenly on top of each other instead of conventional spindles. 'We love the robustness of the architecture,' says Philippe enthusiastically. 'Nothing is delicate or understated, and no expense was spared in its construction.'

A series of small rooms, including a reception area – the chalet was once a small hostel – used to occupy the space that is now the large, open-plan living room. All the exposed wood was stained dark brown, which Annick found claustrophobic. 'Once we had opened up the space to make one big room and bleached the wood to this pleasant honey shade, it felt much more welcoming.'

The room has three defined areas. At one end, a trio of sofas covered in alpaca throws is grouped around a double-sided fireplace. In the

LEFT A Forties-style pedestal table is placed by a window in the sitting room.

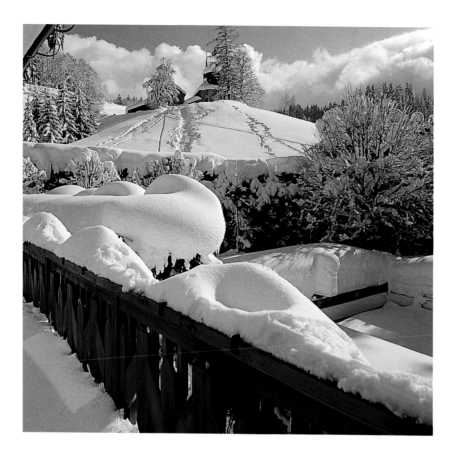

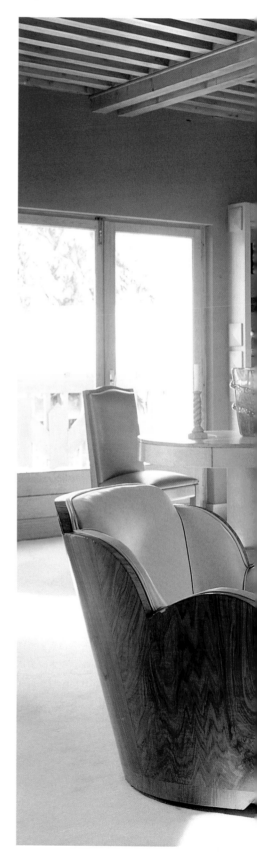

opposite corner, a Forties-style oak table is perfect for playing cards and board games; next to it, another sitting area includes a group of Forties leather tub chairs and a matching sofa.

To counter the stark white winter landscape outside, viewed through enormous windows and glass doors, Annick has chosen a brilliant red, satin-weave wool wall-covering divided into panels by stripes of hand-woven Jacquard. French interior decorator Janie Las helped her choose appropriate fabrics and coordinate design details to suit the period of the chalet. 'We were keen to use colours and textures that would enhance the natural oak framework.'

When the Charriols were obliged by local town planners to visit the elderly Le Même to seek his permission to extend the property, Janie accompanied them and helped to argue their case. 'In fact it was Le

ABOVE The view from an upstairs balcony is over the lowest of the fourteen oratories of Le Chemin du Calvaire.

RIGHT The walls in the sitting room are hung with satin-weave, scarlet wool, divided into panels by stripes of hand-woven Jacquard, to complement the honeyed tones of the original woodwork and Forties seat furniture. The coffee table was made by a local carpenter.

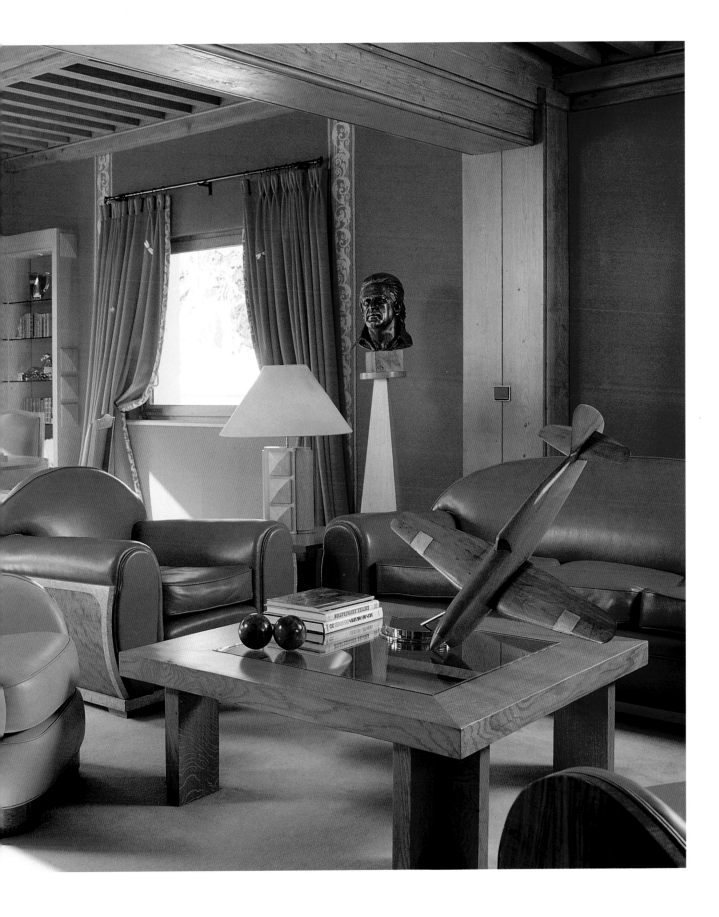

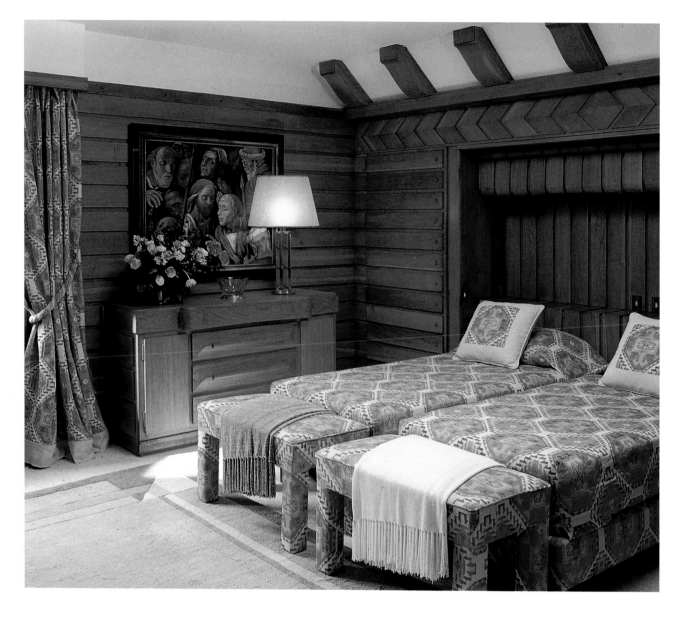

ABOVE The vertically boarded recess in this spare bedroom has been designed with an integrated bed-head.

Même himself who suggested lengthening the roof line to accommodate the extension; this means that the effect of his original design has barely been changed.' From the outside, particularly the front elevation, the extension is not noticeable, but the extra space gained inside allows for a larger kitchen and a dining room reached through sliding doors from the sitting room. In here, up to sixteen guests can be seated at two dining tables with solid oak bases and circular glass 'lazy Susan' turntable tops.

Architectural details used by Le Même in the original design – like the wooden pyramidal capitals – have been faithfully echoed in any new joinery made for the chalet. The Charriols commissioned a local carpenter, Lucien Allard, to make bookcases, cabinets, coffee tables and lamp bases all in an appropriate Forties style.

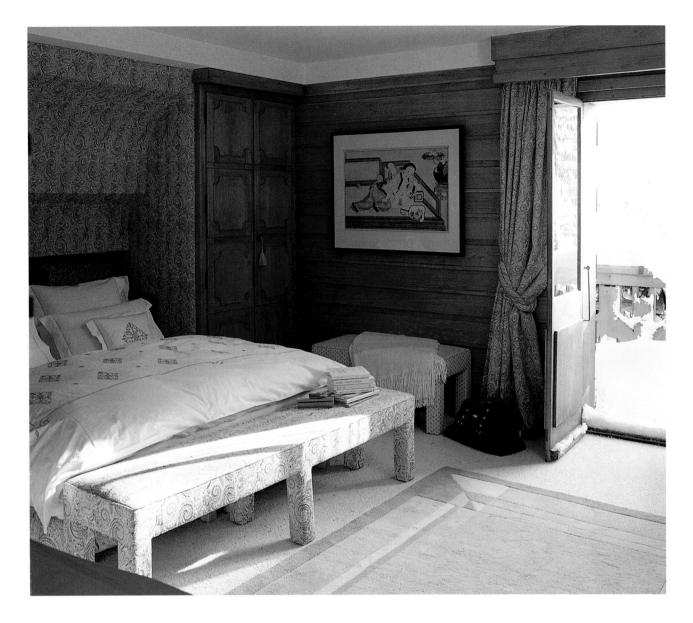

On their travels worldwide, the Charriols have searched for just the right furniture and objects from the Forties. Antiques dealers in London, Paris, the Far East and New York have been fruitful sources, but so, too, have antiques shops in Mégève where Annick found the quirky architect-designed chair at the foot of the stairs. Another prototype which causes discussion among visitors to the chalet is the Thirties model aeroplane – a French 'Saunier'. It sits alongside leather armchairs, its sleek, polished lines a calculated foil for the decoration, and characteristic of Philippe Charriol's taste for the unusual stylishly executed.

The welcome and comfort guests enjoy at Chalet le Sarto have not been compromised by the Charriols' quest for period authenticity. It is essentially a relaxed family home – but one with a character all its own.

ABOVE Paisley cashmere adds pattern to the main bedroom. The same fabric is used for the curtains as well as to upholster the bed and stools and to line the bed recess.

Above the crowd

John and Kathleen Rivers's Hickory House sits so high on the flank of Little Terrapin Mountain in Cashiers, North Carolina, that even insects find the elevation challenging – the windows and doors that stand open all day seldom admit anything more disturbing than an occasional stray hummingbird. Across the valley, Whiteside Mountain, one of the most ancient peaks in North America, rises like an island out of the surrounding waves of azure and lapis and deep turquoise. Clad in shingles of silvery hickory bark – chestnut-shingled houses were once common here, but a blight killed the chestnut trees – the long rambling house seems to merge with the surrounding forest.

'We had built two or three houses before, but never anything like this,' says Kathleen, a Charleston, South Carolina decorator. 'The foundations alone took nearly a year to get in because the house is literally hanging over a cliff. But the site was so spectacular it was all worth it.'

Building the house and developing the surrounding property turned out to be a delicious exercise in memory for Kathleen, who spent childhood summers at the nearby High Hampton Inn. 'I learnt to play tennis

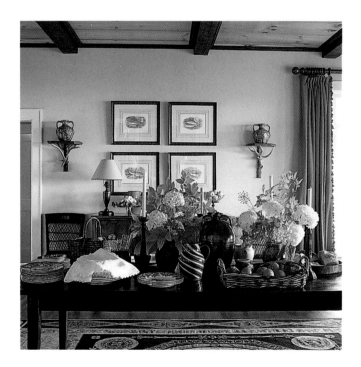

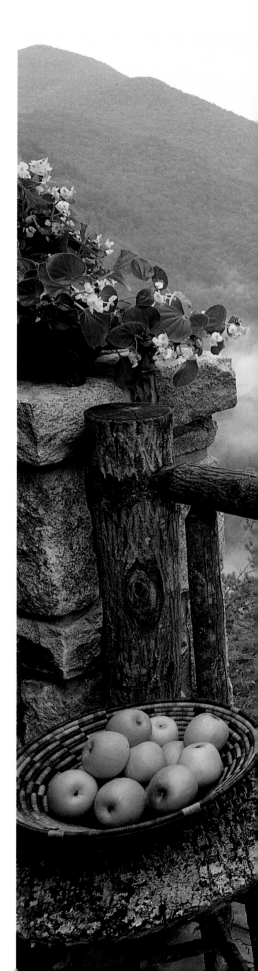

ABOVE The dining room incorporates many rustic touches but the effect is sophisticated.
RIGHT Clinging to the steep flank of Little Terrapin Mountain, the house has breathtaking views across the valley.

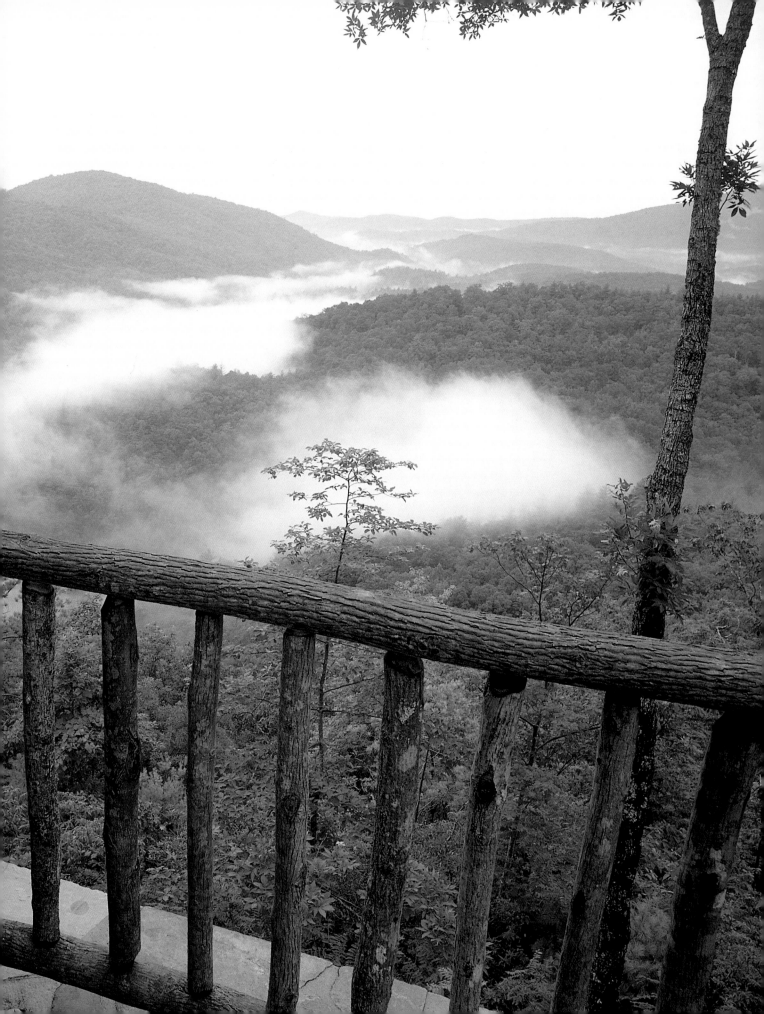

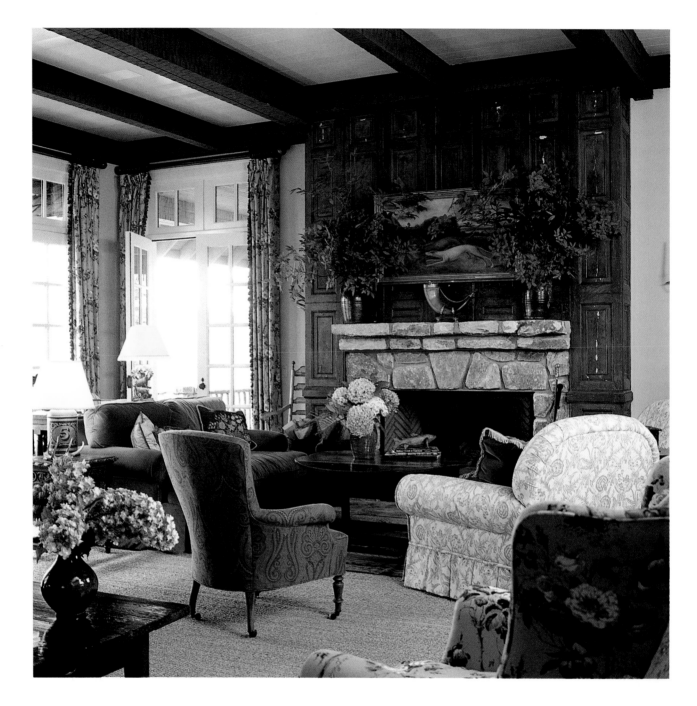

ABOVE The stone chimneypiece in the living room is surrounded by carved, dark-wood panelling.

there, I learnt to ride, I hiked – every active part of my life I first learnt up here in the mountains,' she says.

Working with Jim Meyer, an architect from Charlotte, North Carolina, the Rivers designed a sunny, high-ceilinged house with a broad veranda and an open-air 'sitting room' paved in flagstones and sited to take full advantage of the ever-changing view. In collaboration with fellow decorator and old friend Amelia Handegan, Kathleen filled the house with an earthy, tactile mix of European and American antiques,

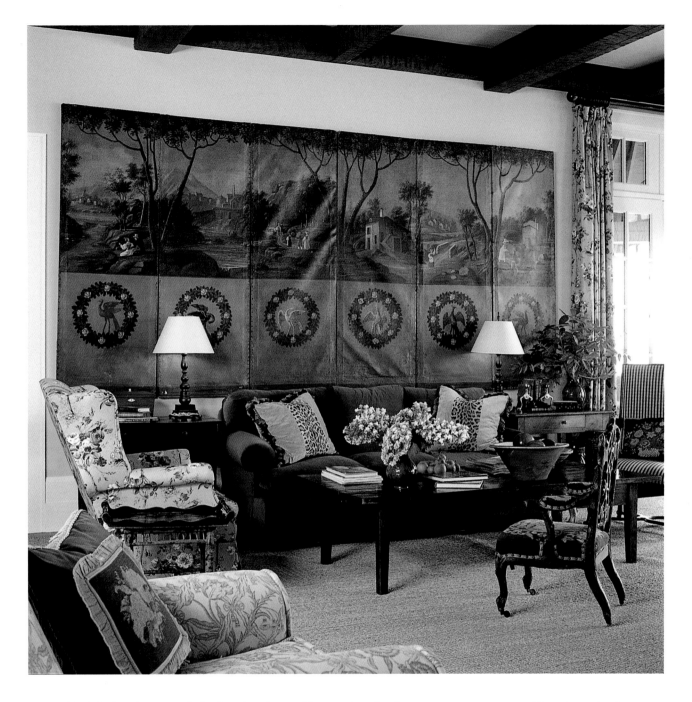

and with folk furniture made by local artisans. Conventional rules were happily broken: rustic beds are dressed in formal toiles, primitive earthenware jugs sit next to Turkish olive pots. 'Amelia and I have an unbelievably powerful synergy,' says Kathleen.

While the house was rising over the tree tops, Kathleen and Amelia combed through the antiques shops and flea markets of Atlanta and Charleston. 'We bought furniture for two years before we had a house to put it in,' says Kathleen. 'We knew where most of the things would go,

ABOVE The antique painted screen prompted the living room's mellow colour scheme. A traditional chintz was chosen for the curtains and a chair.

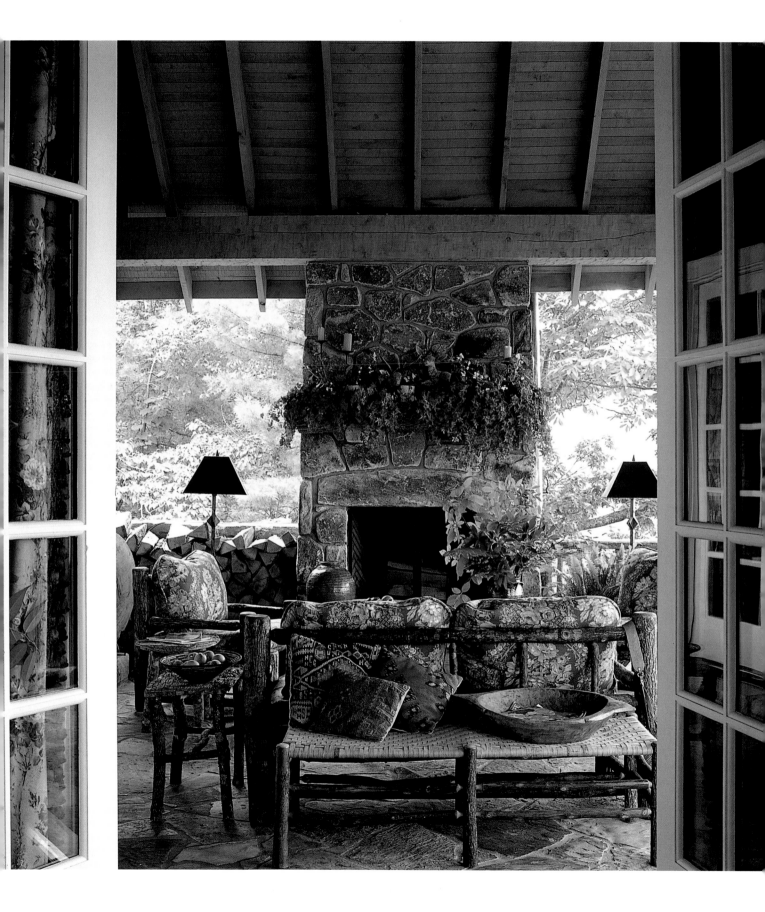

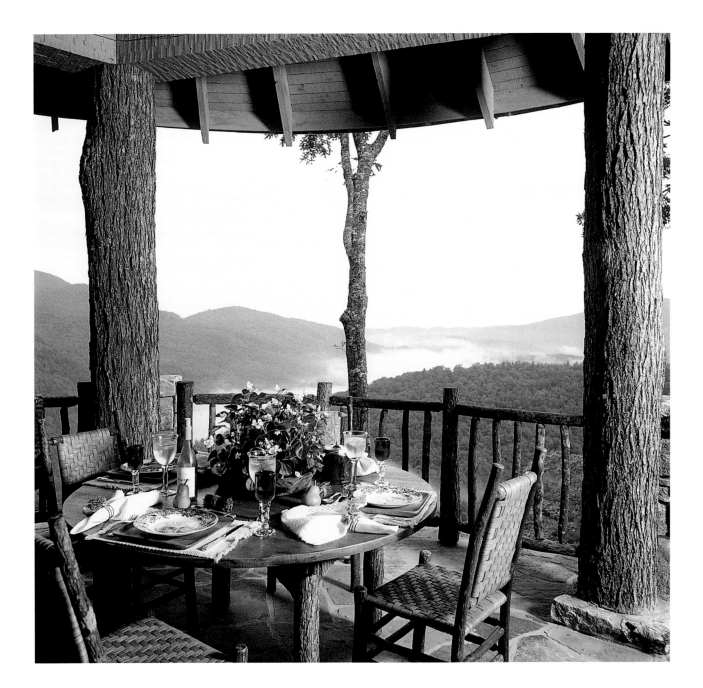

but sometimes we just bought something we loved and figured that we would find a place for it. And we did.'

The result is a five-year-old house that looks as though it has been there for generations. Subtle architectural decisions aid the illusion: ceiling heights, for instance, vary throughout, from eleven-and-a-half feet in the living room to just under ten feet in the nearby dining room, suggesting a building that has been added to over time. The dimensions of the living room were designed around a wall of panelling salvaged from a 1760 Charleston house and stored for years in Amelia's basement until

ABOVE The veranda, enclosed by a balustrade of rough hickory poles and furnished with a rustic table and chairs, is a spectacular spot for alfresco lunches.
OPPOSITE The open-air porch-cum-sitting-room blurs the distinction between indoors and outdoors.

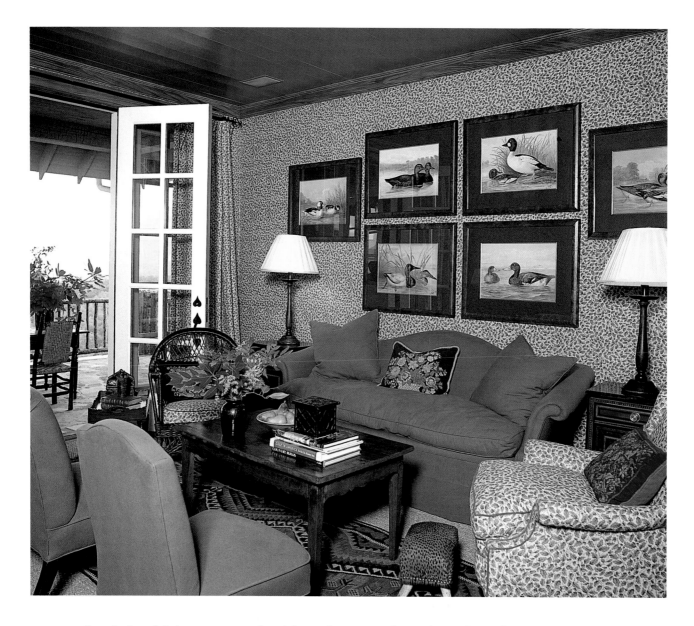

ABOVE Framed prints of ducks are grouped above the sofa in the library.

the right project came along. An antique, six-panel screen painted with a rustic landscape stretches across one wall, a charming counterpoint to the real landscape that lies opposite it, just beyond the room's generous French windows. 'As soon as I saw the screen I knew it belonged up here,' says Kathleen.

The house's soft, mossy colours were inspired by the palette of browns and greens outside the open windows. Next door to the living room, the library, wrapped in a soft brown printed cotton, is an intimate family retreat filled with comfortable chairs and an inviting sofa. A collection of framed prints pays tribute to John's love of duck shooting; book shelves are filled with memorabilia from Kathleen's childhood in Atlanta and in the mountains. In the dining room, furnished with a long

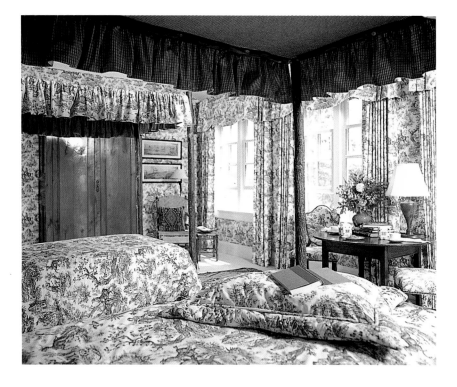

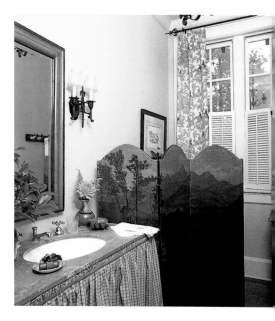

ABOVE LEFT A specially produced toile de Jouy is all-embracing in one of the bedrooms.
ABOVE RIGHT The painted screen in this bathroom depicts, appropriately, a mountain landscape.

rustic table and set with an attractive mix of primitive pottery, the ceiling is panelled with planks of sassafrass wood.

Through the open doors, the wide veranda enclosed by a balustrade of rough hickory poles overlooks the mountains and misty valleys. On cool summer evenings a fire in the outdoor fireplace warms the open-air 'sitting room', furnished with a set of rough furniture made locally from trees harvested from the nearby forests. 'We wanted a feeling of comfort and cosiness with a playful twist,' says Kathleen.

In fact, the whole house is a charming mix of fantasy, sophistication, and modern comfort, from the fairy-tale setting to the delightful pastoral scenes repeated in a favourite toile in an upstairs spare room. Although it sits unobtrusively within its surroundings, the house is roomy enough for a houseful of friends or visiting family, with six bedrooms, as well as an apartment over the garage. On the lower level, however, there is a no-nonsense home office which enables John and Kathleen to keep abreast of their many enterprises, including commercial real-estate ventures in Charleston, as well as the famous Chattooga Club which is located at Hickory House.

But the house is, above all, a retreat for just the two of them. For the main bedroom Kathleen deviated from her earthy palette, and chose a bright floral print on a crisp white background for the windows and walls. 'It rains here nearly every afternoon,' she says, 'and the bedroom is a bright, happy place – just right for curling up with a good book.'

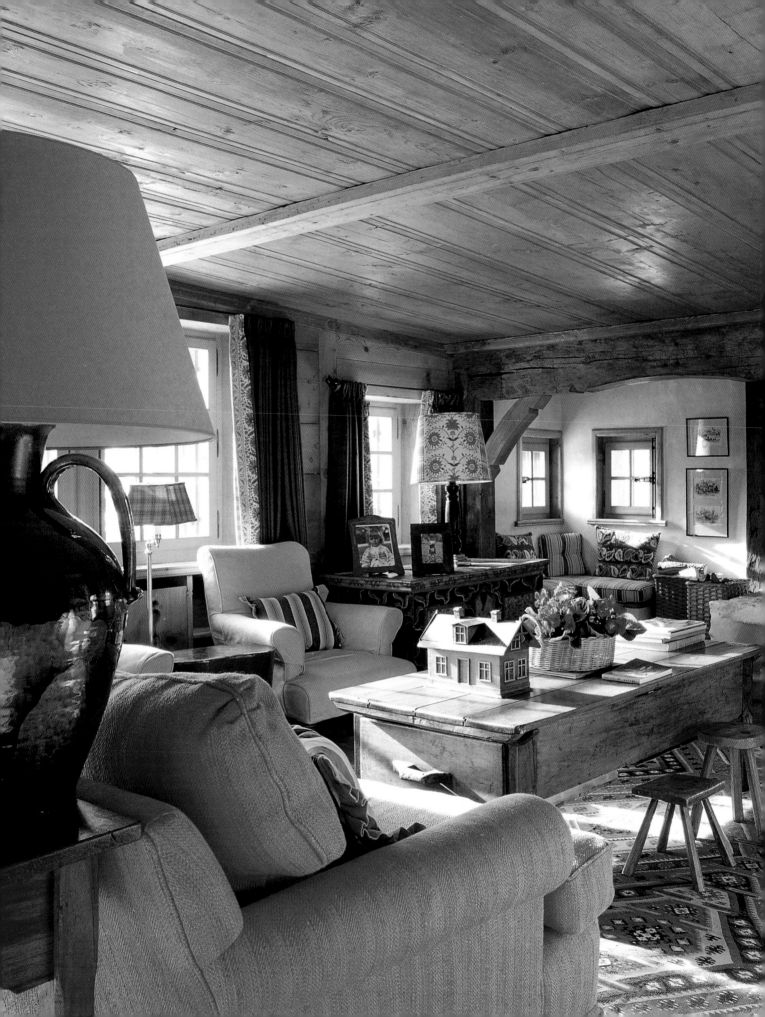

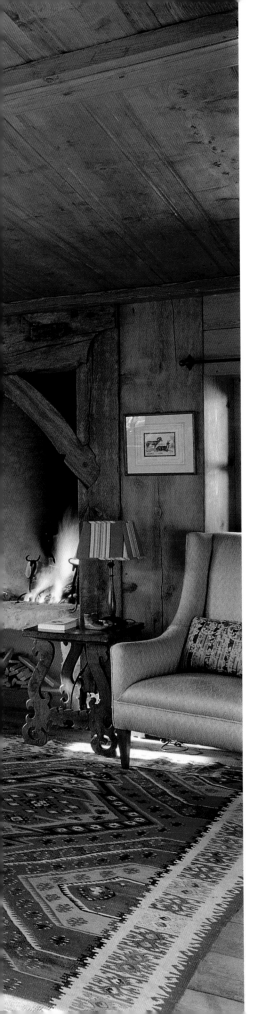

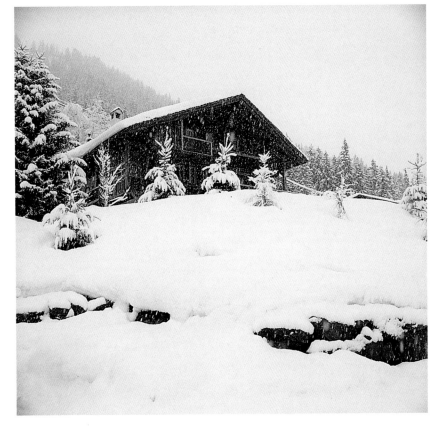

Coming of age

Some houses delight the senses the moment you walk into them. This splendid chalet overlooking Verbier in the canton of Valais in Switzerland is one such: not only is it appealing to look at but it is suffused with the delicious scents of wood-smoke from the enormous fireplace in the sitting-room, and of beeswax from the ancient pine ceilings, polished floorboards and fine old furnishings. Deep, down-filled cushions on sofas and chairs beckon you close to the crackling warmth of the fire; the light is muted; the decoration of the room is richly comfortable; the atmosphere cosy, inviting, timeless. It is a perfect retreat from the vivacity of the ski-slopes.

ABOVE The chalet, though recently built, was designed in the traditional style and constructed of reclaimed timber wherever possible.
LEFT The warm tones of the wood in the sitting room are complemented by the colours and textures of the fabrics and kilims. Seating includes a corner banquette with striped cushions.

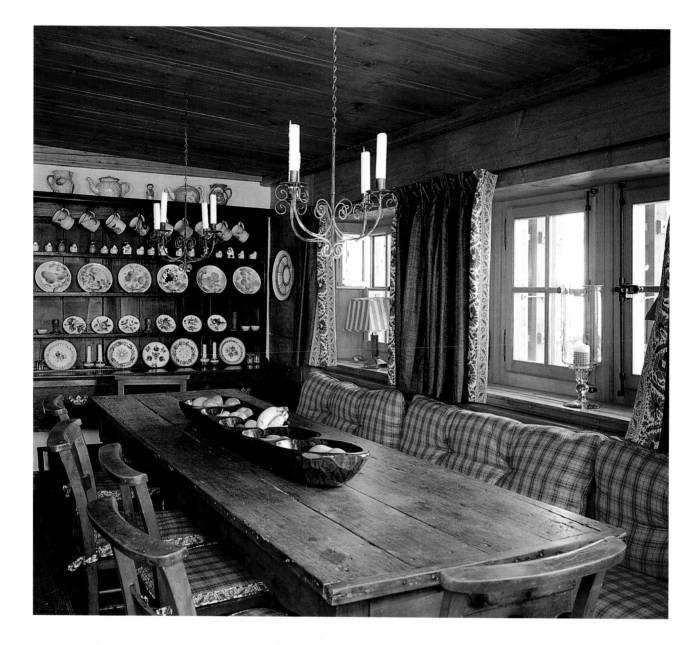

How surprising, then, to learn that this house was finished only a few years ago. Before they built it, the discerning owners – she is American, he is Swiss – already knew the area well, having travelled to Verbier around a dozen times a year over a long period. They used to share the next-door chalet with other members of the family, but when they found they were rapidly outgrowing that establishment, they decided to build something of their own on a site which has a glorious view of the village and the mountains, from the Grand Combin to the Dents du Midi.

They commissioned local architect, Raymond Bruchez of Bruchez and Fellay, to draw up a set of plans. Although he had worked exten- sively in Verbier, this was his first mandate to design in the style of a Val

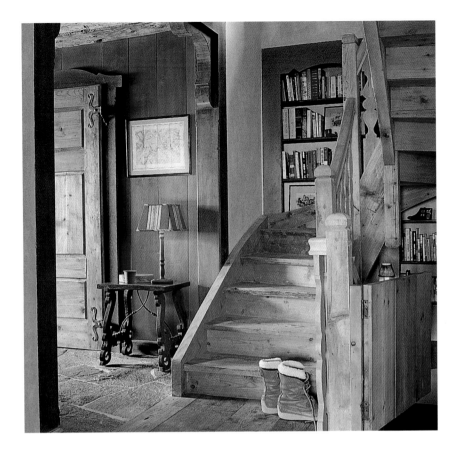

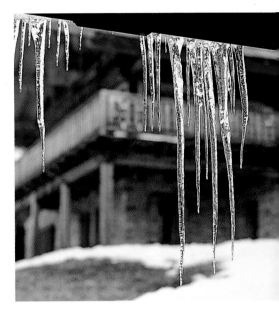

d'Illiez chalet. The main stipulation in the owners' brief was that the new house should fit sympathetically into the landscape, provide lots of space for family and friends and – especially important – to look as though it had been there for ages.

To help realize this aspiration, they enlisted the aid of Emily Todhunter, the London-based interior designer, who had worked on their London home. A happy result of the English commission was that Emily and the owner's wife had become firm friends. Thus, when it came to planning the decoration of the new house in Switzerland, there was an air of shared fun and enthusiasm.

Perhaps the most remarkable aspect of the decoration of this chalet is that the entire scheme was worked out from floor plans. Every colour, every piece of furniture, the lampshades, curtains, rugs, pictures were bought and 'positioned' before the house was finished. 'We did it all using a model of the building, which had sections that flipped up to show a 3-D view of each room from above,' explains Emily. 'It worked like a dream. It was one of those wonderful projects which went without a hitch and Raymond Bruchez and I got on famously. The only slight hiccup was when I flew out to measure up for the curtains and found that there were no windows in place.'

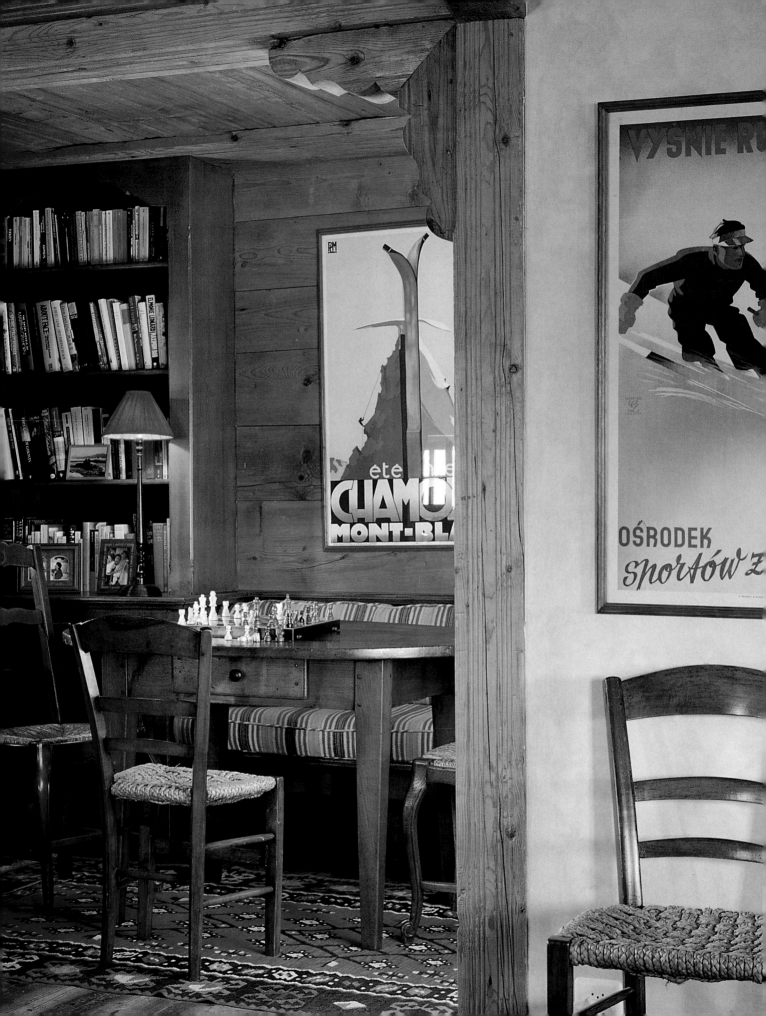

Much of the furniture for the chalet was found by Emily and her client during foraging trips to antiques shops in England and Europe in search of suitable pieces. Meanwhile, the client's husband made several trips to Verbier. Throughout the whole construction project, which took a year, he worked closely with the architect, suggesting a modification here, an addition or subtraction there, keeping an eye on everything as the building took shape.

The secret of the chalet's charmingly bygone look is that all the exterior timbers and as many as possible of the interior ones are old pieces taken from abandoned barns. Instead of the listless, grey driftwood colour that new timber rapidly takes on after exposure to the elements, here the colour has a warm and glowing, reddish hue.

Any new pieces of timber were washed down with a walnut stain, applied hot in the traditional way, and then distressed before being either waxed or painted. A team of specialist painters led by Adam Calkin flew out from England, finishing the whole project in six weeks.

In a spot such as Verbier, where there are many new chalets, this building differs from its neighbours in that it does not have the enormous picture-windows which characterize almost all the others. Instead, the windows have been made traditionally small and intimate. 'There certainly are spectacular vistas but the owners felt that if you want to see

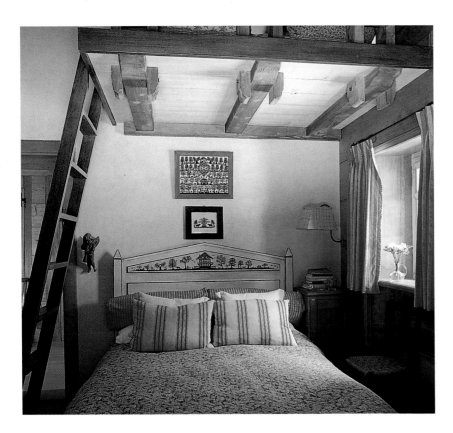

LEFT The decorated headboard in one of the guest bedrooms picks up the character of the silhouettes above.
OPPOSITE The library has rush-seated fruitwood chairs and a small table. Alpine posters, including one proclaiming the delights of Chamonix in summer, decorate the walls.

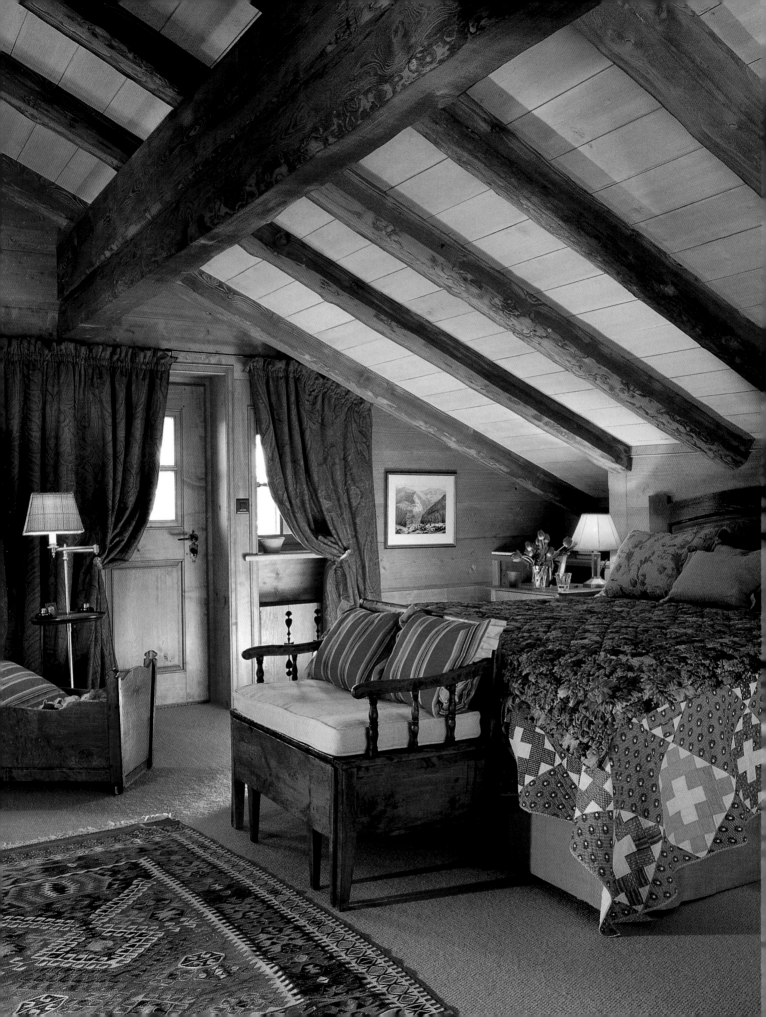

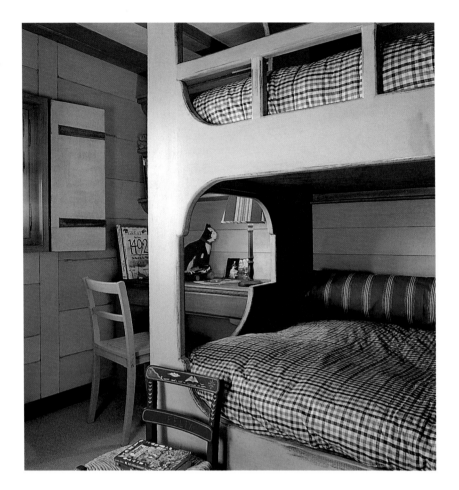

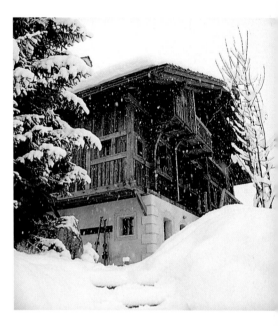

extensive views, you go outside,' explains Emily. 'This means that after being out on the slopes all day, you come back home to lovely, warm and cosy rooms where the focus is internal and not external.'

As the chalet – which sleeps eleven in seven bedrooms – took shape, the shopping expeditions began to reap rewards. Much of the furniture is fruitwood collected in Provence and Spain. The mixture of different woods gives the chalet a faintly rustic ambience. There are no pretensions about these pieces: they are solid, practical and easy to live with, but still immensely attractive. It is the same story with the fabrics used for the sofas, chairs, curtains and lampshades. Some of the most-striking are old French ticking.

For Emily, one of the most anxious moments of the commission was when she went to Verbier to await the arrival of the furniture van. 'The tension as this enormous lorry came gingerly down the icy roads was awful. Until we got everything into the chalet we didn't know for sure that it would fit where we wanted it to go.' Miraculously, save for one enormous cupboard which wouldn't go in until the door had been removed, everything slotted exactly into place.

ABOVE LEFT Bunk beds and a built-in desk in one of the children's bedrooms. ABOVE RIGHT The wide, overhanging gable shelters the balconies below. OPPOSITE The main bedroom, with its heavily beamed ceiling and warmly timbered walls, has a box-seated sofa at the end of the bed.

Acknowledgments

The photographs and text reproduced in this book are derived from features previously published in *House & Garden* magazine.

PHOTOGRAPHERS:

Anita Calero: 34-41; 42-47
Tim Clinch: 2-3; 94-101; 144-51
Michael Dunne: 84-93
Andreas von Einsiedel: 124-33
Brian Harrison: 184-91
Richard Labougle: 9; 58-63
Keith Scott Morton: 6; 14-27; 48-57; 112-23
Jonathan Pilkington: 10; 134-43

Sue Royle: 153; 154-61
Christian Sarramon/Inside/The Interior Archive: 28-33
Fritz von der Schulenburg: 183; 200-07
Fritz von der Schulenburg/The Interior Archive: 11; 162-69
Christopher Simon Sykes: 8; 13; 64-71; 170-81
Simon Upton: 4-5; 73; 102-11
Simon Upton/The Interior Archive: 74-83
Peter Woloszynski: 192-99

AUTHORS:

Olinda Adeane: 154-61
Darleen Bungey: 42-47
Victor Carro: 58-63
Caroline Clifton-Mogg: 34-41; 48-57
Quentin Crewe: 162-69
Susan Crewe: 170-81
Jonathan Dawson: 200-07
June Ducas: 64-71
Liz Elliot: 102-11

Anne Hardy: 144-51
Carolyn Harrison: 184-91
Suzanne Lowry: 124-33
Sophie Lund: 94-101
David Mlinaric: 134-43
Lorenza Bianda Pasquinelli: 74-83
Anthony Roberts: 28-33
Caroline Seebohm: 14-27; 84-93; 112-23
Liz Seymour: 192-99

Lavinia Bolton, House & Garden Locations Editor, researched several of the houses illustrated in this book.

The house on Lamu (pages 162-69) can be rented by the week.
For details contact Shela House Management, PO Box 39486, Nairobi, Kenya, fax: +254 244 5010.